WASSERSTROM

Seal of the Saints

Seal of the Saints

PROPHETHOOD AND SAINTHOOD IN THE DOCTRINE OF IBN ʿARABĪ

Michel Chodkiewicz

Translated by

Liadain Sherrard

Golden Palm Series

THE ISLAMIC TEXTS SOCIETY

CAMBRIDGE · 1993

Translated from the French by Liadain Sherrard
First published as *Le Sceau des Saints* by Michel Chodkiewicz
Editions Gallimard 1986

This edition published 1993 by The Islamic Texts Society
5 Green Street, Cambridge, CB2 3JU, UK.

ISBN 0 946621 40 3 *paper*
ISBN 0 946621 39 X *cloth*

British Library Cataloguing in Publication Data
A catalogue record of this book is available from
The British Library

Typeset by Goodfellow & Egan, Cambridge
Printed by The Alden Press, Oxford

Contents

SYSTEM OF TRANSLITERATION FOR ARABIC CHARACTERS

ʼ	ء	z	ز	q	ق
b	ب	s	س	k	ك
t	ت	sh	ش	l	ل
th	ث	ṣ	ص	m	م
j	ج	ḍ	ض	n	ن
ḥ	ح	ṭ	ط	h	ه
kh	خ	ẓ	ظ	w	و
d	د	ʿ	ع	y	ي
dh	ذ	gh	غ		
r	ر	f	ف		

The article: al- and l- (even in front of sun letters)

Short vowels		*Long vowels*		*Diphthongs*	
ـُ	u	ا ى	ā	ـَو	aw
ـَ	a	و	ū	ـَي	ay
ـِ	i	ي	ī	ـيّ	iyy
				ـُوّ	uww

EDITIONS AND ABBREVIATIONS

EDITIONS

Fuṣūṣ al-Ḥikam, Ibn ʿArabī, edited A. A. Affifi, Beirut, 1946.

Al-Futūḥāt al-Makkiyya, Ibn ʿArabī, Būlāq, 1329AH (4 vols.). There is also reference to Osman Yahya's critical edition in progress (Cairo: al-Hay'a al-Miṣriyya al-ʿĀmma lī'l-Kitāb, 1972–).

ABBREVIATIONS

EI: *Encyclopaedia of Islam* (*EI*^{1} first edition, *EI*^{2} second edition).

GAL: C. Brockelmann, *Geschichte der Arabischen Literatur*, Leiden, 1945–49.

GAS: Fuat Sezgin, *Geschichte des Arabischen Schrifttums*, Leiden, 1967– .

Iṣṭ.: Ibn ʿArabī Kitāb *Iṣṭilāḥ al-ṣūfiyya*, Hyderabad, 1948.

R.G.: the 'Répertoire général' in Osman Yahya's *Histoire et classification de l'oeuvre d'Ibn ʿArabī*, Damascus, 1964. The letters R.G. are followed by the number of the work as it is to be found in O. Yahya's classification.

It is reported in Muslim's *Ṣaḥīḥ* that the Messenger of God said: 'God is beautiful and He loves beauty'. It is God who made the world and endowed it with existence. The entire universe is therefore supremely beautiful. There is nothing ugly in it. On the contrary, in it God has brought together all perfection and all beauty . . .. The gnostics see it as being nothing other than the form of the divine Reality . . .: for God is He who is epiphanized in every face, He to whom every sign refers back, He upon whom all eyes rest, He who is worshipped in every object of worship . . .. The whole universe offers up its prayers to Him, falls down before Him, and sings His praises. All tongues speak of Him alone, and Him alone all hearts desire . . .. If it were not so, no Messenger and no Prophet would ever have loved woman or child.

Ibn ʿArabī, *al-Futūḥāt al-makkiyya* III, pp. 449-50.

Foreword

In 1845, at Leipzig, Gustav Flügel, a student of Silvestre de Sacy, published as an annex to Jurjānī's *Taᶜrīfāt*[1] a short treatise entitled *Definitiones theosophi Muhjied-din Mohammed b. Ali vulgo Ibn Arabī dicti*. With these few pages, which were written at Malatya in the year 615/1218, the work of Ibn ᶜArabī made its discreet entrance into the field of Oriental studies.[2] However, the first studies of any importance were long in appearing. It was not until 1911, in London, that Nicholson brought out his edition and translation of the *Tarjumān al-ashwāq (The Interpreter of Desires)*. It is true that another work attributed to Ibn ᶜArabī, the *Treatise on Unity*, had been translated into English by Weir in 1901, and by Ivan-Gustav Agueli (Abdul-Hādī) into Italian (1907) and French (1910); but this attribution, which gave rise to much misunderstanding, was unfortunately mistaken.[3] The year 1919 was particularly fruitful: in Leyden, Nyberg published his *Kleinere Schriften des Ibn al-Arabī*, together with a long introduction; and at the Royal Spanish Academy, Asín Palacios gave a notable talk which constituted the initial version of his *La Escatologia musulmana en la Divina Comedia*. In it he put forward the hypothesis that Dante had

1. The Flügel edition of the *Taᶜrīfāt* has been published with the title *Definitiones Sejjidi Sherif Alī b. Mohammed Dschordshani*.

2. This is the *Kitāb al-Iṣṭilāḥāt al-ṣūfiyya* or *Kitāb Iṣṭilāḥ al-ṣūfiyya* of which at least two other editions are in existence (Cairo 1357, Hyderabad 1948). It was translated by Rabia Terri Harris in the *Journal of the Muhyiddin Ibn Arabī Society*, Oxford 1984, vol. III, pp. 27-54. A misinterpretation of a mention of the colophon relating to the completion of the copy (and not to the writing of the treatise itself) leads the translator to say that it is only partially the work of Ibn ᶜArabī, whereas in reality the authenticity of the attribution of the *Iṣṭilāḥāt* is beyond doubt. The autograph manuscript Şehit Ali 2813/24 is incomplete, but the text of the treatise exists in full in Chapter 73 of the *Futūḥāt* (II, pp. 128-34), of which we possess a manuscript written by Ibn ᶜArabī himself.

3. On this problem, see the introduction to our translation of the *Epître sur l'Unicité absolue* by Awḥad al-Dīn Balyānī, Paris 1982.

been influenced by Ibn ᶜArabī, thereby arousing a controversy which continues to this day.[4] His subsequent studies led him to publish, in 1931, *El islam cristianizado*, a work which despite its unindicative title is entirely devoted to Ibn ᶜArabī.[5] The year 1939 saw the appearance in Cambridge of *The Mystical Philosophy of Muhyiddin Ibnul Arabī* by A. A. ᶜAfifi, an Egyptian researcher, which is, as far as I know, the first thesis on the author of the *Futūḥāt* to be written in a Western university. The post-war years were to see a succession of texts, translations and studies, most of which will find mention in the course of the present book.[6] For the moment, we should bear in mind two of the most important works in this field of research: Henry Corbin's *Creative Imagination in the Sūfism of Ibn ᶜArabī* (London 1970), and Toshihiko Izutsu's *Sufism and Taoism* (Berkeley and London 1984), a comparative study of Ibn ᶜArabī and Lao-Tzŭ, to which must be added William Chittick's more recent work, *The Sufi Path of Knowledge* (Albany 1989).

The reception initially accorded to Ibn ᶜArabī by those engaged in Islamic studies was one of extreme reserve. Massignon vowed an enduring hostility towards him which his students often inherited. Other more well-disposed authors spoke of Ibn ᶜArabī with rather comical condescension: Clément Huart, while agreeing that he is reputed to be 'the greatest mystic of the Muslim East', expresses concern about his 'disorderly imagination'.[7] Carra de Vaux acknowledges that 'in the East, even in our own times, his popularity is on the increase', but says of him, 'such syncretism has its charm, and his work in its entirety is earthy, full of life and movement'[8]—an ambiguous commendation, and one which

4. In 1924 Miguel Asín Palacios published his *Historia critica de una polemica*, which was added to the 1924 edition of the *Escatología musulmana* (Madrid-Granada). For an account of this issue, see M. Rodinson, 'Dante et l'Islam d'après les travaux recents', in *Revue de l'histoire des religions*, vol. CXL, no. 2, 1951, pp. 203-36.

5. Only the subtitle, which does not figure on the cover, describes the subject matter: *Estudio del 'sufismo' a través de las obras de Abenarabi de Murcia*. A French translation, which leaves much to be desired, has been published under the title *L'Islam christianisé*, Paris 1982.

6. A well-informed critical inventory, covering the last 15 years of Western language publications on the subject of Ibn ᶜArabī, may be found in James W. Morris' article 'Ibn Arabī and his Interpreters', published in the *Journal of the American Oriental Society*, vol. CVI, iii, iv; vol. CVII, i (1986-87).

7. Clément Huart, *Littérature arabe*, Paris 1923, p. 275.

8. Alexandre Carra de Vaux, *Les Penseurs de l'Islam*, Paris 1923, IV, pp. 218-23.

does not point to much depth of understanding. That pious ecclesiastic Asín Palacios skilfully practises what we would today call the art of rehabilitation: Ibn ʿArabī is a Christian without Christ and owes to the Desert Fathers what all unknowingly he was to restore to Catholic spirituality. ʿAfīfī, and later the far more comprehensive Izutsu, suggest an interpretation of the work which is primarily philosophical and hence very reductionist: Ibn ʿArabī is not a 'thinker' among other thinkers, and nor is his doctrine the systematic exposition of merely intellectual speculation. Corbin, by far the most subtle of all these exegetes, does not commit such an error of perspective. Nevertheless, in his persistent attempts to uncover a clandestine Shīʿite in the writings of this self-confessed Sunnī, he presents a picture of him which in many respects needs correction.

The combination of sainthood and genius in the person of Ibn ʿArabī, and the fusion in his work of the most diverse sciences and literary forms, do indeed make it extremely difficult to grasp, and to enable others to grasp, the nature and stature of the man and his work. The bibliography of Ibn ʿArabī, although not yet definitive, has been firmly established, thanks to the labours of Osman Yahia: when the apocryphal or dubious texts have been discounted, there remain over four hundred works. Some of these are no more than short opuscules. Others consist of several hundreds or, in the case of the *Futūḥāt Makkiyya*, several thousands of our pages. But the list would lengthen considerably if we were able to include in it the works considered lost, among them a commentary on the Qur'ān which even though uncompleted comprised 'sixty-four volumes'.

A serious bibliography of Ibn ʿArabī remained to be written. The biographical notes on him written by Muslim authors or orientalists are full of gaps, and do not make use, in any exhaustive or critical manner, of the many sources available, beginning with his own works. Now, however, we have Claude Addas' indispensable study of him.[9] Here we will confine ourselves to a few salient points. Muḥyī al-Dīn Abū ʿAbdallāh Muḥammad b. ʿAlī b. Muḥammad b. al-ʿArabī al-Ḥātimī al-Ṭā'ī was born at Murcia on the 27th day of Ramaḍān 560 (7th August 1165). In France, where Louis VII was king, the construction of Notre-Dame de Paris had been under way for two years. In Muslim Spain, the power of the Almoravids was in decline, to be succeeded

9. Claude Addas, *Quest for the Red Sulphur: The Life of Ibn ʿArabī*, Cambridge U.K. 1993.

shortly by the Almohads. In Egypt, another dynasty was ending, the dynasty of the Fatimids that Saladin was preparing to supplant. On the banks of the Onon in Eastern Siberia, Gengis Khān was born; less than a century later his grandson, Hūlāgū, would destroy Baghdad and have the last Abbasid caliph put to death.

Ibn ᶜArabī spent his childhood in Seville, where his family settled in 568/1172. At about the age of sixteen he 'entered upon the Way'[10] and began to keep company with the spiritual masters of Andalusia (later on, in his *Rūḥ al-Quds*, he describes fifty or so of them). His meeting with Averroes must have taken place at this time and not, as Corbin thinks, when he was nearer twenty years old. His initial 'conversion', however, was succeeded by a period of laxness (*fatra*) 'well-known to men of God and which no one who takes this path can avoid'.[11] He had a vision which rekindled his zeal; he gave up all his worldly goods, practised asceticism, and went on retreats in graveyards.[12] By the age of twenty he had already passed through a whole series of the 'stations' (*maqāmāt*) which in Ṣūfi terminology punctuate the journey towards God, and had received exceptional gifts of grace.[13] Athough at first his travels were confined to Andalusia, they extended after 590/1193 to the Maghrib. Until he reached the age of sixty, in fact, he was constantly on the move. Thus in 590 he was in Tunis and Tlemcen, in 591 at Fez, in 592 at Seville, in 593 and 594 once more in Fez, and in 595 at Cordoba. In 597 he returned to Morocco. In 598 he went to Murcia, then to Salé, and then to Tunis, where the period of his life spent in the West came to an end, and by which time he had certainly written almost sixty works. A vision which came to him at Marrakesh[14] directed him to go to the East, and he left the Maghrib, never to return. During this same year 598 (1201-1202 of the Christian era) he went successively to Cairo, Jerusalem and finally Mecca, where a major spiritual event took place of which we will give an account later. In 599-600 he stayed in the Hijaz, before resuming his way: Mosul, Baghdad, Jerusalem (601), Konya, Hebron (602), Cairo (603). In 604 he was in Mecca, in 606 at Aleppo, in

10. A passage in the *Futūḥāt* (II, p. 425) appears to give the date of this 'entry upon the Way' as 580. Other scattered references, however, seem to indicate that Ibn ᶜArabī's 'conversion' took place several years earlier.

11. *Futūḥāt* IV, p. 172.

12. *Futūḥāt* III, p. 45.

13. *Futūḥāt* II, p. 425.

14. *Futūḥāt* II, p. 436.

608 at Baghdad. Some of his disciples accompanied him, while others were waiting for him wherever he stopped. Princes sought his company; doctors of the Law desired to take issue with him. A contemplative anchored in immutability, Ibn ʿArabī nevertheless travelled without pause over Anatolia and the fertile Muslim East, tirelessly imparting as he went his initiatic teaching and his metaphysical doctrine. The journeys continued, with several sojourns in Asia Minor, until 620/1223, when he settled in Damascus. Here he completed a preliminary version of the *Futūḥāt*, his *summa mystica* begun at Mecca twenty-one years previously (a few years before his death he was to write a second version, of which we possess the autograph manuscript in thirty-seven volumes). Here, too, he wrote his *Fuṣūṣ al-ḥikam* after having had a dream which we will describe in due course.

He was surrounded by an assembly of disciples, continuing to teach and to expound his work up to the end: the last 'attested reading' in his presence known to us (of the *Tanazzulāt mawṣiliyya*, a treatise on the esoteric meaning and spiritual results of ritual practices which was written at Mosul in 601/1204) is dated the 10th Rabīʿ al-awwal 638. In Damascus a few weeks later, on the 28th Rabīʿ al-thānī (16th November 1240) this 'Revivifier of the Religion' (a translation of his name Muḥyī al-Dīn) whom posterity was also to know as *al-Shaykh al-Akbar*, the 'Greatest Master', and *Sulṭān al-ʿārifīn*, 'Sultan of the Gnostics', died.[15]

At the beginning of Chapter Four of his *Futūḥāt Makkiyya* (*The Illuminations of Mecca*), Ibn ʿArabī, addressing his Tunisian teacher and friend ʿAbd al-ʿAzīz Mahdawī—to whom the work is dedicated—recalls the occasion when he stayed with him in 598/1201, and tried to persuade him to join him in the Holy City, 'most noble of all the dwellings of stone and earth'. He then goes on to speak about the nature of one's place of residence and whether it is more or less favourable to contemplation. 'Places', he says, 'produce an effect in subtle hearts, and a hierarchy therefore exists of corporeal dwelling places (*manāzil jismāniyya*), just as there is a hierarchy of spiritual dwelling places

15. More biographical details can be found in the first part of *El islam cristianizado* by Asín Palacios, and in Henry Corbin's *Creative Imagination in the Sufism of Ibn Arabī*. A brief but accurate biographical outline is in R. W. Austin's introduction to his translation of the *Rūḥ al-quds* (*Sufis of Andalusia*, London 1971).

(*manāzil rūḥāniyya*).' He reminds ᶜAbd al-ᶜAzīz that the latter had refused to shut himself away in one of the rooms in a lighthouse east of Tunis, and had preferred to make his retreat a little further off among the tombs, saying that 'he was better able to find his heart there than in the lighthouse'. 'I too', he adds, 'experienced there the truth of what you said.' He explains that the special character of certain places owes its existence to those who have stayed or are staying there, be they angels, *jinn* or men. This is so, for example, in the case of the house of Abū Yazīd Bisṭāmī, which was nicknamed the 'house of the Just', *bayt al-abrār*; of the *zāwiya* of Junayd, the great Ṣūfī of ninth century Baghdad; of the cave of the ascetic Ibn Adham; and of all places generally which have some connection with the pious dead (*al-ṣāliḥīn*).[16]

Earthly space is therefore not neutral: the passage of a saint or his posthumous sojourn in a place somehow establishes in it a field of beneficent power. With this personal testimony the Shaykh al-Akbar presents us both with a warning and with the basis of one of the most visible forms of the 'cult of the saints'. As we shall see, he has much more to say on this subject.

The text we have just been citing was written by Ibn ᶜArabī shortly after his arrival in the East at the start of the thirteenth century. A century later, the Ḥanbalite polemicist Ibn Taymiyya launched a relentless campaign against *ziyārat al-qubūr*, the visiting of tombs and similar practices, and also condemned the practice of seeking the intercession of saints, or even of the Prophet.[17] The celebration of the *mawlid* (birthday) of the Prophet and *a fortiori* of the saints was likewise condemned by him as *bidᶜa*, a deplorable innovation.[18]

16. *Futūḥāt* I, pp. 98-99.

17. Ibn Taymiyya, *Majmūᶜat al-rasā'il wa 'l-masā'il* (*MRM*), ed. Rashīd Riḍā, v, pp. 85, 93; *al-Fatāwā al-kubrā, Beirut* 1965, I, pp. 93, 127, 344, 351; II, pp. 218, 226. See also in M. V. Memon's *Ibn Taimiya's Struggle against Popular Religion* (The Hague-Paris 1976) chapters 18 and 19 of the *Kitāb Iqtiḍā' al-ṣirāṭ al-mustaqīm*. In connection with the visits to the Prophet's tomb and the prayers for his intercession, cf. the answer given by his contemporary Taqī al-Dīn al-Subkī, the Shāfiᶜite jurist, in his *Shifā' al-siqām* (Beirut 1978), who finds justification for this practice in a series of *ḥadīth*. The later compilation by Yūsuf Nabhānī, *Shawāhid al-ḥaqq fī istighāthat sayyid al-khalq*, Cairo 1974, gives a summary of several centuries of polemics on this subject and on the intercession of the saints.

18. Cf. Ibn Taymiyya, *MRM* v, pp. 81-104, *Risālat al-ᶜibādāt al-sharᶜiyya wa 'l-farq baynahā wa-bayna 'l-bidaᶜiyya*.

Although he was not the first to engage in polemics on this subject, Ibn Taymiyya was by far the most violent, and for centuries the most influential: it is he who is responsible, through the Wahhābīs, for the destruction of places in the Arab world which had been venerated by countless generations of Muslims. His work, even today, is the source of vehement campaigns against the 'deviations' which have distorted the original purity of Islam.

Needless to say, the 'cult of the saints' did not arise in the thirteenth century. It was initially addressed, very early on, to members of the Prophet's family (*ahl al-bayt*) and to his Companions (*ṣaḥāba*). From the fourth century of the Hegira at least, funeral monuments were being erected at Baghdad in honour of the illustrious saints of the third century.[19] The accounts of journeys, such as that written by Ibn Jubayr in the twelfth century, the collections of *faḍā'il* (the 'claims to fame' of a city or a region), like the *Faḍā'il al-Shām* by Rubaᶜī,[20] the 'pilgrim's guides', of which a model example is Harawī's *Kitāb al-Ishārāt ilā maᶜrifat al-ziyārāt*, edited by Janine Sourdel-Thomine,[21] all bear witness to local traditions which are without doubt very ancient, even though they can rarely be dated with any accuracy. Finally, this fervour was both produced and nourished by the literature of hagiography, whose major works include Sulamī's *Ṭabaqāt* and the ten volumes of the *Ḥilyat al-awliyā'* (*The Ornament of the Saints*), written in the eleventh century by Abū Nuᶜaym al-Iṣfahānī. Before proceeding, we should note that, for the most part, neither at this time nor at a later date was this hagiography 'popular' literature. This label cannot be applied either to the works we have just mentioned or even to the more modest compilations of strictly regional interest like the *Tashawwuf* by Tādilī (the learned author of a respected commentary on Ḥarīrī's *Maqāmāt*) about the saints of southern Morocco of the fifth and sixth centuries AH,

19. Cf. L. Massignon, 'Les saints musulmans enterrés à Baghdad', in *Revue de l'histoire des religions*, 1908, reprinted in *Opera minora*, Beirut 1963, III, pp. 94-101. See also his article dealing with Cairo, 'La cité des morts' in *Bulletin de l'Institut français d'archéologie orientale*, Cairo 1958, reprinted in *Opera minora*, III, pp. 233-85.

20. Abu 'l-Ḥasan al-Rubaᶜī, *Faḍā'il al-Shām wa-Dimashq*, ed. S. al-Munajjid, Damascus 1951.

21. ᶜAlī b. Abī Bakr al-Harawī, *Guide des lieux de pèlerinage*, ed. J. Sourdel-Thomine, Damascus 1953. See also J. Sourdel-Thomine, 'Les anciens lieux de pèlerinage damascains', in *Bulletin d'études orientales*, XIV, Damascus 1954, pp. 65-85.

or like the *Maqṣad* written by his successor Bādisī.[22] It would be *a fortiori* incongruous to attach such a label to later works of this type written by great poets such as ᶜAṭṭār or Jāmī.

Nevertheless, and without succumbing to the perverse taste for dividing things up into periods, the age of Ibn ᶜArabī must be regarded as the start of a new era. It witnessed the appearance both of the theoretical formulations and of the institutions that were to dictate all later developments in Islamic mysticism down to our day. It was a period of transition in the political history of the community of believers, the more dramatic aspects of which are sufficiently indicated by the taking of Baghdad by the Mongols in 1258 and the fall of the Abbasid caliphate. It is no accident that this was also the period of transition in Ṣūfi doctrine from implicit to explicit, and the start, sociologically speaking, of its transition from informality to formality, fluidity to organisation. Its fundamental concepts were defined and organized, in the work of Ibn ᶜArabī, into a comprehensive synthesis; and from then on, viewed as a summit or as a target, acknowledged or unacknowledged, for followers and adversaries alike this work constituted an essential landmark and a fruitful source of technical terminology.[23] At the same time the *ṭuruq* ('brotherhoods') came into being and began to codify the practices they had inherited into rules and methods. Although the 'cult of the saints' is not necessarily related to these brotherhoods, nevertheless the veneration of the founding *shaykh* and his more eminent successors played an important part in its development. Its forms were progressively structured along the lines taken by the Muslim community in its devotion to the Prophet—a devotion which was itself marked by the official recognition of the *mawlid* under the Ayyubids. Ibn Taymiyya was not wrong in thinking that the actions which he censured and the concepts underlying them were gaining an ever-wider influence.

His critique is not limited to a furious inventory of the ravages brought about by these 'innovations': he sets out to explain them, the

22. The edition of the *Tashawwuf* by Aḥmad Tawfīq, Rabat 1984, is more complete and more accurate, especially with regard to place-names,than the edition by Adolphe Faure, Rabat 1958. The *Maqṣad* by Bādisī, formerly translated by G. S. Colin (*Les Saints du Rif*, Paris 1926), is now available in a critical edition by Saᶜīd Aᶜrāb, Rabat 1982.

23. For this see the introduction (pp. 17-37) of my *Un océan sans rivage: Ibn Arabī, le Livre et la Loi*, Paris 1992.

better to eradicate them. In his eyes, these aberrant devotions on the part of the *ᶜāmma*, the ignorant masses, are purely and simply evidence of polytheism (*shirk*). They are foreign as well as heterodox: their existence and diffusion are due to the pernicious influence of the Jews, the Sabians, the Zoroastrians and above all of the Christians, who, in the guise either of insidious guests or of ambiguous converts, are present at the very heart of the Muslim community.[24] What we are seeing here is the emergence of the 'two-tiered model', a theme which has been brilliantly discussed by Peter Brown in relation to Christianity.[25] Here as there this model, in all its various forms, and often enriched by concepts borrowed from Ibn Khaldūn, was to become popular in later interpretations of the 'cult of the saints'. Classic Islamology, whose sights are set on the empyrean, the dwelling-place of Islam as it ought to be, tends to be condescending towards those mental attitudes and patterns of behaviour which are irreducible to this paradigm, and to treat them as residual archaisms or unconscious borrowings which, in spite of being eventually canonized *a posteriori* by the religious authorities, are nevertheless corrupting influences. Colonial ethnography is formed by the same dichotomy, but tends to overestimate the importance or even to exalt the positive qualities of the indigenous substrata (Berber, African, Malay) at the expense of a universalist orthodoxy which, in the hands of the pan-Islamicists, could threaten the peace of mind of the empire's loyal subjects. 'Progressive' interpretations, which are obviously based on very different principles, are torn between a reluctance to defend 'superstitious' practices and 'reactionary' social structures, and the temptation to see an emerging class consciousness in everything that opposes the ideology of those who represent or are allied to the powers that be. There is no need to extend this list: whether 'authenticity' is viewed as attachment to the Islam of the *ᶜulamā'* or else to the more or less exuberant forms of popular piety, the presence of the 'two-tiered model' is everywhere

24. Similarly, Abraham b. Maimonides, son of the author of the *Guide of the Perplexed* and one of the great figures of thirteenth century Jewish pietism (*ḥasiduth*), was accused by his co-religionists of introducing practices into Judaism which were an imitation of Gentile customs (in this case of the Muslims). A complaint was even lodged against him with the Sultan al-Malik al-ᶜĀdil with the aim of obtaining a condemnation of these reforms. Cf. Paul Fenton, *Deux traités de mystique juive*, Paris 1987, p. 87.

25. Peter Brown, *The Cult of the Saints, its Rise and Function in Latin Christianity*, Chicago 1981.

apparent. It is beginning, in fact, to be questioned, thanks above all to the response that Peter Brown's work has elicited among some American researchers in the field of Islamology and anthropology, and the opposition between Great Tradition and Folk Tradition, Scripturalism and Maraboutism, is no longer a question of dogma.[26] But much work remains to be done.

There is, of course, no question of ignoring the differences that separate the rational, legalistic piety of the *fuqahā'* city-dwellers from the turbulent faith of the illiterate mountaineers, unconcerned with the interdicts of the jurisprudents. But it is important to be at least as aware of the continuities as of the ruptures. It is important to remember that within the spectrum of religious attitudes there was always a place, between these two extremes, for a large number of doctors of the Law and traditionalists who justified and encouraged devotion to the saints. One example is the extraordinary ʿAbd al-Qādir al-Jīlānī, a twelfth century Ḥanbalite lawyer and *muftī*, of whom we will speak later.[27] The history of a *ṭarīqa* like the Naqshbandiyya, famous for its attachment to the Qur'ān and the *sunna*, will serve later on to illustrate the artificial nature of the diametrical opposition that has been postulated between the Islam of the *ʿulamā'* and the Islam of the brotherhoods, between an Islam which is pure and one which is hybrid or deviant: for centuries the Naqshbandiyya retained its coherence while bringing together attitudes which some would consider irreconcilable. Its spiritual masters included

26. See for example vol. XVII of *Contributions to Asian Studies*, entitled *Islam in local contexts*, ed. Richard C. Martin, Leiden 1982, in which explicit reference is made to Peter Brown both in the preface and in several of the articles. It is significant that the title of this collection, like that of the original symposium held in 1980 in Dallas, was initially going to be *Islam and Popular Religion*. The title which was chosen instead wisely avoids any *petitio principii*. Cf. also Henry Munson Jr., *The house of Si Abd Allah*, Yale University Press 1984, p. 28; Warren Fusfeld, 'Naqshbandi Sufism and Reformist Islam', in *Ibn Khaldun and Islamic Ideology*, Leiden 1984, pp. 89-110; Jon W. Anderson, 'Conjuring with Ibn Khaldūn', ibid. pp. 111-21.

27. It has come to be thought by some people that ʿAbd al-Qādir was no more than a pious *faqīh* and that his reputation for sainthood merely reflected a later legend. But we possess sources of information about him other than the work of Shaṭṭanūfī, which can assuredly be challenged by historians in spite of its chain of transmission. The judgement of Ibn ʿArabī—of which we will speak later—who arrived in the East a mere forty years after ʿAbd al-Qādir's death, is based on the evidence of several of the latter's immediate followers, particularly Yūnus al-ʿAbbāsī, from whom he received the *khirqa qādiriyya* in Mecca.

many distinguished scholars, rigorous upholders of orthodoxy, and so actively opposed to innovations (*bidaᶜ*) that certain modern authors have represented them under this aspect alone. Yet these same masters were not only wholehearted members of the brotherhoods, but taught and practised initiatic techniques which were based on an extreme concept of sainthood, where the saint, living or dead, is perceived as the pivot of all spiritual realisation.[28]

Many things, moreover, lead us to question the theory of a popular origin for the 'cult of the saints'. Sufism and sainthood are inseparable. In the absence of saints there is no Sufism: it is born of their sainthood, nourished by it, and led to reproduce it. In one sense, although there is no lack of saints from distinguished backgrounds, Sufism has always been 'popular'. The *ahl al-ṣuffa* of Medina, exemplary figures in the nascent community, were mendicants; the great saints of later hagiography were often, like their disciples, blacksmiths, cobblers, or even slaves. They were often poor and frequently unlettered. This is true equally of the most renowned figures of the 'golden age' in the third century of the Hegira as of Ibn ᶜArabī's masters whom Asín Palacios, translating the *Rūḥ al-quds*, calls 'santones', and who were extraordinary men of God. The new element in the twelfth and thirteenth centuries was not the different proportion of saints among the patricians and the plebeians, the learned and the ignorant. In any case, the saints, whether scholars or illiterate, are always those who possess knowledge, the true *ᶜulamā'*, not just miracle-workers and rain-makers. This knowledge, in fact, is their most essential feature. Abū Yaᶜzā, a rough Berber who was unable to speak Arabic, never led the prayers himself; yet if the *imām* whom he had ordered to do so made a mistake in reciting the Qur'ān, he would immediately replace him with another.[29] ᶜAbd al-ᶜAzīz al-Dabbāgh, also illiterate, amazed the learned author of the *Kitāb al-ibrīz*, who was a great reader of Ibn ᶜArabī, by explaining to him some of the difficult passages in the *Futūḥāt*.[30]

What was new was the fact that little by little, within an *umma* riddled with dissension, while on its Eastern as on its Western borders storms were brewing or bursting, Sufism was openly becoming a focus

28. Cf. my 'Quelques aspects des techniques spirituelles dans la *tarīqa naqshbandiyya'* in the proceedings of the *Table ronde sur l'ordre naqshbandī*, Istanbul-Paris 1990.

29. Tādilī, *al-Tashawwuf ilā rijāl al-taṣawwuf*, ed. A. Tawfiq, p. 323.

30. Aḥmad b. al-Mubārak, *Kitāb al-ibrīz*, Cairo 1961 (e.g., pp. 179-80).

of communal integration, which until then it had never been and had never needed to be. Hence the progressive appearance of the *ṭuruq* which, in comparison to the past, were mass organisations. Hence too the clearer affirmation, in doctrinal teaching, of the reasșuring, mediating function of the saints. And hence the progressive transition from free personal practices to collective and formal ones. But there is plenty of evidence to suggest that this was a deliberate adaptation engineered from above—meaning, in the first instance, by the princes. Ibn Taymiyya was not wrong. He railed against the *ᶜāmma*, but he was addressing the sovereigns or the agents of their authority; and the precaution of his discourses does not hide the fact that in inciting them to prohibit the abominations he denounces, he is accusing them of more than negligence: he sees them as veritable adversaries. And it is true that, either through personal conviction or through policy, the Ayyubids, the Mamluks, the Mughals and the Ottomans regularly protected the saints, living or dead, and encouraged the devotion surrounding them.[31] But behind the princes were the princes' counsellors: a spiritual aristocracy whose faith and knowledge are evident in their actions and writings, and whom we have no reason to suspect of coming under the sway of pagan revivals or corrupt idolatries. The part played by ᶜUmar Suhrawardī in the case of the caliph al-Nāṣir, or by Shaykh Manbijī in the case of Baybars, or by Ibn ᶜArabī in the case of Kaykā'ūs the Seljukid or, later, of several members of the Ayyubid family—all these are worth considering as indications of the conscious or deliberate influence exerted by an élite on the changes that occurred. Here again, Ibn Taymiyya is more perceptive than his statements give us reason to believe at first sight, and his vehement heckling is unerringly aimed at judiciously chosen culprits: Karīm al-Dīn Āmulī, the *shaykh al-shuyūkh* of the *khanqā Saᶜīd al-Suᶜadā'*; the influential Shaykh Manbijī; Ibn ᶜAṭā' Allāh, second in succession to Abu-Ḥasan al-Shādhilī and the real founder of the *ṭarīqa* which bears the latter's name; but above all Ibn ᶜArabī, first expounder of a global doctrine of sainthood—a doctrine whose foundation at this particular moment in time can scarcely be conceived as coincidental.

31. In particular, they were often responsible for the mausoleums built on the saints' tombs (the one on Ibn ᶜArabī's tomb was constructed on the orders of Salim I after the conquest of Damascus in 972/1516) and which became centres of devotion for the faithful. They patronized and regulated the *mawālid*, whose prototype was the *mawlid* of the Prophet, first celebrated at the Fatimid court and later, on the initiative of one of Saladin's brothers-in-law, institutionalized in Sunnī Islam.

The debate is open, and it would be premature to do more than call attention to it. Since the researches carried out by Goldziher a hundred years ago, the material has accumulated. But the existing monographs leave many gaps to be filled and are often permeated by pre-conceived ideas (usually the result of the 'two-tiered model') which distort the interpretation of the facts. They certainly disallow any attempt to write a history of sainthood in Islam which would be both a history of the saints and an account of the community's relationship with its saints—a history both of the doctrines and of the practices and attitudes. The present book is no more than a simple documentary contribution to this vast enterprise, one which we hope at a later date to supplement by researching into the function of the saints with respect to the inception of the *ṭuruq*. If the reader comes away with the conviction that in any investigation into Islamic sainthood, the writings of Ibn ᶜArabī constitute a major reference point, which the researcher ignores at the risk of laying himself open to many misinterpretations, our labours will not have been in vain.

But the present work was not conceived with a view to this perspective alone. The saints belong to history. Sainthood, in the understanding of the Shaykh al-Akbar, overshadows history. It has seemed worthwhile, for the sake of those who, indifferent to the controversies we have mentioned, nevertheless sense the importance of Ibn ᶜArabī but have no access to his work, to attempt an organised and faithful presentation of his teaching based solely on the texts—a teaching which merits study on the grounds of its singular greatness alone. On certain points, the succeeding pages furnish facts which have already been indicated by previous writers who have explored the vast corpus of writings by the Shaykh al-Akbar. On others, it is our belief that we have introduced elements which have either escaped their attention or whose correct significance they have failed to appreciate. Although our aim has been to define the main points of the doctrine, we have not attempted to give an exhaustive description of it. It would not be untrue to say that in one sense Ibn ᶜArabī, from the first to the last line of his work, never spoke of anything other than sainthood, of its ways and its goals; and that 'ocean without a shore' (to use a formula dear to the Ṣūfīs) will never be charted in its entirety.

Here I must acknowledge, with no hope of repaying, the debt that I owe to Michel Vâlsan. It was he who, forty years ago, introduced me to the work of Ibn ᶜArabī, of which his own knowledge was both extensive and penetrating, and aided my groping attempts at understanding. It was he, too, who enabled me to grasp the fundamental aspects of his hagiology. My gratitude therefore is addressed first and foremost to his memory.

Several of the themes that will be touched upon here were first broached during the course of a seminar at the École des Hautes Études en Sciences sociales in the years 1982-83 and 1983-84. Thanks are due in particular to François Furet, then president of the École, who so kindly received me into it, and to all those who, like him, encouraged me in my work—Alexandre Bennigsen, Pierra Nora, Lucette Valensi among others—or who agreed to take part in our discussions, notably James W. Morris, J.-L. Michon and Alexandre Popović. Many more were assiduous participants under conditions which were not always comfortable. I cannot name them all, but they should know that this book is a tribute also to their tenacity.

The present edition takes account of remarks and suggestions made to me by some readers of the original edition, among whom I must mention my friend Hermann Landolt and my daughter Claude Chodkiewicz-Addas. She likewise corrected the odd *lapsus calami* or typographical error which had escaped my vigilance.

CHAPTER

1

A Shared Name

I contemplated all the prophets, from Adam to Muḥammad, and God made me contemplate also all those who believe in them, so that there is no one whom I did not see of those who have lived or will live until the Day of the Resurrection, whether they belong to the élite or to the common body of believers. And I observed the degrees of this assembly and knew the rank of all who were in it.[1]

THIS vision, according to the *Fuṣūṣ al-ḥikam*,[2] took place at Cordoba in 586/1190. Ibn ʿArabī, who was born in 560/1165, was thus twenty-five years of age (twenty-six lunar years), and his 'entry upon the way' had taken place only six years previously.[3] Several other texts, written by Ibn ʿArabī himself or by his disciples, furnish us with additional details about this event, of which we will have occasion to speak at greater length. One of these texts[4] tells us that the vision unfolded in two stages. On the first occasion, Ibn ʿArabī saw the Prophets by themselves; on the second, he saw them in the company of all their followers, a fact which enabled him to conclude that the saints (*awliyā'*) walk *ʿalā aqdām al-anbiyā'*), 'in the footsteps of the prophets'—an expression which, as we shall see, is not metaphorical but possesses a precise technical meaning; and in this connection he cites the example of his teacher, Abū 'l-ʿAbbās al-ʿUryabī, who was *ʿalā qadam ʿĪsā*, 'in the footsteps of Jesus'.[5]

This vision, however, important as it is, is only one of many. According to Ṣadr al-Dīn Qūnawī, Ibn ʿArabī's step-son and disciple, 'our teacher had the ability to encounter the spirit of whomsoever he wished among the prophets and saints of the past, in three ways: sometimes he caused those who inhabit that world [of the spirits] to

1. *Futūḥāt* III, p. 323.
2. *Fuṣūṣ al-ḥikam* I, p. 110.
3. *Futūḥāt* II, p. 425.
4. Ibid. III, p. 208.
5. For references to this shaykh, who will be discussed at greater length in Chapter Five, see note 8, p. 76.

descend and perceived them in a subtle corporeal form; sometimes he caused them to be present to him in his sleep; and sometimes he would cast aside his own material form.'[6] It is a fact that the writings of the Shaykh al-Akbar speak of innumerable occasions when he met with the prophets[7] or—especially in the subtle dialogues of the *Book of Theophanies* (*Kitāb al-tajalliyāt*)—with the saints of the past,[8] in a manner as natural as when he speaks of the *awliyā'* of his time whom he knew and visited. Thus it goes without saying that the word 'doctrine' in the title of the present work refers to the written translation of a visionary knowledge and a personal experience of sainthood: we do not find in Ibn ᶜArabī, in connection with this or with any other subject, the systematic exposition of a theory such as a theologian might write. He warns us of this often enough, moreover, when speaking of the conditions under which his works were written: 'I have not written one single letter of this book save by divine dictation (*imlā' ilāhī*) and dominical vouchsafing (*ilqā 'rabbānī*)'.[9] Elsewhere he insists that even the ordering of his subject-matter does not proceed from his own will. If that were the case, he says, the order would be different: for example, the chapter in the *Futūḥāt* on the *sharīᶜa*, the divine Law, should logically speaking come before the chapters on ritual prescriptions, whereas in fact it occurs some way after them.[10] Thus, only a tortuous progress through the thousands of pages which make up his work, and a comparative reading of texts which may at first sight appear contradictory, make it possible to demonstrate the coherence of his teaching and to understand

6. Quoted by Ibn al-ᶜImād, *Shadharāt al-dhahab*, Beirut, n.d., v, p. 196 (year 638).

7. See for example *Futūḥāt* I, p. 151; IV, pp. 77, 184.

8. The *Kitāb al-tajalliyāt* was edited at Hyderabad in 1948, and again in Beirut (n.d.). Osman Yahia has brought out a new edition of it with two commentaries, one by Ibn Sawdakīn (a disciple of Ibn ᶜArabī, who simply transcribes the commentary delivered by the Shaykh al-Akbar himself), and the other anonymous (attributed by Brockelmann to ᶜAbd al-Karīm al-Jīlī), entitled *Kashf al-ghāyāt* (in the review *al-Mashriq*, 1966-67). Several chapters of the *Kitāb al-tajalliyāt* give an account of meetings with a whole series of people who lived several centuries prior to Ibn ᶜArabī, such as Junayd, al-Ḥallāj, Dhu' l-Nun al-Miṣri, Sahl al-Tustarī, etc.

9. *Futūḥāt* III, p. 457.

10. Ibid. II, p. 163. On the inspiration for Ibn ᶜArabī's writing, see also—among other texts—*Futūḥāt* I, p. 59; ibid. III, p. 334; and the prologue to the *Fuṣūṣ*: a work which, according to him, was delivered to him, during a vision he had at Damascus in 627/1229, by the prophet Muḥammad himself (*Fuṣūṣ* I, p. 47).

its implications. The reader must not be surprised if at times in the course of this journey the wood cannot be seen for the trees.

Ibn ᶜArabī's claim to be divinely inspired (either directly or, as in the case of the *Fuṣūṣ al-ḥikam* which he received from the Prophet's own hands, indirectly), his recourse, on almost every page, to the evidence of the invisible world, the difficulty, ultimately, of grasping his doctrine in all its breadth and shades of meaning through the profusion of its statements and the diversity of its successive points of view—these are sufficient, doubtless, to explain in part the violent attacks made on his doctrine of sainthood. Blindness and bad faith would do the rest. 'The spirit from whom the writer of the *Futūḥāt* claims to have received this work is a devilish spirit', declared Ibn Taymiyya (d. 728/1328); and in support of this view he cites an account given by Shaykh Najm al-Dīn ibn al-Ḥakīm, who was present at the funeral of Ibn ᶜArabī in 638/1240: 'My arrival in Damascus coincided with the death of Ibn ᶜArabī. I saw his funeral procession and it was as though covered with a rain of ashes. I realized that it in no way resembled the funeral processions of the *awliyā'*.'[11] But Ibn Taymiyya, not content with such impressionistic observations, wrote a lengthy pamphlet in which he systematically criticized the ideas of Ibn ᶜArabī and his school on the *awliyā'*, and which he entitled *al-Farq bayna awliyā' al-Raḥmān wa awliyā' al–Shayṭān*: 'On the difference between the saints of God and the saints of Satan'.[12] He could not have made it more clear! Against this, as against certain other themes (Ibn ᶜArabī's supposed 'pantheism', his interpretation of the Qur'ānic verses concerning Pharaoh in the story of Moses, and of the verses relating to infernal punishment etc.), a polemical campaign was unleashed at the end of the thirteenth century, just at the time when, in Paris, two hundred and nineteen propositions of the 'Latin Averroists' (among them Siger of Brabant, whom Dante was to place in Paradise) were being branded as 'heretical' by Etienne Tempier.[13] The campaign continues to this day. Osman Yahia lists

11. Ibn Taymiyya, *Majmūᶜ fatāwā Shaykh al-Islām Aḥmad b. Taymiyya*, Riyadh 1340-82, XI, p. 511 (the account of Shaykh Najm al-Dīn comes in the *Majmūᶜat al-rasā'il wa l-masā'il*, ed. Rashīd Riḍā, IV, p. 77).

12. Ibn Taymiyya, *Majmūᶜ fatāwā*, XI, pp. 156-310.

13. The accusations made in both cases have many points of resemblance: the heretical interpretation of scriptural and traditional teaching on the pains of hell, the eternity of the world, sexual licence (a constantly recurring theme in Sakhāwī's work. Cf. *al-Qawl al-munbī*, ms. Berlin 2849, Spr. 790, e.g. fos. 17a, 97b). The accusation of *ibāḥa* (antinomianism), a classic anti-Ṣūfī allegation, formalized by

thirty-four works and one hundred and thirty-eight *fatwās* (jurists' *responsae*) between the seventh century of the Hegira and the end of the ninth which are hostile to Ibn ᶜArabī; and this list is not exhaustive for it does not take into account many authors of merely local repute, nor the literature written in Persian.[14] These diatribes were repeated from generation to generation, and usually derived the essential part of their argument from the register of 'reprehensible propositions' compiled by Ibn Taymiyya;[15] and, although they never came to an end, they acquired renewed vigour at the end of the last century with the *salafiyya* movement.[16] More recently, they have been revived with considerable violence in Egypt, where the debates in the press, on the radio and even in Parliament resulted in a ban being imposed (it has since been lifted) on the critical edition of the *Futūḥāt Makkiyya*, undertaken by Osman Yahia. This campaign started with an open letter published in the daily newspaper *al-Akhbār* on the 14th November 1975. Here as elsewhere, one of the *questiones disputatae* which obsessed Ibn ᶜArabī's critics concerned the nature and forms of sainthood.[17]

The critics of the Shaykh al-Akbar usually opposed those of his ideas which they judged heretical with facts taken from the scriptures and with the opinions or practices of 'pious men of the past'—meaning the Prophet's companions and the Sufis of the early Islamic era. Before embarking on an exposition of Ibn ᶜArabī's doctrine, therefore, we must

---

Ibn al-Jawzī in his *Talbīs Iblīs* (Cairo n.d., pp. 351-56), and often lodged against Ibn ᶜArabī, is directly contradicted by his views on the divine Law (*sharīᶜa*), to which we will return.

14. Osman Yahia also lists thirty-five *fatwās* which are favourable to the Shaykh al-Akbar. With regard to the hostile *fatwās*, we should note that Yahia's principal source is the *Qawl al-munbī* by Sakhāwī (died 902/1497). But the 500 or so folios of this work are frequently reduced to a catalogue of gossip or spiky remarks which cannot easily be regarded as *fatwās stricto sensu*. Of course, this does not make the polemic less violent and far-reaching.

15. On this subject, see the PhD thesis of Cyrille Chodkiewicz, Paris IV, November 1984, 'Les Premieres Polemiques autour d'Ibn ᶜArabī: Ibn Taymiyya', and on the subject of sainthood in particular, see. pp. 142-221 of the same work.

16. On the position adopted by the *salafiyya* with regard to the saints, and on the cult of saints in Sufism, see J. Jomier, *Le Commentaire coranique du Manār*, Paris 1954, chapter 7.

17. See the articles by Shaykh Kamāl Aḥmad ᶜAwn (Dalālāt fī kitāb al-Futūḥāt) in the review *Liwā' al-islām*, first five numbers of 1976, especially May-June, pp. 32-39, and September-October, pp. 23-30.

return to the source *par excellence*, which is the Qur'ān. But first we must draw attention to a tricky problem of terminology.

The word *walī*, plural *awliyā'*, from the root *w.l.y.*, is translated here, in conformity with established usage and for lack of a better term, by the word 'saint'. Without anticipating the analogies or the differences which will come to light later between the nature and function of a *walī* in the economy of Islamic spirituality and those of the saints in other religions, we must observe at once that, from a strictly etymological point of view, the true equivalents of the terms 'saint' or 'sainthood' should be formed from the root *q.d.s.*, which expresses the idea of purity and inviolability, and hence corresponds appropriately to the Greek *hagios* and the Latin *sanctus* (Hebrew *qādōsh*). Alternatively, they should be formed from the root *ḥ.r.m.*, which, while expressing a notion different in principle (the notion of 'sacredness', translated in Greek by *hieros* and in Latin by *sacer*), in practice is not always distinguishable from the idea of sainthood: in English 'the holy' means 'the sacred', but 'the holy man' usually means 'the saintly man'. Now, neither the words derived from the root *q.d.s.* nor those derived from the root *h.r.m.*, are normally applied to a person designated by the term *walī*, with the exception, in the case of *q.d.s.*, of the posthumously spoken traditional eulogy, *qaddasa 'Llāhu sirrahu*, 'May God sanctify his secret!' On the other hand, it is interesting to note that in Christian Arabic terminology, the word *qiddīs* is used to designate the saints. This discrepancy between two vocabularies within the same language, although easily explained by historical considerations, is nevertheless worth bearing in mind.

The primary meaning of *w.l.y.* is proximity or contiguity, and this in turn gives rise to two further meanings. One of these is 'to be a friend', and the other is 'to direct, to govern, to take in charge'. Thus, the *walī*, properly speaking, is the 'friend', he who is close; but, as Ibn Manẓūr emphasizes in the *Lisān al-ʿarab*, he is also the *nāṣir*, 'he who assists', and the *mudabbir*, he who disposes.

Here we must insert a parenthesis. If (for the sake of convenience, and because we will define the analogies and differences between the semantic values of the two terms later on) we translate the word *walī* as 'saint', what is the Arabic word corresponding to 'sainthood'? We find the words *wilāya* and *walāya* used concurrently. For Henry Corbin, who establishes a categorical distinction between the two, the use, current in Sufism, of *wilāya* (which is generally accepted as implying the notion of *auctoritas*) is a spiritual misconstruction which demonstrates the ambiguity of 'an imamology which dares not reveal its name'.[18] We will come back to this assertion, and to similar ones which, especially in the case of Ibn ʿArabī, reduce *taṣawwuf* to nothing more than crypto-Shīʿism.

From the strictly linguistic point of view, it is beyond doubt that the *fiʿāla* pattern (*wazn*) on which the word *wilāya* is constructed is normally used to express the execution of a *function*. Thus, *khilāfa* signifies the function of a caliph, *imāra* the function of an emir; similarly *wilāya*, in political and administrative terminology, signifies the function of a *wālī* (with a long *ā*)—a governor or prefect—and by extension his realm of competence. The *faʿāla* pattern on which *walāya* is modelled expresses a *state of being*, and would thus appear to be a more adequate basis for the term denoting the nature of a *walī* (with a short *a*), that which makes him what he is. Nevertheless, the original manuscripts of the Sufi texts, when they are vocalized—for *wilāya* and *walāya* are indistinguishable in the written form—betray a hesitation between the use of the two terms. The spoken language, and particularly that spoken in the *ṭuruq* in the Arab countries, exhibits a clear preference for *wilāya*, a vocalization that appears to be based on a long tradition. In part at least, this preference can probably be explained by a consideration for euphony which often leads Arabic speakers to turn a short *a* into an *i* when it occurs near a long *ā*. But there may be other reasons, and this preference is not unrelated to the way in which the *walī* is perceived in the Muslim community: for the *ʿāmma*, the common run of believers, the powers with which a *walī* is invested are more evident and of a more obviously immediate importance than the essential characteristics from which such powers actually arise. However that may be, the opposition between *walāya* and *wilāya* should not be exaggerated. Arabic lexicographers, for their part, put forward various arguments about the precise meanings to be attached to these two words and the relationship between them; but, after citing the different opinions on the matter, they are manifestly hesitant to come to a decision. Let us observe in passing that for a late Roman, *amicitia*, the usual term for defining one's relationship with a patron saint, also connoted (as Peter Brown says) the idea of 'friendship' in the broad sense, and the idea of protection and power: both *walāya* and *wilāya*.[19]

18. Cf. *En Islam iranien*, Paris 1971, I, p. 48, note 20, and III, pp. 9-10.

19. Cf. *Lisān al-ʿarab*, Beirut, n.d., XV, p. 407; *Tāj al-ʿarūs*, place and date unknown, X, p. 398 ff. On contemporary usage, see also *al-Muʿjam al-wasīṭ*,

The fact remains that the best argument in favour of *walāya*, from the point adopted here, is that this term, unlike *wilāya*, possesses Qur'ānic references—something which for the Sufi masters and certainly for Ibn ʿArabī was sufficient reason for preferring it. It actually occurs twice over: on the first occasion it is applied to men, and is connected (significantly) with the term *awliyā'* which comes into the same verse (Qur'ān 8:72), and on the second occasion it has reference to God (Qur'ān 18:44). We will therefore retain the form *walāya*, without however condemning the concurrent use of *wilāya*. This cautiousness is strengthened by the fact that, just to complicate matters, the scriptural argument is not as conclusive as it might appear: of the seven traditional 'readings' of the Qur'ān retained by Ibn Mujāhid, the Ḥamza reading of these two verses has *wilāya*, whereas the other six have *walāya*.[20]

Furthermore, the occurrences in the Qur'ān of the root *w.l.y.* are manifold: it appears, in different forms, two hundred and twenty-seven times. *Walī* and its plural *awliyā'* occur with widely divergent meanings. The meaning can be positive, as in verse 10:62 where mention is made of *awliyā' Allāh*, the 'saints of God' who are exposed 'neither to fear nor to affliction': *Lā khawfun ʿalayhim wa lā hum yaḥzanūn*. This expression, by a subtle play of echo, reveals that the establishment of *walāya* is coincident with the starting point of the human cycle, for it is found again in the text (Qur'ān 2:38) in the divine speech addressed to Adam after his fault is pardoned (God has 'come back to him': *fa-tāba ʿalayhi*), when he is sent to earth in order to carry out his mandate as *khalīfa* or *locum tenens*. Other verses carry a negative connotation, such as verse 4:76 which speaks of the *awliyā' al-shayṭān*, the 'saints of Satan'—an expression which was to furnish Ibn Taymiyya with the title of the work already referred to, and which holds the mysterious suggestion of a 'counter-sainthood', a hierarchy which is the symmetrical inversion of the hierarchy of the 'saints of God' and which likewise possesses a Pole.[21]

---

published by the Arabic Academy in Cairo, 1961, p. 1070. Orientalists are themselves divided on the question: Massignon sometimes employs *wilāya* and at other times *walāya*; ʿAfifī, in his thesis on Ibn ʿArabī, and P. Nwyia in his *Exegèse coranique et langage mystique* (both of them native Arabic speakers) employ *wilāya*. On the use of *amicitia* in Christian terminology, cf. Peter Brown, *Society and the Holy in Late Antiquity*, London 1982.

20. Rāzī's *Tafsīr*, Tehran, n.d., vx, p. 210, in connection with verse 8:72.

21. The 'pole' of the 'saints of Satan' is no other than the *Dajjāl* or impostor, who is not only identified with the Antichrist but also represents a function of which the Antichrist is the ultimate possessor. (Cf. Shaʿrānī, *Mukhtaṣar tadhkirat*

On the other hand, although *walī* can be applied to man, it is also one of the divine Names; and for Ibn ᶜArabī, as we shall see, this point is of enormous importance: 'Allāh is the *Walī* of those who believe; He causes them to come out of darkness into the light' (Qur'ān 2:257). 'Allāh is the *Walī* of the pious' (45:19). The Muslim exegetes, although unable at times to resist the inclusion of somewhat arbitrarily distinguished shades of meaning, attempted to classify the different meanings of *walī* in the sacred Book. Muqātil (eighth century) detected ten meanings[22] which can in fact be reduced to two. The first is directly related to the idea of proximity which, as we saw, is the primary meaning of the root, and signifies, according to the context, 'friend', 'companion', 'relative', 'ally', 'counsellor'. The second meaning is 'protector' or 'governor'. The existence of these two classes of meaning is connected with the very nature of the word *walī*. This word is constructed on the ambivalent *faᶜīl* pattern which in Arabic can possess both an active sense (normally expressed by the form *fāᶜil*) and a passive sense (corresponding to the form *mafᶜūl*). Thus the *walī* is simultaneously one who is close, the beloved, he who is protected, taken in charge, and the protector, the 'patron' (in the Roman sense), the governor (*al-walī*, the active participle constructed on the *fāᶜil*) paradigm. Ibn ᶜArabī was, moreover, to extract major doctrinal consequences from the ambivalence of the *faᶜīl*-based divine Names in the Qur'ān, demonstrating for example that *al-ᶜAlīm*, usually translated as 'the Knower', signifies God in His capacity as both *al-ᶜĀlim* (He who knows) and *al-Maᶜlūm* (He who is known): the sole Knower and the sole Known in all known things.[23]

All the doctrinal developments of the concepts *walī* and *walāya* arise

---

al-Qurṭubī, Aleppo 1395 AH, p. 179, where he quotes a *ḥadīth* according to which the number of *dajjālūn* approaches thirty; cf. also Suyūṭī, *al-Jāmiᶜ al-ṣaghīr*, Cairo 1954, II, p. 78, who quotes another *ḥadīth* which states that there will be twenty-seven, 'four of them women').

22. P. Nwyia, *Exegèse coranique et langage mystique*, Beirut 1970, pp. 114-15.

23. *Futūḥāt* III, p. 300. There is another word from the root *w.l.y.* which is frequently employed in the Qur'ān and which possesses, for different reasons, the same ambivalence as *walī*, so that it can be applied sometimes to God and sometimes to man. This is the word *mawlā*, an approximate translation of which may be either 'patron' or 'client'—in the Roman sense—and which is part of the 'false *aḍdād*'; the words, that is, which can be used impartially to designate either side of a relationship, as in the French 'hôte'.

out of the Qur'ān and lead back to it. But meditation on the revealed Book is enriched through meditation on the *ḥadīth* (pl. *aḥādīth*), the words spoken by the Prophet. Here again derivatives from the root *w.l.y.* are frequent.[24] For the moment, we will limit ourselves to a few of the most-quoted *aḥadīth* in the writings of *taṣawwuf*, ignoring the slight variations present in the different readings. It should be noted that in most cases these are *aḥadīth qudsiyya*, where God Himself speaks in the first person through the mouth of the Prophet. 'The most enviable of My *awliyā'* close to Me is a believer whose possessions are few, whose joy is prayer, who accomplishes the service of his Lord to perfection and obeys Him in secret. He is obscure among men and no one points at him . . ..'[25] 'Know that God has servants who are neither prophets nor martyrs and who are envied by the prophets and martyrs for their position and their nearness to God . . . on the Day of Resurrection thrones of light will be placed at their disposal. Their faces will be of light . . .. These are the *awliyā'* of God.'[26]

Another *ḥadīth—man ʿādā lī waliyyan . . .*—is repeated over and over in countless texts and plays a major role in Ibn ʿArabī's teaching on *walāya*. Since we give the full text later on, together with the Shaykh al-Akbar's commentary, the first line only is quoted here: 'I declare war on him who is my *walī*'s enemy'.[27] Mention should also be made of two further *aḥadīth* which are of importance in defining the *walī*: 'Among My servants, My *awliyā'* are those who remember Me' (or 'who invoke Me', *yadhkurūna bi-dhikrī*);[28] 'For My *awliyā'* I have set aside ninety-nine Mercies . . ..'[29] In the course of this work we will come across many other prophetic traditions, and the interpretation of these by the Sufi masters will prove essential to an understanding of the *walī*. But we may as well say at once that it is the Prophet's very *being* which is the definitive key to the secret of the name that is shared between God and man.

24. Cf. Wensinck, *Concordances et indices de la Tradition musulmane*, VII, pp. 322-36.

25. Tirmidhī, *zuhd*, 35; Ibn Ḥanbal, V, pp. 252, 260; Ibn ʿArabī, *Mishkāt al-anwār*, *ḥadīth* no. 3.

26. Tirmidhī, *zuhd*, 53; Ibn Ḥanbal, V, pp. 229, 239, 341, 342, 343.

27. Bukhārī, *riqāq*, 38; Ibn Māja, *fitan*, 16; Ibn ʿArabī, *Mishkāt*, no. 91.

28. Ibn Ḥanbal, III, p. 430.

29. Ibid., II, p. 514.

CHAPTER

2

'He who sees thee sees Me'

OUR first brief survey has allowed us to glimpse in the words *walī* and *walāya* two complementary meanings. The most general of these attaches to the notion of 'proximity' (*qurb*)—hence the use of these words to express kinship; and the other, which derives from the first, to the notion of 'taking in charge' or 'governing'. These two series of semantic values, conveyed by the root and confirmed by scriptural references, determine, implicitly or explicitly and to the exclusion of neither, each and every definition of the word *walī*, 'saint'. For Ibn Taymiyya,[1] the *awliyā'* are purely and simply the *muqarrabūn*, 'those who are close': a Qur'ānic term signifying the highest category of the chosen, beyond the binary distinction of the 'People of the Right' and the 'People of the Left'; it is a category also called in the Qur'ān (56:10-11) *sābiqūn*, 'those who go before', or the 'forerunners'. In the fourteenth century, Jurjānī (who, in his *Taᶜrīfāt*, clearly distinguishes between *walāya* and *wilāya* making them correspond respectively to the state of the *walī* and to his cosmic functions) defines *walāya* as the proximity [of God].[2] Similarly, in the eighteenth century, Ibn ᶜAjība gives *al-uns* as the equivalent of *walāya*: intimacy (with God).[3] Ibn ᶜArabī, on the other hand, sometimes emphasizes the idea of divine assistance (*nuṣra*). 'The *awliyā'*,' he writes, 'are those of whom God has taken charge by aiding them (*hum al-ladhīna tawallāhum Allāh bi-nuṣratihi*: the verb *tawallā* used here is derived from the root *w.l.y.*) in their battles against the four enemies: the passions (*al-hawā*), the ego (*al-nafs*), the world (*al-dunyā*) and the devil (*al-shayṭān*).'[4]

But the texts we have been quoting are, relatively speaking, late. What was the position at the beginning of the Islamic era? According to

1. Ibn Taymiyya, *Majmūᶜat al-rasā'il* I, p. 40.
2. Jurjānī, *Taᶜrīfāt*, Istanbul 1327 AH, p. 172.
3. J.-L. Michon, *Le Soufi marocain Aḥmad Ibn ᶜAjība et son miᶜrāj*, Paris 1973, p. 204.
4. *Futūḥāt* II, p. 53.
5. Hujwīrī, *Kashf al-maḥjūb*, trans. R. A. Nicholson, London 1911, p. 44.

a sarcastic comment reported by Hujwīrī,[5] *taṣawwuf* (a word that, since publication in 1821 by Tholluck of his *Ssufismus, sive theosophia Persarum pantheistica,* has been rather awkwardly translated as 'Sufism') 'is today a name without reality, whereas it was once a reality without a name'. Bearing in mind the spiritual brilliance of the era in which this curt judgement was pronounced, the first part of this statement must be seen as a mere paradox intended to stimulate the zeal of novices, but the second part has a basis in history: the first recorded appearance of the term *ṣūfī* dates from the middle of the second century of the Hegira (eighth century CE), when it was applied in Kufa to the famous Jābir ibn Ḥayyān, a follower of Jaᶜfar al-Ṣādiq. In the same way, in the case of *walāya,* the thing existed before the word. According again to Hujwīrī, it was actually al-Ḥakīm al-Tirmidhī who in the ninth century introduced the term into the technical vocabulary of Sufism, where it had not previously existed.[6] Hujwīrī was aware, of course, that the terms *walāya, walī,* and *awliyā',* which were part of the vocabulary of the Qur'ān and the *ḥadīth,* could not have been totally unknown for two centuries; but any evidence we possess of their use prior to this date does not contradict his statement. This is corroborated, indeed, by a fact of more importance than the mere introducing of a term: although some of Tirmidhī's contemporaries, such as Sahl al-Tustarī in his *Tafsīr* (of which more later) and Abū Saᶜīd al-Kharrāz in his *Rasā'il* throw light on the concept of *walāya,* Tirmidhī himself is indeed the first author to provide a greatly expanded doctrinal exposition of it, which is sufficient to explain the place occupied by his work in the writings of Ibn ᶜArabī on this subject.

Tirmidhī was born in Khorasan, and died at a very advanced age at the beginning of the fourth century of the Hegira. According to his pupil Abū Bakr al-Warrāq, he had been a disciple of al-Khaḍir (or Khizr, to transcribe the Persian form of his name), the immortal itinerant initiator, who used to visit him every Sunday.[7] His view on the problem of *walāya* apparently led him to be accused of being a *mutanabbī*—of laying claim, that is, to the dignity of the prophets; he was denounced to the governor of Balkh and underwent painful trials. His major work,

6. Ibid., p. 210. This section of the *Kashf al-maḥjūb* on the *ḥakīmiyya,* the followers of al-Ḥakīm al-Tirmidhī, illustrates the confusion which surrounds the meaning to be attributed to the terms *walāya* and *wilāya* respectively.

7. Ibid., p. 141. See also p. 142, the anecdote reported by Abū Bakr al-Warrāq, in which Khaḍir also figures.

the *Kitāb Khatm al-awliyā'* (*The Book of the Seal of the Saints*, probably written around 260/873), was long thought to be lost, and was known only through the quotations from it in Ibn ʿArabī's *Futūḥāt Makkiyya*. The discovery of two manuscripts in Istanbul about thirty years ago (a third has since been identified in London) has enabled Osman Yahia to bring out a first critical edition of this work.[8]

The *Khatm al-awliyā'* is far from being a treatise containing a systematic exposition of the author's ideas on *walāya*. Thus, in Osman Yahia's division of it into twenty-nine chapters, the idea of a 'Seal of the Saints' appears in chapter eight, recurs in chapter thirteen, and is the subject of chapter twenty-five. The remarkable text, which takes the form of a tortuous dialogue between Tirmidhī and one of his followers, is first and foremost the record of a spiritual experience that is discreetly veiled by an impersonal tone. The subject of it is defined in the first lines:

> You have just mentioned the debate aroused by some people on the subject of *walāya*. You have asked questions about *walāya*, about the dwellings of the *awliyā'*, about the implications of putting one's faith in them. You asked whether the *walī* is conscious or not of his state of being, because you have heard it said that those who possess *walāya* have no awareness of it. Finally, you asked about those who think that they are in possession of it even though they are in fact far from being so. Know, in truth, that those who talk about *walāya* know nothing about it

8. *Kitāb Khatm al-awliyā'*, Beirut 1965. Osman Yahia, in his dissertation for the diploma of the École pratique des Hautes Études, has made an (unpublished) translation of this work. The dissertation contains (pp. 41-69) a bibliography of Tirmidhī's works (cf. also *GAL* I, p. 199, and *S* I, 355; *GAS* I, pp. 653-59). To our knowledge, the only published works of his, apart from the *Khatm al-awliyā'*, are the *Kitāb al-riyāḍa wa adab al-nafs*, ed. Arberry, Cairo 1947; the *Bayān al-farq bayna 'l-ṣadr wa 'l-qalb wa 'l-fu'ād wa 'l-lubb*, ed. Nicholas Heer, Cairo 1958; and *al-Ḥajj wa-asrāruhu*, ed. Ḥusnī Naṣr Zaydān, Cairo 1969. On Tirmidhī himself see the translation of the principal passages from his spiritual autobiography, *Bad' al-sha'n*, in Osman Yahia's introduction to his translation of the *Khatm*; ʿAṭṭār, *Tadhkirat al-awliyā'*, ed. Nicholson, London 1905-7, II, pp. 91-99; L. Massignon, *Essai sur les origines du lexique technique de la mystique musulmane*, Paris 1954, pp. 286-94 (a superficial and somewhat malicious piece, written, moreover, at a time when Massignon had no access to the text of the *Khatm*); ʿAbd al-Muḥsin al-Ḥusaynī, *al-Maʿrifa ʿinda 'l-Ḥakīm al-Tirmidhī*, Cairo, n.d. (in any case prior to the following work in which it is quoted); ʿAbd al-Fattāḥ ʿAbdallāh Baraka, *Al-Ḥakīm al-Tirmidhī wa-naẓariyyatuhu fī 'l-walāya*, Cairo 1971, 2 vols. (of which the first is biographical); M. I. el-Geyoushi, 'Al-Tirmidhī's Theory of Saints and Sainthood', *Islamic Quarterly* XV (1971), pp. 17-61; B. Radtke, *Al-Ḥakīm al-Tirmidhī, Ein islamischer Theosoph des 3/9 Jahrhunderts*, Freibourg 1980; Aḥmad ʿAbd al-Raḥīm al-Ṣabīḥ, *al-Sulūk ʿinda 'l-Ḥakīm al-Tirmidhī*, Cairo 1988.

whatsoever. They try to perceive it with a knowledge which is external, and they express only their personal opinions or else rely on fallacious analogies. Such people do not find favour with their Lord. They have no access to the dwelling places of *walāya* and have no conception of the way in which Allāh operates.[9]

A fundamental distinction is made at the beginning of the work. It is based on the idea of *Ḥaqq Allāh,* which strictly speaking means 'the right of Allāh', that right which is the consequence of His Absolute suzerainty over all beings. For Tirmidhī, it is essential not to confuse the *walī ḥaqq Allāh* with the *walī Allāh ḥaqqan.* These are actually two modalities, or, rather, two stages of the spiritual life. One is founded on the practice of *ṣidq*—veracity or sincerity, the greatest of all the virtues—which involves the total fulfilment of all obligations, both inner and external, arising out of the 'feudal' relationship between the vassal and his lord. The other is based on the operation of grace (*minna*). In the first of these cases the person is characterised by *ᶜibāda,* 'observance'; in the second he is characterised by *ᶜubūdiyya,* a word derived from the same root but which can be rendered as 'servitude' and which, in Tirmidhī as in Ibn ᶜArabī, signifies the awareness of a radical ontological indigence. *ᶜIbāda,* which is situated on the level of action, does not totally exclude the illusion of autonomy; *ᶜubūdiyya,* which has reference to being, does away with this illusion once and for all. The 'right of God' over a created being has as its implicit corollary the right of the created being over the Creator: the *walī ḥaqq Allāh,* whose sainthood consists in serving the right of God, gives in order to receive. The *walī Allāh,* on the other hand, serves God alone and has nothing to exchange. But his absolute servitude constitutes the empty space within which Absolute Plenitude is displayed; and this is why one of the characteristics of authentic *walāya,* or rather the guarantee of its authenticity, is, according to Tirmidhī, the descent of *sakīna*: the 'Peace' and also, in accordance with the etymology, the 'Presence' of God. It is not surprising, therefore, that one of the external signs whereby we may recognize a true *walī* is as expressed in the *ḥadīth*: 'The saints among you are those whom one cannot see without remembering Allāh'.[10] The essential feature of the *awliyā'* is the transparency which makes them the privileged vehicles of theophany.

9. The translation used here corresponds, with very slight modifications, to that of Osman Yahia, op. cit., pp. 100-1 (pp. 114-16 of the Arabic text).

10. Ibid., p. 166 (p. 361 of the Arabic). Cf. also pp. 177-79 (pp. 372-74 of the Arabic). On this *ḥadīth*, cf. Suyūṭī, *al-Fatḥ al-kabīr*, Cairo 1351 AH, I, p. 214.

A question arises here which had inevitably to be confronted in Islam by any doctrine of spiritual perfection, whatever the terms used to describe its forms and stages: what is the relationship between the *walī* on the one hand, and the *nabī* (prophet) or *rasūl* (messenger) on the other? Here we touch on the particular point in Tirmidhī's doctrine which aroused the ire of some *fuqahā'* and which caused him, throughout a whole period of his life, to be persecuted, as he says in a short autobiographical document entitled *Bad' al-sha'n*. According to him, both *nubuwwa* and *risāla* have an end, which coincides with the end of the world. When the Day of Resurrection dawns, the eschatological message and the promulgation of the divine Law, which are the respective missions of the *nabī* and the *rasūl* (we may recall that every *rasūl* is a *nabī* but not vice versa) will no longer have a point: with the consummation of the centuries, the time of faith and of the law is over. *Walāya*, on the other hand, subsists to eternity, which explains why God himself is called *walī* although neither *nabī* nor *rasūl* have a place among the divine Names. This does not in the least mean that the *awliyā'* are superior to the prophets and the messengers: every *rasūl* and every *nabī* is above all and by definition a *walī*. *Walāya* is superior to *nubuwwa* or *risāla* in the *persons* of the prophets and messengers; it is the hidden and enduring face of their being; and the mandate which they execute here below represents only its external and transitory aspect. An initial link is thus clearly established between prophetology and hagiology, which Ibn ᶜArabī was later to elucidate.

What is meant, however, by the 'Seal of the Saints', the title of Tirmidhī's work? Here again, it was Ibn ᶜArabī who defined its nature and function. Tirmidhī, although he speaks of it several times both here and elsewhere, only gives vague hints as to the meaning of the term, which no one before him appears to have used. It is

> 'the proof of God before the *awliyā'*. To these God will say: 'Oh you assembled *awliyā'*! I bestowed my *walāya* upon you but you did not protect it from the interference of the ego. Now behold, it has been given to the weakest and youngest among you to contain truly within himself *walāya* in all its wholeness, to the total exclusion of his ego. And this is from all eternity, by virtue of a special grace from God with regard to his servant, on whom He will confer the Seal so as to rejoice the heart of Muḥammad [literally: to refresh his eye] and to put Satan aside . . . [On the day of Resurrection] Muḥammad will come furnished with the Seal [of Prophethood] and will be a surety for created beings against the terror of the Judgement; and this saint will come, likewise furnished with his seal, and for the

awliyā' who have need of him he will be the guarantee of the authenticity of *walāya.*[11]

In another text quoted by Osman Yahia,[12] Tirmidhī gives a lyrical description of the *Khatm al-awliyā'* which deserves to be recorded:

He is a servant whom God has taken into his charge.
He is under the divine aegis; he speaks through God, hears
 through God,
He listens, sees, acts and meditates through God.
God has made him famous throughout the world
And has established him as the *imām* of created beings.
He is the keeper of the emblem of the *awliyā'*
The surety of the inhabitants of the earth,
The spectacle of the beings of heaven.
Flower of paradise, chosen one of God, object of His gaze,
Mine of His secrets, scourge of His justice,
Through him God quickens hearts,
Through him He guides created beings along the Way,
Through him He enforces the divine laws.
This being is the key to the right direction,
The flaming torch of the earth
Guardian of the registers of the Saints
And their guide.
He alone gives God the praises that are due to Him . . .
He is the lord of the saints
He is the Wisest of the Wise . . .

While this may appear fairly enigmatic, the *Kitāb Khatm al-awliyā'* contains an even more mysterious section: the long questionnaire which makes up the fourth chapter of Osman Yahia's edition of the book. Challenging the claims of those who 'talk like the *awliyā'*' without possessing the necessary qualifications, these one hundred and fifty-seven questions are given with no answers and no commentary. 'What is *sakīna*?' 'What is meant by the *ḥadīth*: God created creatures in a darkness? What was their condition in this darkness?' 'What is

11. O. Yahia, ibid., pp. 232-33 (p. 422 of the Arabic). The translation has been slightly modified. At the end of the second paragraph of the Arabic text, the reading which makes most sense is *fa-ḥtāju ilayhi 'l-awliyā'*, not *fa-ḥāju ilā 'l-awliyā'*.

12. Ibid., p. 91 (adapted from the *Nawādir al-uṣūl*, pp. 157-58).

meant by the *ḥadīth*: Allāh has one hundred and seventeen qualities? What are these qualities?' 'What words will Allāh address to the Messengers on the Day of Resurrection?' 'What are the Keys of Generosity?' 'How many stages are there in prophethood?' 'What is prostration? How did it begin?' 'What is the primordial Name from which all other Names proceed?' 'Where is the door which reveals the hidden Name to created beings?' In most cases, there is no obvious logical sequence to these questions, whose very form is often so cryptic that before envisaging a reply one would like to be sure of having understood the nature of the question. As far as we know, for three centuries no one ventured to pass this test, which the sage of Tirmidh imposed on any person who thought himself worthy to attain to the secret of *walāya*. It fell to Ibn ʿArabī, first in a short unedited treatise entitled *al-Jawāb al-Mustaqīm ʿammā sa'ala ʿanhu al-Tirmidhī al-Ḥakīm* (*The Reply to the Questions of Tirmidhī al-Ḥakīm*), and then at greater length in chapter seventy-three of the *Futūḥāt*, to take up the challenge triumphantly.[13] It was a spiritual tournament between two solitaries, confronting each other across the ages.

In spite of its sometimes sybilline statements and the apparent lack of organization, for those who knew how to read it, the *Kitāb khatm al-awliyā'* clarified certain essential aspects of *walāya*. Yet this first step towards a doctrinal exposition remained for a long time without a successor. This may possibly have been because the subject-matter cannot be handled without seeming to call into question prophetic privilege, and therefore needed to be approached with extreme caution as regards language.

The scandal raised by Tirmidhī's assertions, and perhaps by his followers' imprudent remarks, may serve to explain the circumspection of later writers on this theme. We will leave the theologians out of it: one might expect, for example, a writer such as Bāqillānī (tenth century) to come up with some definitions. He devoted a work to the difference between *muʿjizāt* (miracles of the prophets), *karāmāt* (miracles of the saints), sorcery, and prestidigitation.[14] Yet he confines himself to affirming, as against the Muʿtazilites, the possibility of

13. *Futūḥāt* II, pp. 40-128; O. Yahia, in his edition of the *Khatm*, gives the text of the replies in the *Jawāb mustaqīm*, as well as excerpts from the corresponding text in the *Futūḥāt* (pp. 142-326).

14. Bāqillānī, *Kitāb bayān al-farq bayna 'l-muʿjizāt wa' l-karāmāt wa 'l-ḥiyāl wa 'l-siḥr*, ed. Richard McCarthy, Beirut 1958, p. 56.

karāmāt. As far as he is concerned, the *awliyā'* are the *ṣāliḥūn*, the pious—an equivalent which is no substitute for a definition.

If one turns to the Ṣūfis one discovers, it is true, some allusions which can be most illuminating; but there is also an evident desire to be discreet on the subject of what constitutes *walāya per se*. Needless to say, many texts where the word *walāya* does not occur make mention of *ʿārif* (gnostic), *ṣūfī* or other similar terms, and thereby contribute to a definition of the nature of *walāya*. But we may well be surprised that a term which, unlike the others, possesses Qur'ānic references, is either omitted altogether or only given a brief mention. Also surprising is a curious remark of Hujwīrī's in his *Kashf al-maḥjūb*, where he says: 'Certain shaykhs in the old days wrote works on this subject, but these became rare and quickly disappeared.'[15] Surely this remark, which may be deliberately vague, can only be an allusion to the writings of Tirmidhī or of his followers, the *Ḥakīmiyya*, whose characteristic features are described by Hujwīrī in the chapter from which this quotation is taken. In this chapter, in fact, the author simply recalls, with the help of a few anecdotes, what we find in Tirmidhī's own writings (stressing the fact that all prophets are *awliyā'* but that not all *awliyā'* are prophets), and does not discuss the concept of a 'Seal of the Saints'. This can hardly be an accident, considering that Hujwīrī mentions the work of that title (calling it *Khatm al-wilāya*).[16]

The great texts of *taṣawwuf*, whose authors are themselves frequently acknowledged to be *awliyā'*, prove on investigation to be equally lacking in precision.[17] In one section of his *Qūt al-qulūb* (*The Nourishment of Hearts*), Abū Ṭālib al-Makkī (died 380/990) speaks of the 'People of the spiritual stations among the Proximate' (*ahl al-maqāmāt min al-muqarrabīn*)[18] and distinguishes three categories of

15. Hujwīrī, *Kashf al-mahjūb*, trans. Nicholson, p. 212. A little further on (p. 216), Hujwīrī observes again, 'All the Masters have *alluded* to the true meaning of *walāya*'—an observation which highlights the exceptional character of Tirmidhī's far more specific teaching on the subject.

16. Ibid., p. 141. It is possible that Hujwīrī feared that confusion might arise between the doctrine of the Seal of the Saints and certain Ismaili teachings. As Herman Landolt has pointed out, it was during this same time that the *dāʿī* al-Mu'ayyad fī 'l-Dīn al-Shīrāzī (died 470/1077) formulated the notion of the 'Seal of the Imāms', which was evidently suspect in the eyes of the Sunnis.

17. Apart from the examples given here, there are the quotations collected by O. Yahia in the Appendix to his edition of the *Khatm*, p. 449 ff.

18. Abū Ṭālib al-Makkī, *Qūt al-qulūb*, Cairo 1350 AH, I, pp. 111-12 (*faṣl* 29).

awliyā'. In ascending order, these are: the 'People of the knowledge of Allāh' (*ahl al-ʿilm bi'Llāh*), the People of Love (*ahl al-ḥubb*), and the People of Fear (*ahl al-khawf*); and he cites, in relation to the saints, a remark attributed to Jesus which enumerates their characteristic virtues. Another great Ṣūfī classic, the *Kitāb al-Lumaʿ* by Abū Naṣr al-Sarrāj (died 377/987), contains a chapter[19] which issues a strict warning against those who situate *walāya* above *nubuwwa*. We may ask ourselves whether this could be an indirect criticism of Tirmidhī, who is not mentioned by name, or of certain *Ḥakīmiyya* who deviated from him or who at any rate gave ill-considered expression to their teacher's doctrine. Another chapter[20] is devoted to the 'miracles of the saints' (*karāmāt al-awliyā'*) and criticizes those (in this case the Muʿtazilites) who persist in denying them. Yet here again, we will look in vain for any detailed account of *walāya*.

Among the authors contemporary with those we have just mentioned, the work of one is also considered to contribute fundamentally to our knowledge of Sufism: Kalābādhī (died 385/995), whose *Kitāb al-Taʿarruf*, with its methodical construction, can truly be considered a treatise. Once again, and not for the last time, the subject of Chapter Twenty-Six is the problem of miracles.[21] Predictably, it is a defence both of the possibility and of the legitimacy of *karāmāt*: the miracles of the saints, in relation to the prophet whose authority the latter acknowledge, are not of a competitive but of a confirmative nature (*ẓuhūr al-karāmāt ta'yīd li 'l-nabī*)—a statement which is based on a remark of Abū Bakr al–Warrāq, mentioned above as one of Tirmidhī's immediate followers, to the effect that 'the miracle does not make the prophet'. Kalābādhī goes on to reply in the affirmative to the question which Tirmidhī had already been asked by the student to whom the *Khatm al-awliyā'* is addressed: can or cannot the saint be aware of his sainthood? Finally, he distinguishes between two types of *walāya*: in its

19. Abū Naṣr al-Sarrāj, *Kitāb al-Lumaʿ*, ed. ʿAbd al-Ḥalīm Maḥmūd and Ṭāhā ʿAbd al-Bāqī Surūr, Baghdad 1960, pp. 535-37. (Nicholson's edition is more reliable but less complete; but the editors, unfortunately, give no indication as to what manuscripts they have used).

20. Ibid., pp. 390-408.

21. Kalābādhī, *Kitāb al-Taʿarruf li-madhhab ahl al-taṣawwuf*, ed. ʿAbd al-Ḥalīm Maḥmūd and Ṭāhā ʿAbd al-Bāqī Surūr, Cairo 1960 (copied from the Arberry edition, Cairo 1953), pp. 71-79. There is now an excellent French translation of this work by R. Deladrière, entitled *Traité de soufisme*, Paris 1981. Chapter 26 corresponds to pp. 74-83.

more general sense it can be applied to all believers, and in the more limited sense which it possesses in the vocabulary of Sufism it is the privilege of the elect. 'He who possesses it is preserved from all concern with his ego (*maḥfūẓan ᶜanal-naẓar ilā nafsihi*) . . . and from all afflictions pertaining to the human condition (*min āfāt al-bashariyya*).' This passage contains two points, not new but important enough to bear in mind. One is the relationship between *walī* and *nabī*: the saint's role in relation to the prophet is confirmatory, and consequently any ideas of autonomy with regard to the Law, and of equality or superiority with regard to the prophet, are ruled out; and the other is the definition of the saint as a being who has lost sight of his *nafs* or ego.

We come now to the authors of a somewhat later date. Sulamī died in 412/1021. In the introductory doxology of his *Ṭabaqāt al-ṣūfiyya*,[22] there is a brief reference to the saints as the successors of the prophets (*wa atbaᶜa 'l-anbiyā' bi 'l-awliyā'*), but even though the words *walī*, *awliyā'*, *walāya* occur often in this hagiographic compilation, there is an absence of doctrinal expositions even where one might logically expect to find them. It is in fact extraordinary that the note about Tirmidhī[23] does not refer to one single remark of his about *walāya*. Still on this subject, Sulamī also quotes a severe judgement made by Jaᶜfar al-Khuldī (died 348/959): when asked whether he possessed any works by Tirmidhī, he replied 'that he did not number him among the Ṣūfis'[24]—a remark which should probably be interpreted as meaning that he numbered him among the philosophers. Needless to say, the *logia* compiled by Sulamī raise the classic questions (concerning *karāmāt*, whether the *walī* knows that he is a *walī*), recommend frequent visits to the *awliyā'* and their tombs, describe their distinctive features and, in particular, speak of their earthly status as an anticipation of their condition in paradise: 'It has been given to the *awliyā'* by Allāh in advance to enjoy His *dhikr* and to have access to His proximity. The life of their body is that of earthly beings and the life of their spirit is that of heavenly beings.' This quote is taken from Abū Saᶜīd al-Kharrāz (died 286/899).[25] But the most attractive definition of a saint to be found in the *Ṭabaqāt* and the one which best sums up many of the ideas expressed by the Shaykh al-Akbar is undoubtedly the following by Abū

22. Sulamī, *Ṭabaqāt al-ṣūfiyya*, ed. Nūr al-Dīn Sharība, Cairo 1953, p. 1.
23. Ibid., pp. 217, 220.
24. Ibid., p. 434.
25. Ibid., p.229.

Yazīd al-Bisṭāmī (died 261/874 or 234/857), for whom 'the saint of Allāh has no feature by which he is distinguished nor any name by which he can be named.'[26] We can compare this statement with another made by Bisṭāmī, and quoted by Sahlajī:[27] 'I asked Abū Yazīd, "How are you this morning?" He answered, "There is no morning or evening. Morning and evening exist only for the man to whom one can assign a quality; but I am without a quality (*wa anā lā ṣifata lī*)".' Neither morning nor evening, but the *lux perpetua* of the Eternal Day which has already dawned for the man who, having shed both name and attributes, is henceforth beyond all forms.

Another monument of Islamic hagiography, the *Ḥilyat al-awliyā'* (*The Jewel of the Saints*) by Abū Nuᶜaym al-Iṣfahānī (died 430/1038), leaves us, despite its title, still unsatisfied, although it contains elements of interest. This ten-volume catalogue, containing no fewer than six hundred and eighty-nine biographies, includes a notice on al-Ḥakīm al-Tirmidhī;[28] and here again there is an omission which must be intentional, for it says nothing about the teachings on *walāya* which were his major contribution to the doctrines of *taṣawwuf*. Thus, from scattered allusions and at times conflicting descriptions of character, a picture emerges of the *walī* and a typology of the *awliyā'* starts to take shape. But the actual essence of sainthood escapes structured definition. It is significant that the introduction to the work simply describes the external characteristics (*al-nuᶜūt al-ẓāhira*) of the *walī* using a series of *ḥadīth* and 'sayings' (*akhbār*) of the ancients.[29] According to these, the saints remember God (or invoke Him: *yadhkurūna 'Llāha*), and through their mere presence arouse the desire to remember Him. They are preserved from error during times of sedition (*fitna*). They live in poverty and obscurity ('Many a man', said the Prophet, 'with unkempt hair, whose possessions amount to no more than a couple of dates, whom no one wants to look at, may, if he adjures God, have his prayers answered').[30] The theme of the saint's occultation is consistently

26. Ibid., p. 103.

27. A.R. Badawi, *Shaṭaḥāt al-ṣūfiyya*, I, *Abū Yazīd al-Bisṭāmī*, Cairo 1949, p. 70.

28. Abū Nuᶜaym al-Iṣfahānī, *Ḥilyat al-awliyā' wa ṭabaqāt al-aṣfiyā'*, Beirut 1967, X, pp. 233–35.

29. Ibid., I, pp. 5-17.

30. This *ḥadīth* occurs in a slightly different form in Muslim, *birr*, 138, and *janna*, 48.

emphasized. Another *ḥadīth* quoted by Abū Nuᶜaym says: 'The servants whom God loves best are the pious and the hidden. When they are away no one misses them, and when they are present they are ignored. These are the imāms of good guidance and the torches of Knowledge.'[31] Mention is also made of the hierarchy of the saints and of asceticism (*zuhd*), and sayings are quoted about the latter which are attributed to Jesus, as well as the advice which God is supposed to have given Moses and Aaron before their meeting with Pharaoh. Further on is a reference to Dhū'l-Nūn al-Miṣrī's marvellous phrase, 'the Qur'ān has mingled with their flesh and blood',[32] which clearly echoes the words of ᶜĀ'isha, the Prophet's wife, who in answer to questions about his nature (*khuluq*), said, 'His nature was the Qur'ān'. Another *ḥadīth* which comes into this introduction says: 'Among the best in my community, as the supreme Pleroma has taught me, the highest ranks contain people who laugh outwardly because of the immensity of their Lord's Compassion and weep inwardly for fear of the harshness of their Lord's punishment.'[33] Among the features to which Abū Nuᶜaym wished to give prominence by his considered choice of quotations, we may note in particular the fact that *walāya* does not necessarily involve spectacular manifestations; on the contrary, the saint—the 'man without a quality' as Bisṭāmī terms him—often avoids being seen. Yet paradoxically, this effacement (which cannot be reduced to the mere practice of the virtue of humility but is the result of a *metamorphosis* in the etymological sense of the word) has the consequence that when the *walī is* seen, an anamnesis (*dhikr*) takes place, be it only a fleeting one, in the being of the beholder. Moreover, Dhū'l-Nūn's remarks subtly introduce a reflexion, the fruits of which will appear later, on the identification of the divine word itself—an identification of which the Prophet is both the example and the guarantee.

The *Risāla* of Qushayrī (died 465/1072) is one of the classics of Sufism. *Walāya* has a chapter to itself,[34] but here as in the other works we have mentioned, discretion prevails. After referring to verse 10:62, which, as we saw, is the most frequently invoked reference in the

31. Suyūṭī, *al-Fatḥ al-kabīr*, Cairo 1351AH, I, p. 47, mentions this *ḥadīth* —which does not occur in the canonical collections—with reference only to Abū Nuᶜaym's *Ḥilyat al-awliyā'*.

32. *Ḥilyat al-awliyā'* I, p. 14.

33. Ibid. I, p. 16. This *ḥadīth* does not appear in the canonical collections.

34. Qushayrī, *Risāla*, Cairo 1957, p. 117-19.

Qur'ān on the subject of the *awliyā'*, Qushayrī, like his predecessors, quotes the *ḥadīth qudsī 'Man ᶜādā lī waliyyan. . . .'* ('I declare war on him who is the enemy of My *walī*'). He then goes on to emphasize that *walī* is a word in *faᶜīl* and hence, as we pointed out earlier, possesses two meanings, passive and active. For the author of the *Risāla*, *walī* in the first sense is he of whose affairs God takes charge, and, in the second sense, he who takes charge of the service of God and the obedience due to Him. Furthermore, *walāya* presupposes a condition to be fulfilled: just as the true prophet must be without sin (*maᶜṣūm*), the true *walī* must be 'preserved' (*maḥfūẓ*) from all that is contrary to the Law.

We come next to the usual question: does the saint know that he is a saint? Qushayrī speaks of the arguments aroused by this problem and cites the affirmative answer to it given by his own teacher and father-in-law, Abū ᶜAlī al-Daqqāq. The chapter continues with a series of quotations which give us a brief glimpse of themes that we have already encountered: the saint's occultation, together with a remark of Abū Yazīd al-Bisṭāmī on the *awliyā'* as the 'brides' (*ᶜarā'is*) of God whom He conceals from alien eyes; the continuity between *walāya* and *nubuwwa*, and words of Sulamī (who was also one of Qushayrī's teachers) to the effect that 'the prophets begin where the saints end'; and the dissolution of the ego, accompanied by a definition of *walī* by Abū ᶜAlī al-Juzjānī. Qushayrī concludes with a short commentary on the verse from the Qur'ān with which the chapter begins. In a famous phrase, slightly transposed (and more often applied to the Ṣūfī), the *walī* is 'the son of the moment': he has no past and no future, and therefore, as the Qur'ān says, is not subject either to fear or to unhappiness.

Another chapter of the *Risāla* treats, as usual, of the 'miracles of the saints' (*karāmāt al-awliyā'*) but has nothing new to say about them. Similarly, if we turn to Qushayrī's commentary on the Qur'ān, published for the first time in Cairo a few years ago, it contains few additional elements, apart from a definition of the difference between *maᶜṣūm* and *maḥfūẓ*: the prophet's freedom from sin lies in the fact that he does not even experience the desire to commit a sin. The saint, on the other hand, is not shielded from temptation and may yield to it; but divine grace preserves him from persevering in his fault (*wa-lākin lā yakūnu lahu iṣrār*).[35]

35. Qushayrī, *Laṭā'if al-ishārāt*, ed. Ibrāhīm Basyūnī, with a preface by Ḥasan ᶜAbbās Zakī, Cairo, n.d., 6 vols. For the commentary on verse 10:62, see III, p. 105. The commentary on verse 4:76 gives no clue as to the *awliyā' al-shayṭān*.

Despite the fact that his father had been a follower of a shaykh from Tirmidh through whom he claimed spiritual descent from al-Ḥakīm al-Tirmidhī, ʿAbdallāh Anṣārī (died 481/1089), in what is known to us of his work, does not appear to have devoted particular attention to the subject of *walāya*.[36] The same is true of al-Ghazālī (died 505/1111) who, as was standard practice in treatises on *taṣawwuf*, criticizes in his *Iḥyā'* those who deny the *karāmāt al-awliyā'*.[37] Who then are the *awliyā'*? It is *walāya* that can explain *karāmāt*, not the reverse. Sainthood is concealed behind its manifestations and symbols, and it is in this roundabout way that Najm al-Dīn Kubrā (died 617/1270) for example, approaches the problem in his *Fawā'iḥ al-jamāl*.[38] Thus, among the *ʿalāmāt al-walī*, the saint's distinguishing features, Kubrā singles out the facts that he is *maḥfūẓ* (stressing the difference between this relative immunity and the *ʿiṣma*, the prophet's absolute freedom from sin), that the requests he makes of God are granted, that he knows the Supreme Name of God as well as the names of the *jinns* and the angels, and so on. For him, *walāya* is the third and final stage of the spiritual journey, whose division into three parts is expressed by a series of ternaries: 'service' (or the act of worship, *ʿibāda*), 'servitude' (*ʿubūdiyya*), and lastly 'absolute servitude' (*ʿubūda*);[39] the 'knowledge of certitude' (*ʿilm al-yaqīn*) which is acquired (*muktasab*), the 'truth of certitude' (*ḥaqq al-yaqīn*) which is a permanent state, and the 'eye of certitude' (*ʿayn al-yaqīn*), which is the extinction (*fanā'*) of the knower in the Known;[40] 'instability' (*talwīn*), 'stability' (*tamkīn*), and the 'existentializing power' (*takwīn*) conferred on him whose own will has been entirely annihilated in the divine Will and through whose mouth the divine Command itself of 'Be!' (*kun!*) is expressed—an allusion to verse 16:40 ('The Word that We say to a thing when We wish it to be is:

36. On Anṣārī, see S. de Laugier de Beaurecueil, *Khwādja Abdullāh Ansārī, mystique hanbalite*, Beirut 1965.

37. Ghazālī, *Iḥyā' ʿulūm al-dīn*, Cairo, n.d., IV, pp. 355-59.

38. Najm al-Dīn Kubrā, *Fawā'iḥ al-jamāl wa-fawātiḥ al-jalāl*, ed. Fritz Meier, Wiesbaden 1957, p. 82 ff. of the Arabic text.

39. Ibn ʿArabī also distinguishes in principle (cf. *Futūḥāt* II, p. 519) between *ʿubūdiyya* and *ʿubūda*, without always taking account in his writings of this theoretical distinction. Tirmidhī uses both of them impartially.

40. This hierarchy of degrees of certainty, which is classic in Sufism, is a reference to verses 5 and 7 in *sūra* 102, where the expressions *ʿilm al-yaqīn* and *ʿayn al-yaqīn* occur. But the usual order of these three terms is *ʿilm al-yaqīn*, *ʿayn al-yaqīn*, *ḥaqq al-yaqīn*.

Be! and it is'). 'The spiritual traveller', says Kubrā, 'will acquire the qualification of sainthood only when he has been accorded this "Be!"' Unlike Ibn ᶜArabī later, Najm al-Dīn Kubrā makes no attempt to justify metaphysically this seemingly extravagant appropriation of the creative word for the benefit of a created being; he simply finds support for it in the scriptures, citing verse 76:30 of which the translation must now run: 'And you wish nothing which Allāh does not [also] wish.'[41]

Even though Najm al-Dīn Kubrā does not furnish us with a discursive account of *walāya*, he does tell us more about it than any of the others. What we know of his spiritual life through his own writings justifies us in thinking that, had he wished, he could have gone a great deal further. But apart from his personal experience, he was undoubtedly also familiar with the problem of *walāya* as defined by Tirmidhī: his teacher ᶜAmmār Bidlīsī (died 590/1194), from whom he borrows several of his expressions, actually refers several times in his writings to the author of the *Khatm al-awliyā'*. Like Tirmidhī, Bidlīsī stresses the relationship between *walāya* and *sakīna*, the divine Peace or Presence. Again, like Tirmidhī, he distinguishes various stages of sainthood: there is, he says, a limited sainthood (*muqayyada*) and an absolute sainthood (*muṭlaqa*). The saint who possesses the latter is no longer subject to natural appetites, nor to desires of the soul. He knows neither personal will nor passion. He acts through God and God through him.[42] Bidlīsī also derives from Tirmidhī the idea of the Seal of the Saints, and paraphrases his definition without going any deeper into it. But at least he bears witness to the fact that, however discreetly, the teaching of the master of Tirmidh was still being passed on.

The great saints of the twelfth century, among whom are included those we have been quoting, prove through their writings that the question of *walāya* concerned them and, no doubt, that they were asked about it. At first glance, however, their laconic answers tell us nothing,

41. The usual translations give it as: 'And you wish for nothing if it is not what God wants.' Metaphysically speaking, these two possible interpretations of the verse are not contradictory, since the two wills (of God and of His creations), for the man who attains to the supreme stage of *walāya*, are neither successive nor distinct from each other in any relation. This is expressed by Kubrā when he says that then, 'God wishes for nothing without the servant wishing for it, and the servant wishes for nothing without God wishing for it' (ibid., p. 86).

42. The passages here referred to from Bidlīsī's *Bahjat al-ṭā'ifa* have been published by Osman Yahia as an annex to the *Khatm al-awliyā'*, pp. 469-71, copied from a manuscript in Berlin.

and only a patient exegesis of their words and actions, to which Ibn ʿArabī holds the key, reveals their coherence and depth. One of the greatest figures of the time, ʿAbd al-Qādir al-Jīlānī, whose death in Baghdad in 561/1165 coincided with the birth in Andalusia, to the west of the Muslim world, of Ibn ʿArabī, says only (as ʿAmmār Bidlīsī also says, using another image of a tree and its branches) that *walāya* is 'the shadow of the prophetic function' (*ẓill al-nubuwwa*), as the prophetic function is the shadow of the divine function[43]—a metaphor which, while it confirms the close link between prophetology and hagiology, is too vague to provide us with an adequate doctrinal perspective. We will have occasion to return to ʿAbd al-Qādir al-Jīlānī; but in order to conclude this brief survey of the texts on *walāya* which appeared during the three centuries that separate Tirmidhī from the author of the *Futūḥāt*, we must turn to a spiritual teacher contemporary with the latter: Rūzbehān Baqlī, who died in 606/1209, a dozen years after Ibn ʿArabī's arrival in the East. Henry Corbin has written a great deal about Baqlī,[44] as well as editing his *Le Jasmin des Fidèles d'Amour*.[45] At the risk of overlapping with him on certain points, we feel it would be useful to draw attention to some sections of his work of which we now possess more recent editions than were available to Corbin. There also exists at present[46] a slightly different and more complete version of Baqlī's spiritual autobiography, the *Kashf al-asrār*. First, however, we will quote from another work, the *Mashrab al-arwāḥ (The Watering-place of Spirits)*, in which Baqlī, taking his cue from the systematic description suggested by Anṣārī both in his *Book of a Hundred Lands* and then in his *Book of the Travellers' Stages*, embarks on the analysis of one thousand and one stations (*maqāmāt*), which he divides into twenty chapters. Among them is a section on *walāya*.[47] 'The start of the Way', writes Rūzbehān Baqlī,

43. Shaṭṭanūfī (died 713/1314), *Bahjat al-asrār*, Cairo 1330 AH, p. 39.

44. See especially *En Islam iranien*, III, pp. 9-146.

45. H. Corbin and M. Mo'in, *Le Jasmin des Fidèles d'Amour*, Tehran-Paris 1958.

46. Dr Nazif Hoca, *Rūzbihān al-Baklī ve kitāb kaşf al-asrār*, Istanbul 1971. The text of the *Kashf* has been established from a manuscript preserved at Konya. We should note in passing that the Shīʿite tone that Corbin detects in Baqlī can in no way be reconciled with the mention of Abū Bakr which occurs in the account of the vision on p. 104.

47. *Kitāb mashrab al-arwāḥ*, ed. Nazif Hoca (=*Khwādja*), Istanbul 1973, p. 377 of the Arabic text plus 8 pages of introduction in Turkish, chapter four, section 48, p. 89.

is the will [or desire, *irāda*], and it is accompanied by spiritual battles. The middle of the Way is love (*maḥabba*), and it is accompanied by miraculous graces (*karāmāt*). The end of the Way is gnosis (*maʿrifa*), and it is accompanied by contemplation (*mushāhadāt*). When a being is firmly established in these stages, when the laws of change (*talwīn*) are no longer operative for him and he swims in the oceans of unicity and the secret of solitude (*tafrīd*), then he is a *walī*, a deputy of the prophets and truly pure among the pure. The word *walāya* is a synthetic term encompassing all the dwelling places of men of spiritual realisation [*al-ṣiddīqūn*, literally: those who confirm the truth because they have experienced it for themselves]. . . . A wise man has said: *walāya* is the fact of appropriating the divine attributes to oneself (*al-takhalluq bi khuluq al-ḥaqq*).

This abstract text is illustrated by the account left to us by Rūzbehān, aged fifty-five years, of his personal experience of the Way in the *Kashf al-asrār* (*The Unveiling of the Secrets*)—an account so significant and so moving that we have no hesitation in quoting a few passages from it:

I saw God—may He be blessed and exalted!—clothed in Magnificence and in eternal Majesty, while I was on the terrace of my house. It seemed to me that the entire universe was transformed into a shining light, abounding and immense. He called to me out of the heart of this light and said to me in Persian: 'O Rūzbehān, I have chosen thee for *walāya* and I have selected thee for love (*maḥabba*). Thou art My *walī* and thou art My lover (*muḥibb*). Do not fear and do not be unhappy [an allusion to verse 10:64, quoted above], for I will make thee perfect and I will help thee in all that thou desirest.' And I saw as it were from the Throne to the earth[48] an ocean like the rays of the sun. Then my mouth opened without my will and this entire ocean entered into me until there remained no drop which I had not drunk.[49]

The words *walī* and *walāya* which we have left untranslated are obviously to be understood here in the sense of 'proximity', which is, as we saw, the primary meaning attaching to the root. But insofar as *walāya* applies to God, it is also *al-nuṣra*, the divine Assistance from which the *walī* benefits and which is promised to Rūzbehān during the course of this vision.

The texts which follow, while not referring explicitly to *walāya*, nevertheless contain very valuable indications as to its nature:

I saw God under His attributes of Majesty and Beauty and the angels were with Him. I said to Him, 'O my God, how wilt Thou take my spirit?' He said to me, 'I will come to thee from the inmost depths of the Eternity which has no beginning and I will take thy spirit into My hand. Then I will bring thee to the station of

48. *Al-tharā*; Corbin—or the copyist of the Mashhad manuscript whom he used—reads *al-thurayyā*, the Pleiades, by mistake.

49. *Kashf al-asrār*, p. 103.

"My home". I will give thee the drink of proximity and I will reveal to thee for ever My Beauty and My Majesty, as thou desirest and without a veil.'[50]

One night, I saw an immense ocean and this ocean was composed of a drink that was red in colour.[51] And I saw the Prophet seated, drunk, in the midst of the depths of this ocean. He held a cup of the drink in his hand and was drinking it. When he saw me, he took some of that ocean into the palm of his hand and gave me to drink. And that which was opened to me was opened! Then I understood that the Prophet was above all other creatures, who die thirsty while he stands intoxicated in the middle of the ocean of divine Majesty.[52]

I saw, in the universe of non-manifestation, a world illuminated by a blazing light. And I saw God—to Whom be Glory!—clothed in the garment of Majesty, Beauty and Splendour. He poured out the sea of Tenderness for me to drink and honoured me by according me the station of Proximity. When I was immersed in the clarity of eternity, I stopped at the gate of Magnificence and saw all the prophets there—Peace be upon them! I saw Moses holding the Torah, Jesus holding the Gospel, David holding the Psalms and Muḥammad with the Qur'ān. Then Adam made me drink 'the most beautiful names'[53] and the Supreme Name. Then I understood what I understood of the high reserved knowledge with which God favours His prophets and saints.[54]

In another vision, Rūzbehān Baqlī sees a yellow lion (the solar symbolism is doubly obvious here) walking on top of Mount Qāf, the inaccessible emerald mountain which marks the limit of the terrestrial world. This lion has devoured all the prophets and their blood is still dripping from its mouth. Rūzbehān realizes that this is a subtle reference (*ishāra*) to the overwhelming power of divine Unity (*qahr al-tawḥīd*) and that it is God Himself who is epiphanized in the form of a lion.[54]

A little further on there is a long account of a spiritual event that occurred when Rūzbehān was in his *ribāṭ* ('convent') at Shiraz. 'Then He clothed me in His Attributes and made me one with His Essence. Then I saw myself as though I were He (*thumma ra'aytu nafsī ka-annī huwa*) . . .. Afterwards I returned from this state and I descended from the rank of Lordship (*rubūbiyya*) to that of servitude (*ʿubūdiyya*)'.[56] We will cite one more of Rūzbehān's communications, in relation to

50. Ibid., p. 104.

51. The frequent occurrence of oceanic images and the colour red is characteristic of the visions reported in the *Kashf*.

52. *Kashf al-asrār*, p. 107.

53. This is a double Qur'ānic allusion, to verse 2:31 ('And He taught Adam all the names'), and to verse 7:180 ('And the most beautiful Names belong to Allāh').

54. *Kashf al-asrār*, p. 107.

55. Ibid., p. 109.

56. Ibid., p. 111.

what was said earlier about the saint's 'transparency' and his role as a favoured vehicle of theophany:

Once, I was sitting during the first part of the night beside my son Aḥmad who was ill with a violent fever; and my heart was almost breaking with anxiety. Suddenly I saw God in His aspect of Beauty. He gave evidence of Goodness towards my son and myself. Ecstasy and agitation seized hold of me . . . . I said to Him, 'O my God, why dost Thou not speak to me as Thou didst speak to Moses?' He replied, 'Is it not enough that he who loves thee loves Me and that he who sees thee sees Me?'[57]

As we saw, only the prophets are completely shielded from temptation (such at any rate is the Sunnī attitude in this regard; the Shīᶜite doctrines extend this impeccability to the imāms). While the life of Rūzbehān Baqlī allows us to perceive the nature of the divine Grace accorded the *walī*, it also gives us a striking example of the dangers attendant upon the Way. In the chapter of the *Futūḥāt Makkiyya* which treats of the Station of Knowledge (*maqām al-maᶜrifa*), Ibn ᶜArabī speaks of the spiritual lapses which teachers must know how to remedy in their disciples. After speaking of 'the illnesses which affect actions' (*amrāḍ al-afᶜāl*), he describes 'the illnesses which affect the spiritual state' (*amrāḍ al-aḥwāl*), and refers to an episode in the life of the saint of Shiraz which occurred during his visit to Mecca:

It is related of Shaykh Rūzbehān that he was smitten by love for a woman, a singer, and was carried away by transports of passion. It was his custom, when he experienced ecstasies inspired by God, to utter such cries that he disturbed people who were walking around the Kaᶜba at the time when he was staying in Mecca and walking on the terrace of the Holy Mosque. But his spiritual state was genuine.

When he was smitten with love for this singer, no one perceived it; for the state that had been inspired in him by God was now inspired in him by the woman. When he realized that people thought that his ectasies were still being inspired by God, as had originally been the case, he took off his *khirqa* [the Ṣūfī 'habit'], threw it towards them and related his story to everyone, saying, 'I do not wish to tell lies about my condition.' Then he placed himself at the service of the singer. She

57. Ibid., p. 117. This divine reply is the same as the answer craved by Abū Yazīd Bisṭāmī when he addresses God as follows: 'Raise me up to Your Unity, that when Your creatures see me they will see You' (*Kitāb al-Lumaᶜ*, p. 461). And four centuries later, Shaykh Ibn Qaḍīb al-Bān (died 1040/1630) was to hear himself called by God in the same terms as Baqlī, during a vision in which he beheld himself invested with the station of divine Viceregency (*maqām al-khilāfa*): *Man ra'āka ra'ānī wa 'l-ladhī turīduhu irādatī* ('He who sees you sees Me, and what you wish is My will'). Cf. Ibn Qaḍīb al-Bān, *Kitāb al-Mawāqif al-ilāhiyya*, ed. by A. R. Badawī in his *al-Insān al-kāmil fī 'l-islām*, 2nd edition, Kuwait 1976, pp. 175-76.

was then told of what had happened to him, of the transports that he experienced for her and that he was one of the greatest of holy men. The woman was ashamed and asked God to forgive her her faults through the *baraka* of Rūzbehān's sincerity. She placed herself at his service and God caused the attachment that Rūzbehān felt for her in his heart to cease. He returned to the Ṣūfis and put on his *khirqa* again.[58]

The example of Baqlī reveals some aspects of *walāya* which, in appearance at least, contrast strongly with those aspects of it that we encounter in the case of other people. Mad love—and its eventual aberrations—is one of the elements that make up *taṣawwuf*. Eminent men like Shiblī or Ḥallāj in the ninth century, or Jalāl al-Dīn Rūmī in the thirteenth, and many more, bear witness to this fact. Such love is distinguished by verbal lyricism—always threatened by hyperbole or staleness but which sometimes attains a heart-rending beauty—and by rather ostentatious irregularities of behaviour. However, it would be too simple to oppose a 'way of knowledge' and a 'way of love': spiritual life is not a choice between light and warmth. Both of them exist in the case of all those who are recognized in Islamic tradition as *awliyā'*, including Ibn ᶜArabī whose *Tarjumān al-ashwāq* (*The Interpreter of Desire*) was inspired by a woman, as was Rūzbehān Baqlī's *Le Jasmin des Fidèles d'Amour*.[59] Although it is common, especially for those who pay a pious visit (*ziyāra*) to their tombs, to designate Ibn ᶜArabī as *Sultān al-ᶜārifīn*, 'Sultan of Gnostics', and Ibn al-Fāriḍ or Jalāl al-Dīn Rūmī as *Sulṭān al-muḥibbīn*, 'Sultan of Lovers', yet it is the case that every *walī* is both a *ᶜārif*, a gnostic, and a *muḥibb*, a lover. In a text quoted above, Rūzbehān Baqlī likens *walāya* to the 'appropriation of the divine characters'—an equivalence which, although not always so clearly formulated, is present in all the Ṣūfi writings on *walāya* and is corroborated by the fact that the word *walī* is a name shared between God and created being. God is both *al-ᶜAlīm*, He who knows, and He who loves: *yuḥibbuhum*, 'He [i.e. Allāh] loves them', says the Qur'ān (5:54) in a passage which is immediately followed (5:55) by the statement 'God is your *walī*'.

Knowledge and love are indissolubly linked. The predominance of one or the other is just one of the many criteria determining a typology of the saints—a typology that we will later come to understand in all its

58. *Futūḥāt* II, p. 315.

59. On the circumstances in which the *Tarjumān al-ashwāq* was written, cf. the Beirut edition, 1961, pp. 8-10, and Nicholson's translation, London 1911, pp. 3-5. On the *Jasmin des Fidèles d'Amour*, cf. Corbin, *En Islam iranien*, III, p. 71 ff.

richness. In all cases the Way has dangers which, however diverse, are merely forms of the ultimate temptation of idolatry. There is idolatry of the self on the way of gnosis, if the seeker, aiming at knowledge of the One, pauses on the road in the belief that the One resides within his own soul. There is idolatry of the other on the way of love, for the *muḥibb* may forget that the other is simply an aspect of the One. Rūzbehān Baqlī fell into this trap at least once and possibly twice, for the prelude to the *Jasmin* is ambiguous. He is in love with divine Beauty, but for a time he ends up worshipping a reflection of it. Properly speaking, this is 'infidelity', *kufr* in Arabic: a term, as Ibn ʿArabī often reminds us, which etymologically signifies the act of veiling or hiding something,[60] for by preferring one theophany, it excludes or conceals all the others and hides the *Theos* of whom it is just one of the infinite modes of manifestation. Hence the danger, repeatedly alluded to in the literature of *taṣawwuf*, of taking any human being, whether man or woman, to be a 'witness of contemplation'. Hence also the necessity of observing the rules of prudence which are tirelessly reiterated by the teachers, and which are not the fruit of conventional morality but the dictates of wisdom. Needless to say, transgressions are numerous, and not even exceptional men are immune to the divine guile (*makr*) which is a test of the believer's sincerity. But although the saints can be deceived, they do not deceive. 'He who loves thee loves Me, and he who sees thee sees Me': these are the words heard by Rūzbehān, while he watched, with such human tenderness, over his fever-stricken son.[61]

60. Cf. for example *Futūḥāt* I, p. 415; II, p. 511; III, pp. 27, 92, 406.

61. More valuable information on the concept of *walāya* in Sufism, and on its juridical and political implications, can be found in H. Landolt's article in the *Encyclopedia of Religion*, New York 1987, XV, pp. 316-23.

CHAPTER

3

The Sphere of *Walāya*

DESPITE the fact that the texts to which we have hitherto referred are far from explicit, it is already clear that *walāya* cannot be reduced to a *heroiciton* of the theological and cardinal virtues such as that which defines the criteria of sainthood for Roman Catholic theologians. The concept of *walāya* was to be given definition by Ibn ʿArabī; and later on we will learn what the authority was on which he based his teaching, and which was acknowledged both by himself and by his followers, as well as the providential necessity which called forth his disclosure at that particular moment in time.

The doctrine of *walāya* is the cornerstone of all that is initiatic in Ibn ʿArabī's work (as opposed to what is purely metaphysical),[1] and it comes into many texts where the *walī* does not always go by the name of *walī*. He may also be called *ʿārif* (gnostic), *muḥaqqiq* (a term favoured by Ibn Sabʿīn and meaning 'man of spiritual realization'), *malāmī* 'the one associated with blame', *wārith* (heir), or quite simply *ṣūfī*, *ʿabd* (servant) or even *rajul* (man, in the sense of *vir perfectus*). However, in our preliminary investigation we will confine ourselves to the texts which refer explicitly to *walāya* and to the *awliyā'* as such.

In this connection, and for reasons which will become clear, special prominence must be given to one of Ibn ʿArabī's last works. This is the *Fuṣūṣ al-ḥikam*,[2] a title which has been variously translated as *The*

1. It is scarcely necessary to explain that these two aspects are inseparable from each other, and thus form a unity. The word 'opposed' as it is used here does not, of course, imply the existence of any contradiction between Ibn ʿArabī's metaphysical doctrine and his initiatic teaching; it merely refers to the distinction between the two complementary and alternating perspectives which inform his work.

2. In spite of the title 'Sainthood and Prophethood' given to Hamed Taher's article in *Alif*, no. 5, 1985, Cairo, pp. 7-38, which contains the first edited version of it, the untitled *Risāla*, corresponding to no. 625 and possibly also to no. 632 of Osman Yahia's R.G., and written by Ibn ʿArabī in 590 AH after a visit to Shaykh ʿAbd al-ʿAzīz al-Mahdawī in Tunis, is not a straightforward treatise on *walāya* (in

Wisdom of the Prophets, *The Gems of Wisdom*, *The Seals of Wisdom*,[3] but which strictly speaking means *The Settings of Wisdom*. The book contains a prologue and twenty-seven chapters, each of which has reference to a prophet, of whom the first was Adam and the last Muḥammad. The order followed is not chronological: the chapter about Jesus precedes the one about Solomon, which precedes the one about David. It is worth noting, moreover, that two out of the twenty-seven, namely Seth (Shīth in Arabic) and Khālid ibn Sinān, who is mentioned in a *ḥadīth*, do not come into the Qur'ān, whereas two of the prophets whose names appear in the Qur'ān (Dhū' l-Kifl and al-Yasaᶜ) do not figure in this catalogue. It is also worth noting that Luqmān, whose name is the title of one of the chapters of the *Fuṣūṣ*, appears in the Qur'ān as a sage rather than a prophet.

The setting (*faṣṣ*, plural *fuṣūṣ*) of a ring is the part which encloses the precious stone. The word recurs in the title of each chapter where it is followed by two determinants: a 'wisdom' (*ḥikma*), which is itself qualified by an adjective; and a 'word' (*kalima*) connected with one of the twenty-seven prophets. Thus, for example, we have 'the setting of divine wisdom in the Word of Adam', 'the setting of the wisdom of the heart in the Word of Shuᶜayb', and so on. In this way a series of spiritual types is built up, of whom each is in some sense defined as the

---

fact, as established by ms. BN 6104, ff. 1 to 28b, and by Ibn Sawdakīn's commentary, Fatih 5322, ff. 201-14, it is not an autonomous text at all, but forms the preamble to the *Mashāhid al-asrār al-qudsiyya*, R.G. 432). It deals with other themes as well; and even though, in response to a remark of Mahdawī's which Ibn ᶜArabī undertakes to explain to the latter's disciples, some fundamental ideas about *walāya* are expressed, there are others which are passed over completely. We will refer later to this text, which is, even so, deeply interesting; and our thanks are due to James W. Morris for alerting us to its publication under the title *Risāla fī'l-walāya*. As regards the *Fuṣūṣ al-ḥikam*, we are still using the critical edition by A. A. ᶜAfīfī, Beirut 1946—the best in existence even though it does not take account of the most ancient extant manuscript, copied by Sadr al-Dīn Qūnawī and with an attested reading date of 630 AH (Evkaf Müzesi 1933). The chief commentaries employed are by Jandī (died c. 700/1300), edited by Ashtiyānī (not critical, many faults), Mashhad 1982; by ᶜAbd al-Razzāq Qāshānī (died 730/1330), Cairo 1321 AH; by Dāwūd Qayṣarī (died 751/1350), lithog., Bombay 1300 AH; and by Bālī Effendī (died 960/1553), Istanbul 1309 AH.

3. On the two most recent English translations of the *Fuṣūṣ al-ḥikam*, by R. W. Austin (*The Bezels of Wisdom*, London 1980), and by ᶜĀ'isha al-Tarjumāna (*The Seals of Wisdom*, Norwich 1980), cf. my review in *Bulletin critique des Annales islamologiques*, XX, pp. 334-37.

intersection of an aspect of divine Wisdom with the human vessel which encloses it and thereby imposes its own limits on it. As we shall see, this structure is in no way a mere rhetorical device, but corrresponds symbolically with the actual structure of *walāya*.

We are justified in the importance we accord to the *Fuṣūṣ* by the information given in the prologue about the circumstances of its composition; the prologue likewise contains details about Ibn ʿArabī's function of which the full significance will emerge later on. The essential passages are as follows:

In the name of Allāh, the All-Merciful, the Most-Merciful! Praise be to Allāh, who has caused wisdom to descend upon the hearts of the Words from the station of absolute Eternity by a straight path whose unity is unaffected by the diversity of beliefs and religions, which results from the diversity of human communities. And may Allāh bestow His Grace upon Muḥammad (who by means of the most righteous word pours out upon the aspirations [of created beings] what he draws from the treasure-house of Generosity and Munificence) and upon his family; and may He give him peace.

I saw the Messenger of Allāh in a vision of good augury which was imparted to me during the last ten days of the month of *Muḥarram*[4] in the year 627 at

4. Not 'the tenth day of the month of Moharram' as Henry Corbin states in the French introduction to Ḥaydar Āmolī's *Naṣṣ al-Nuṣūṣ*, Tehran-Paris 1975, p. 4, where he is manifestly obsessed with discovering Shīʿite allusions and believes this date to correspond with the anniversary of the martyred Imām al-Ḥusayn. For an account of Corbin's thesis on the transposition (and the denaturation) of Shīʿite concepts in Sufism, especially the doctrine of the Imāmate, see, in particular, the chapter entitled 'Prophétologie et imāmologie' in *En islam iranien* I, pp. 219-84. A similar thesis is sustained in a more historicist fashion by Dr Kāmil Muṣṭafā Shaybī in *al-Ṣila bayna 'l-taṣawwuf wa 'l-tashayyuʿ*, 2nd ed., Cairo 1969 (see pp. 339-79 on *walāya*). It would of course be absurd to deny that, both in vocabulary and conceptually, Shīʿism and Sufism were connected, and therefore interacted, with each other, especially prior to the coming of the Safavids. But these influences were reciprocal, and the influence of Ibn ʿArabī on the Shīʿite doctrine of *walāya* is obvious, its importance being acknowledged by the Shīʿite authors themselves. The case of Ḥaydar Āmolī who, in his vast commentary on the *Fuṣūṣ*, forcefully expresses his admiration for Ibn ʿArabī and the extent of his indebtedness to him, is particularly significant. Let us merely note that on p. 267 of the Arabic text of the *Naṣṣ al-nuṣūṣ*, in a section devoted to the *awliyā'*, Āmolī justifies the need to explain the ideas he is dealing with by the need to make them understood by the Sunnīs (who refuse to admit them even though it is implied that they are aware of them) and by the Imāmite Shīʿites, for 'statements of this kind have never reached their ears or been uttered by their tongues'. This does not prevent Corbin from saying several times over that, in accepting certain of Ibn ʿArabī's ideas, Shīʿism was merely 'taking back its own'.

Damascus—may God protect it! In his hand he held a book and he said to me, 'This is the book of the *Fuṣūṣ al-ḥikam*. Take it and bring it to men that they may profit by it'.

I replied, 'I hear and obey "Allāh, His Messenger and those among us who are keepers of the Commandment", as it has been laid down' (Qur'ān 4:59).

I therefore undertook to carry out his request. To this end, I purified my intention and aspiration with a view to making known the book as it had been consigned to me by Allāh's Messenger, with nothing added or taken away. And I asked Allāh, in this task and in all my states, to place me among those of his servants over whom Satan has no power, and to favour me in all that my hands write, in all that my mouth speaks, in all that my heart contains, with a projection of His Glory, an inspiration breathed into my spirit and an assistance to protect me, in order that I may be an interpreter and not an author, so that the men of God and the teachers of the heart who read this book will be certain that it proceeds from the station of inviolable Sainthood, which is beyond reach of the deceptive desires of the individual soul. I hope that God, having heard my prayer, has answered it. I have uttered nothing which has not been sent to me, I write nothing which has not been inspired. I am neither a prophet nor a messenger, but simply an inheritor; and I labour for the life to come.[5]

In Chapter Fourteen of the *Fuṣūṣ*, which is under the sign of ʿUzayr[6] (whom Muslim tradition usually compares to the Biblical Ezra), Ibn ʿArabī throws light on some aspects of *walāya* which are of major importance.

'Know', he writes, 'that *walāya* is the sphere which encompasses all the other spheres, and for this reason it has no end in time . . .. On the other hand, legislative prophethood (*nubuwwa*) and the mission of the Messengers (*risāla*) do have an end which they have reached in the person of Muḥammad, since after him there is neither any other prophet—meaning a prophet who brings a revealed Law or submits himself to a previously revealed Law[7]—nor any other legislating

5. *Fuṣūṣ* I, pp. 47-48. Because of the particular nature of the prophetic trust of which the *Fuṣūṣ* is the repository, and concerning which, as we saw, Ibn ʿArabī said that he was the interpreter and not the author, we learn from Jandī (a pupil of Qūnawī, who was an immediate follower of Ibn ʿArabī) that he had forbidden it to be bound together with any other of his books (Jandī, *Sharḥ al-Fuṣūṣ*, p. 5 of the Arabic text).

6. *Fuṣūṣ* I, p. 134 ff. ʿUzayr is only mentioned once in the Qur'ān (9:30).

7. This explanation, which defines prophethood *stricto sensu*, is necessary because of the extended meaning which Ibn ʿArabī, as we shall see, attributes to the term *nubuwwa*. For example, the prophets who submit to a previous Law are the biblical prophets who come after Moses and who do not bring any laws to their community.

Messenger.[8] This news is a terrible blow for the *awliyā'*, for it implies the impossibility of experiencing total and perfect servitude.' This last point, which may appear obscure, is explained by Ibn ʿArabī as follows: since no being can henceforth term himself *nabī* or *rasūl*—names which properly belong to created being because they form no part of the divine Names—the only name which remains available is *al-walī*, which is one of the Names of God. For the spiritual man, awareness of his *ʿubūdiyya* (his servitude or ontological nothingness) goes contrary to such a sharing with God of the same name, for it implies participation in the *rubūbiyya*, or Lordship. But, he adds, if prophethood *stricto sensu* is ended, 'general prophethood' (*nubuwwa ʿāmma*) remains. This is what is more commonly termed *walāya*, and even though it is not accompanied by the legislative authority which characterizes the prophets in the narrow sense of the word, nevertheless it does possess a legislative aspect in that it implies the possibility of interpreting the statutes of the Law. This is why a *ḥadīth* says that the learned (*al-ʿulamā'*)—and the *awliyā'* alone are truly worthy of the name—'are the heirs of the prophets'.[9] As we shall see, the concept of inheritance is crucial.

Next, Ibn ʿArabī broaches a theme which we encountered in Tirmidhī.

When you see a prophet expressing himself in words which do not arise from his legislative authority, it is because he is a *walī* and an *ʿārif* (a gnostic or knower); and the station which he occupies by virtue of being *ʿalīm* (wise) is more complete and more perfect than the station he occupies by virtue of being a messenger or a legislative prophet. Likewise, when you hear a man of God saying—or when someone tells you that they have heard him say—that *walāya* is superior to *nubuwwa*, you must know that he means by this exactly what we have just said. Similarly, if he says that the *walī* is superior to the *nabī* or the *rasūl*, he implies that this is so in the person of one and the same being. In other words, the *rasūl* is more perfect in his capacity as a *walī* than in his capacity as a *nabī*. So this does not mean that the *walī* who follows a prophet is superior to the latter, for he who follows can never catch up with him whom he follows, inasmuch as he is his follower. If it were

8. The case of Jesus, who is one of the messengers (*rasūl*) and who will return on earth at the end of time, apparently contradicts this statement. The attitude adopted by Ibn ʿArabī with regard to this problem, which conforms in every point with the attitude of Islamic exotericism, will be dealt with in the next chapter.

9. Bukhārī, *ʿilm*, 10; Dārimī, *muqaddima*, 32, etc.

otherwise, he would not be a follower. Therefore understand! The source of the *rasūl* and the *nabī* lies in *walāya* and in knowledge.[10]

The preliminary conclusions to be drawn from this passage of the *Fuṣūṣ* may appear hard to reconcile with each other. On the one hand, *walāya* encompasses *nubuwwa* and *risāla* which proceed from it, and hence it is superior to them in the person of him who combines the three qualifications. On the other hand, we have witnessed the emergence of the idea of 'inheritance', which implies the passing on to the *awliyā'* of something which was originally the property of the prophets. Thus *walāya* is in some way dependent on *nubuwwa*, and in short represents a mode of participation in it. This is emphasized in other texts, such as these passages from the *Futūḥāt*: 'If you are a *walī*, you are the heir of a prophet and nothing will reach you [literally, your composition, or constitution, *ilā tarkībika*] which is not in proportion to your share of this inheritance.'[11] 'No one receives a prophet's heritage in full. If this were the case, it would mean that that being was himself a messenger or a legislating prophet in the same way as he whose heir he is.'[12] A similar notion is found in the *Kitāb al-Tajalliyāt* (*The Book of Theophanies*)[13] and the *Risālat al-Anwār* (*The Epistle of the Lights*):

Know that prophethood and sainthood possess three things in common: a knowledge not derived from study intended to acquire it; the faculty of acting through spiritual energy alone (*himma*) in cases where it is normally possible to act only through the body, or even in cases where the body is powerless to act; and finally, the sensible vision of the imaginal world (*ʿālam al-khayāl*). On the other hand, they differ from each other as far as the divine discourse is concerned, for the divine address to the saint is other than that made to the prophet, and it must not be imagined that the spiritual ascensions (*maʿārij*, plural of *miʿrāj*) of the saints are

10. This last passage was the object of a violent attack from Ibn Taymiyya (*Majmūʿat al-rasā'il*, IV, p. 58ff.). In view of Ibn ʿArabī's explanations concerning what should be understood by the superiority of the *walī* over the *nabī* or the *rasūl* (in the person of one and the same being), the remark made by A. D'Souza in his article on Jesus in Ibn ʿArabī's *Fuṣūṣ* ('Ibn ʿArabī, I believe, leaves the question open . . .') is inexplicable (see *Islamochristiana* no. 8, 1982, pp. 185-200). The superiority of the *nabī* over the mere *walī* is affirmed over and over again in the work of the Shaykh al-Akbar. Cf. for example his *Kitāb al-ʿAbādila*, ed. ʿAbd al-Qādir ʿAṭā, Cairo 1969, p. 82.

11. *Futūḥāt*, IV, p. 398.

12. Ibid., II, p. 80 (question 58 of Tirmidhī's questionnaire).

13. *Kitāb al-Tajalliyāt*, ed. Osman Yahia, in the review *al-Mashriq*, 1966-67 (cf. no. 1, 1967, pp. 53-54).

identical to those of the prophets. This is by no means the case . . .. The ascensions of the prophets are effected by means of the principial Light (*al-nūr al-aṣlī*), whereas those of the saints are effected through what is reflected of this principial light.[14]

Before attempting to reconcile these seemingly disparate elements, and at the risk therefore of somewhat confusing the reader, we must refer to some other texts in the work of the Shaykh al-Akbar in which he speaks of the *walī* and *walāya*. Mention was made earlier of Tirmidhī's famous questionnaire. Ibn ʿArabī replies to it in the long Chapter Seventy-Three of the *Futūḥāt*. The first question is: 'What is the number of the dwellings (*manāzil*) of the saints?' These dwellings, writes Ibn ʿArabī, are of two kinds: sensible (*ḥissiyya*) and spiritual (*maʿnawiyya*). The number of the first kind, which in turn is subdivided into sub-categories, is 'higher than one hundred and ten', which means that these *manāzil* are the 114 *sūras* of the Qur'ān. The number of the second kind is two hundred and forty-eight thousand; these belong exclusively to this community and no one has previously attained them. These 'spiritual dwellings' are linked with four types of knowledge (implicitly related to four *sūras*): the 'knowledge through Me' (*ʿilm ladunnī*, an allusion to verse 18:65, where this knowledge, which is related to the divine I, is attributed to Khaḍir); the knowledge of the Light (*ʿilm al-nūr*); the knowledge of union and of separation (*ʿilm al-jamʿ wa 'l-tafriqa*); and the knowledge of the divine Scripture (*ʿilm al-kitāba al-ilāhiyya*). Ibn ʿArabī goes on to say that, according to him, the number of saints is five hundred and eighty-nine; but he adds that he is talking here about the *awliyā'* belonging to the categories described at the start of Chapter Seventy-Three, who correspond to initiatory functions whose titulars are at all times fixed in number: in every epoch, as we shall see, there is a 'Pole' (*quṭb*), four 'Pillars'

14. *Risālat al-anwār*, Hyderabad 1948, p. 15. The distinction between *walī* and *nabī* is constantly emphasized by Ibn ʿArabī in order to avoid the confusion that might be engendered by some of his own statements or by statements to which other Ṣūfis have had recourse. The *Risāla fī 'l-walāya* mentioned in note 2 is a typical example. It is intended first and foremost to clarify a statement made by ʿAbd al-ʿAzīz Mahdawī (died 621/1224). It was for his benefit that Ibn ʿArabī undertook to write the *Futūḥāt*—cf. I, pp. 6-9—and it was for him too that he wrote the *Rūḥ al-quds*—cf. the Damascus edition, 1964, p. 3; in the *Risāla*, pp. 29-32, he enlarges on his merits and says that he will devote a work to him, although no manuscript of it seems to have been identified: cf. R.G. 119. The statement, to the perplexity of his disciples, was as follows: 'The wise (=*awliyā'*) of this community are the prophets of other communities' (*Risāla fī 'l-walāya*, p. 21 ff.).

(*awtād*),[15] and so on. But he also says[16] that the *total* number of the saints in all the categories is, in perpetuity, at least equal to the number of the prophets who have succeeded each other during the course of the human cycle—that is, in conformity with Islamic tradition, one hundred and twenty-four thousand. If the figure amounts to more than this, it is because the heritage of some prophet has been divided up between several *awliyā'*.

In reply to Tirmidhī's nineteenth question ('How is the station of the prophets situated in relation to that of the saints?'), Ibn ʿArabī says that it is its specification, and that, in order to be more precise, one would have first to know what kind of prophethood is meant: legislative prophethood (to which the answer given above applies specifically), or prophethood in an indeterminate sense (*nubuwwa muṭlaqa*)? This last actually represents the highest degree of sainthood, that of the *afrād* or 'solitaries' among whom is the Pole, the supreme authority in the initiatory hierarchy.[17]

Question Sixty-Eight concerns the prophets, but the answer tells us something about the saints. 'What is the lot of the prophets', asks Tirmidhī, 'as far as looking towards Him is concerned?'

> I do not know (for I am not a prophet and what the prophets experience is known only to them) at least if by 'prophet' he [Tirmidhī] means those to whom God has accorded legislative authority, whether general or limited. If, on the other hand, he has in mind those who are 'prophets among the saints' [i.e. those who are mentioned in the preceding texts], their lot is proportionate to the number of forms of belief (*wujūh al-iʿtiqādāt*) that they possess concerning God. For the man who possesses them all, his lot is the sum of the parts corresponding to each belief. He enjoys total felicity. He enjoys what is enjoyed by all the types of believers, and no joy can be greater than that! For the man who only possesses some [forms of belief], his enjoyment is proportional to what he possesses. The man who possesses only one enjoys what is allotted to that form of belief and no more.[18]

In this passage we encounter one of the fundamental themes of Ibn

15. *Futūḥāt*, II, pp. 40-41. The 35 categories (totalling 589 saints) described at the beginning of chapter 73 correspond to permanent cosmic functions; the 49 categories listed afterwards represent types and degrees of sainthood.

16. Ibid., III, p. 208.

17. Ibid., II, p. 53. The expression *nubuwwa muṭlaqa* is one of those terms whose ambiguity requires the kind of elucidation mentioned in note 14, regarding the respective status of *nabī* and *walī*.

18. *Futūḥāt*, II, p. 85.

ʿArabī's doctrine: each belief concerning God is a limited representation—and thus inadequate in that it excludes other 'aspects' of the divine infinity—yet it nevertheless contains a part of the total Truth because it is, of necessity, based on a theophany. 'The perfect gnostic knows Him in all the forms in which He is epiphanized and in which He 'descends'. He who is not a perfect gnostic knows [when he manifests Himself] only in the form of his particular belief, and does not know Him when He is epiphanized under a different form.'[19] The 'looking at Him', that is to say the extent of the vision of God to which a man may aspire, is determined by the image he already has of Him; the most perfect vision, therefore, which is that of the 'prophets among the saints' or *afrād*, is possessed by those who 'have all of the beliefs'. Needless to say, what is in question here is not simply the sum of the mental images corresponding to these beliefs, but a full realisation of the specific modalities of knowledge and worship connected with each of them.

There are ten chapters in the *Futūḥāt* which are of particular interest in this connection.[20] In these, Ibn ʿArabī discusses the 'stations' (*maqāmāt*) of sainthood, of prophethood and of the mission of the Messengers (*risāla*), first in general terms and then in terms of how they relate to the human condition on the one hand and the angelic state on the other. He does not forget to remind us that we are dealing here, in a sense, with three concentric spheres, of which the first, the sphere of *walāya*, encompasses all the others: every *rasūl* is a *nabī* and every *nabī* is a *walī*.[21] He concludes his discussion with a chapter rich in autobiographical detail, where he speaks of the 'station of proximity' (*maqām al-qurba*) which represents the fullest degree of sainthood, in accordance with the etymology of the Arabic word for it.

In the first of these chapters, however, the Shaykh al-Akbar draws attention to a meaning of *walāya* which has a connection with this etymology but is distinct from it. *Walāya*, he says, is the *naṣr*, meaning help or assistance. This help can be envisaged as active—the help that

19. Ibid., III, p. 132. On this recurrent theme in the teaching of Ibn ʿArabī, see among other texts *Futūḥāt* II, pp. 219-20; III, pp. 162, 309; IV, pp. 142, 165, 211-12, 393; *Fuṣūṣ* I, pp. 113, 122-24. Henry Corbin deals with this subject—in terms concerning which we have certain reservations—in his *Creative Imagination in the Sufism of Ibn Arabī*.

20. Chapters 152 to 161 inclusive (*Futūḥāt* II, pp. 246-62).

21. Ibid., II, p. 256.

one gives—or as passive—the help that one receives. It is help in the active sense that is discussed here, and specifically *walāya* inasmuch as it is a divine attribute. Ibn ʿArabī makes the observation that in verse 2:257, which states, as we have seen, that 'God is the *walī* of those who believe', the reference is to 'those who believe' in general, not just to 'monotheistic believers' (*muwaḥḥidūn*). He concludes that the *walāya* of Allāh extends to the *mushrik*, or polytheist, and that the latter's faith, no matter what its immediate object may be—a stone, an idol, a star—in fact has no object but God. 'All that is in the universe, believing or unbelieving, glorifies God.'[22] This divine assistance accorded to the *mushrik* explains how it is that the latter can triumph over the 'believer' in the usual sense (*al-mu'min al-muwaḥḥid*) who neglects the duties of his faith. This interpretation, he says, is formulated 'in accordance with the language of the spiritual élite': in the language of the majority of believers, when an infidel triumphs over a believer it is perceived solely as a punishment inflicted on the believers, not as a result of positive assistance rendered to the infidels. Only the gnostics know that 'Allāh's *walāya* is universal and extends to all His creatures inasmuch as they are His servants', whether or not they desire it. At the time of the primordial Covenant, when God caused beings to issue from Adam's loins (Qur'ān 7:172), the question He asked them was: 'Am I not your Lord?' He asked them, then, to bear witness to His suzerainty (*rubūbiyya*), not to His unicity. The undertaking that they made to Him in replying 'Truly' (*balā*) is observed by the polytheist as well as by the believer: he may add other lords to this Lord, but he always acknowledges Him as the Lord. God's *walāya* is promised to all those who believe, and 'here below there are only believers and non-belief is an accident' which veils the faith that is inscribed upon the essence of all created beings. This accident is the result of the establishment of revealed Laws which, in accordance with a providential Wisdom, determine the particular ways in which human communities represent and therefore worship God at certain moments of their history. Grave as the consequences may be of

22. This concept, which needless to say is closely related to the concept mentioned above of the 'god created in beliefs', is often discussed by Ibn ʿArabī in relation to his interpretation of verse 17:23 ('And your Lord decreed that you should worship Him alone'), as for example in the *Futūḥāt* I, p. 405. For Ibn Taymiyya's criticism of this interpretation, see *Majmūʿat al-rasā'il*, ed. Rashīd Riḍā, I, p. 173.

disobedience to these Laws, it cannot alter the original, imprescriptible bond established by the Covenant.[23]

In the next chapter the Shaykh al-Akbar turns from discussing *walāya* as a divine attribute to a consideration of it as a human attribute. He makes a clear distinction between *walāya ʿāmma, walāya* in its broadest sense, which consists in the co-operation of created beings, each of them *volens nolens* occupying its place and playing its part in the hierarchy of being, and *walāya khāṣṣa* or *walāya* in the limited sense, which consists in the capacity of the saints to receive, according to the circumstances, the authority and power of one of the divine Names, and to reflect Justice or Mercy or Majesty or Beauty, according to what is required by the state of things at any given moment. Among these saints, we must also distinguish between the *aṣḥāb al-aḥnāl*, the beings who are governed by their spiritual states, and the *aṣḥāb al-maqāmāt*, who master the 'stations' while remaining masters of their states, and are 'the most virile men along the Way'. The former are relatively imperfect, but their *walāya* can be seen by most people. The *walāya* of the latter, in a certain way, is even more evident, but its very brilliance conceals it from man's eyes: 'They manifest themselves endowed with the divine Attributes (*bi-ṣifāt al-Ḥaqq*) and for this reason they are unnoticed.' We have already encountered, and will encounter again, this idea of perfect sainthood as occulted.[24]

Whereas the passages from the *Futūḥāt* which we have been considering envisage *walāya* in terms of 'taking charge' or 'helping', and are thus concerned with the function of the *walī* rather than with what constitutes the *walī* as such, in the concluding chapter of the series Ibn ʿArabī considers *walāya* inasmuch as it is proximity to God.

According to al-Ghazālī, the coming of Muḥammad put the stage of prophethood out of bounds once and for all, the highest level attainable by human beings is the stage of *ṣiddīqiyya*, a word derived from the surname of the caliph Abū Bakr al-Ṣiddīq, 'the truthful'.[25] In this as in other texts[26] Ibn ʿArabī contradicts the author of the *Iḥyā'*, saying that

23. All these remarks are taken from Chapter 152 of the *Futūḥāt* (II, pp. 246-48).

24. Ibid., II, p. 249.

25. *Iḥyā' ʿulūm al-dīn* III, p. 99; IV, pp. 159, 245, etc.

26. The *maqām al-qurba*, which forms the subject of chapter 161 of the *Futūḥāt* (II, pp. 260-62) to which reference is made here, is further discussed in ibid. II, pp. 19, 24-25, 41; III, p. 103. It also comes into the *Kitāb al-Qurba*, Hyderabad

there is a spiritual station which is higher than the *ṣiddīqiyya*, intermediate between that and the 'prophetic station'. This is the 'station of proximity' (*maqām al-qurba*), which represents the ultimate point in the hierarchy of the saints, a point which he also calls the station of non-legislative prophethood or 'prophethood of the saints'. It is accessible only to the *afrād*, otherwise known as the *muqarrabūn*, 'those who are close'—a term which, as we have seen, originates in the Qur'ān. One of these is the Pole, *quṭb*, the one being in this world who is 'the place of Allāh's gaze',[27] and who therefore carries out the 'mandate of heaven' in all the universe. But the superiority he possesses in respect of his function does not make him superior in spiritual rank: he is *primus inter pares* and has no authority over the *afrād*. We will come back to the metaphysical significance of this 'proximity', as well as to the information provided by Ibn ᶜArabī on the subject of the Pole and the initiatic hierarchy, defining and supplementing the information we can gather from *taṣawwuf* in general. But we should note that in this chapter Ibn ᶜArabī gives an account of his own entry into the *maqām al-qurba*. It happened when he was in Morocco, during the month of Muḥarram in the year 597 (October-November 1200)—the same year, that is, in which he had a vision at Marrakesh of the divine Throne during which was revealed to him the name of the companion whom he met later on at Fez, and with whom he finally set out for the East in 598.[28] 'I wandered about this station', he writes, 'without meeting a soul, and the solitude oppressed me.' At that point there appeared to him ᶜAbd al-Raḥmān al-Sulamī, author of the *Ṭabaqāt al-ṣūfiyya*, who had died almost two hundred years previously and who had come, through the operation of divine Grace, to relieve this sense of overwhelming loneliness by his presence and to teach Ibn ᶜArabī the name and nature of this *maqām*.

Prophethood and sainthood, therefore, are related. But there exists another relationship as well, in virtue of which the saints are the heirs of the prophets. The idea of this inheritance existed prior to Ibn ᶜArabī, although it was not much developed: Sahl al-Tustarī, for example, says:

1948, which makes a more cautious mention of Ibn ᶜArabī's arrival at this spiritual station, and also makes a brief reference to some of the general facts concerning *walāya* and its relation to *nubuwwa* and *risāla*.

27. *Iṣṭ.*, definition no. 19.

28. *Futūḥāt*, II, p. 436. This companion, Muḥammad al-Ḥaṣṣār, died in Egypt shortly after their arrival.

'There is no prophet who does not have someone similar to himself in this community, that is to say, a *walī* who shares in his charisma.'[29] Earlier on, the Shaykh al-Akbar was quoted as saying: 'If you are a *walī*, you are the heir of a prophet.' He goes on to explain: 'And if you have inherited knowledge from Moses or Jesus or from any prophet in between, all you have actually inherited is Muḥammadan knowledge.'[30] But if all the saints are in a sense the 'heirs of Muḥammad', there is a crucial difference between those who have received this heritage in full, and the others. Before analysing Ibn ᶜArabī's views on the subject, we must go more deeply into the doctrinal basis of the role assigned to the Prophet Muḥammad.

29. Quoted by Gerhard Böwering, *The Mystical Vision of Existence in Classical Islam*, Berlin-New York 1980, p. 65.

30. *Futūḥāt*, IV, p. 398.

CHAPTER

4

The Muḥammadan Reality

FOR a saint, to be the heir of one of the prophets is always to be the heir of Muḥammad. Indeed, 'the prophets were his deputies in the created world when he [i.e. Muḥammad] was pure spirit, aware of being so, prior to the appearance of his body or flesh. When he was asked, 'When were you a prophet?', he replied, 'I was a prophet when Adam was between water and clay', meaning: when Adam had not yet come into existence. And this was so until the appearance of his most pure body. At that moment the authority of his deputies came to an end . . . the authority, that is to say, of the other messengers and prophets.'[1] As we will see later, other texts by Ibn ʿArabī define more clearly the nature and function of this primordial Muḥammadan Reality (*ḥaqīqa muḥammadiyya*), of which every prophet since Adam, the first prophet, is but a partial refraction at a particular moment of human history.

What is the real meaning of the word *ḥaqīqa*, which we have translated as 'Reality'? According to the *Lisān al-ʿarab*, it signifies the true meaning of a thing as opposed to its metaphorical meaning (*majāzī*); it also signifies the 'heart' of a thing or matter, its true nature, its essence, and thus the inviolable inmost self of a being, its *ḥurma*.[2] The concept of a Muḥammadan reality which is not only fully constituted and active before the appearance in this world of the person named Muḥammad, but is also situated prior to history, has been the subject of heated debate in Islam. Ibn Taymiyya and several other writers, in accordance with their usual practice, attempted to prove its innovative and aberrant nature (*bidʿa*) by challenging the main scriptural reference for it, which is the *ḥadīth* quoted above where Muḥammad says, 'I was a prophet when Adam was between water and clay'. For the Ḥanbalite polemicist, this *ḥadīth* is a forgery and the only permissible version of it

1. *Futūḥāt*, I, p. 243.

2. Ibn Manẓūr, *Lisān al-ʿarab*, Beirut, n.d., x, p. 52. See also the article by Louis Gardet, *EI*², s.v. *ḥaqīqa*.

is the one quoted by Ibn Ḥanbal and Tirmidhī, where the Prophet apparently says, 'I was a prophet when Adam was between spirit and flesh' (*bayna' l-rūḥ wa 'l-jasad*).[3] Without stressing the fact that the differences in phraseology between these two concurrently existing forms of the same statement seem to us, ultimately, to be minor, we should point out that the criteria by which traditionists judge the authenticity of a *ḥadīth* are purely external and have reference essentially to the reliability of the chain of transmission. Yet Ibn ᶜArabī, who, even when an old man, never ceased to study the *ḥadīth* in the usual ways and knew everything there was to know about the traditions, says on several occasions[4] that an 'unveiling' (*kashf*) is the only sure way of judging the validity of a particular remark attributed to the Prophet, and in so saying he challenges the doctrinal authority of the doctors of the Law.

On the other hand, even though the phrase *ḥaqīqa muḥammadiyya* made its appearance late and in this sense is indeed a *bidᶜa* or innovation, the concept that it represents in abstract terms is one of the most traditional in Islam, where it is clearly symbolized as the 'Muḥammadan light' (*nūr muḥammadī, nūr Muḥammad*). Moreover, the association of the Prophet with a symbolism of light is not, in Islamic terms, a human invention, but is based on the actual words of God. In the Qur'ān (33:46), Muḥammad is called 'a torch which illumines' (*sirājan munīran*); another verse (5:15) says that 'a light has come to you from God', which is interpreted by the commentators as a reference to the Prophet.[5] For Muslims, this 'light' is not simply a metaphor. Ibn Isḥāq, who was born only seventy years after the Prophet's death, reports that the Prophet's father ᶜAbdallāh, just before his marriage with Āmina, met a woman who tried in vain to seduce him. When he saw her again on the day after his wedding, and the Prophet had already been conceived, this same woman turned away from him, and on being asked

3. Ibn Ḥanbal, IV, p. 66; V, p. 59; V, p. 379; Tirmidhī, *manāqib*, 1. On Ibn Taymiyya's repeated criticism, see *Majmūᶜat al-rasā'il*, IV, pp. 8, 70-71. Ghazālī (*al-Maḍnūn al-ṣaghīr*, printed in the margin of Jīlī's *al-Insān al-kāmil*, Cairo 1949, II, p. 98) accepts the version when 'Adam was between water and mud', but interprets it more narrowly as a reference to the predestined nature of the Muḥammadan mission. Suyūṭī, in response to Subkī's critique, only cites the version 'between spirit and flesh', but he uses the expression *ḥaqīqat al-nabī* (*al-Ḥāwī li'l-fatāwī*, Cairo 1959, II, p. 189).

4. *Futūḥāt*, I, p. 150; II, p. 376.

5. Cf. Tabarī, *Tafsīr*, ed. Shākir, X, p. 143.

why, said, 'The light which was upon you yesterday has left you'.[6] Ibn Isḥāq explains that his own father told him that this woman had seen between ʿAbdallāh's two eyes a radiant white mark, which disappeared when the Prophet was conceived. According to a slightly different version of this story, as related by Ibn Isḥāq, the woman speaking to ʿAbdallāh was no other than the sister of Waraqa ibn Nawfal—the Christian from Mecca who, when questioned by the Prophet after the first visit of the angel Gabriel, assured him of the authenticity of the Revelation—and had been warned by her brother of the imminent coming of a prophet. What she had perceived in the face of ʿAbdallāh was the 'light of prophethood' of which he was the transmitter.[7]

This story was taken up by later historians such as Ṭabarī (died 310/923)[8] and widely diffused by all the writers who wrote 'histories of the prophets'.[9] The interpretation of it very soon introduced the explicit theme of the *verus propheta*, based, among other things, on a *ḥadīth* quoted by Bukhāri[10] in which the Prophet, 'borne' century after century and generation upon generation (*qarnan fa-qarnan*), appears

6. This account of Ibn Isḥāq's (died 150/767) is transmitted by Ibn Hishām, *al-Sīra al-nabawiyya*, Cairo 1955, I, p. 155. For the latest research on the development of the *sīra* in Ibn Isḥāq and Ibn Hishām, see *La Vie du Prophète Mahomet*, ed. T. Fahd, Paris 1983, the article by R. G. Khoury ('Les sources islamiques de la *sīra* avant Ibn Hishām'), pp. 7-29, and the article by W. Montgomery Watt ('The reliability of Ibn Isḥāq's sources'), pp. 31-43. This last shows the accusations of Shīʿism levelled against Ibn Isḥāq to be baseless.

7. The case of Waraqa ibn Nawfal—in any case a fairly mysterious person—merits a study of its own. The confirmation he gives the Prophet must be understood as the acknowledgement, by the inspired representative of a previous tradition (in this case Christianity) of the validity of a new cycle of tradition. It thereby possesses, on a more restricted scale, a meaning analogous to that of the visit of the Three Kings to Bethlehem (cf. René Guénon, The Lord of the World, Ellingstring U.K., 1983, chapter 6). It bears a particular relation to the Qur'ānic affirmation (61:6) that Jesus foretold the coming of the Prophet—an affirmation which, as understood in Islamic exotericism, is supported only by unconvincing exegeses of Gospel texts (John 14:16 and 14:26) or else by obvious forgeries such as the pseudo-Gospel of Barnabas. (To our mind, the most probable theory on the origin of this work is that put forward by Mikel de Epalza, who attributes it to Moorish writers; cf. his article 'Le milieu hispano-moresque de l'Évangile de Barnabe', in *Islamochristiana*, no. 8, Rome 1982, pp. 159-83).

8. See the excerpt from the Zotenberg translation published under the title *Mahommed, Sceau des prophètes*, Paris 1980, p. 56.

9. Thaʿlabī, *Qiṣaṣ al-anbiyā'*, Cairo 1371 AH, pp. 16-17.

10. Bukhārī, *manāqib*, 23.

to be travelling through time towards the point where his physical nature becomes manifest. Is this journeying of the prophetic Seed to its final birth to be understood as taking place in the 'loins' of his ancestors, of his carnal lineage, or as a series of stopping-places in the persons of the successive bearers of the Revelation, the one hundred and twenty-four thousand prophets of whom he is both the forefather and the final Seal? Ibn ᶜAbbās (died 68/687), the *tarjumān al-qur'ān* or 'interpreter *par excellence* of the Qur'ān', commenting on verse 26:219, seems to favour the second meaning: according to him, Muḥammad goes from prophet to prophet (*min nabiyyin ilā nabiyyin*) until the moment when God causes him to 'emerge' (*akhraja*) as a prophet in his turn.[11] Ibn Saᶜd, who cites this, also refers to a *ḥadīth* which Ṭabarī likewise mentions, and in which Muḥammad says, 'I am the first man to have been created and the last to have been sent [i.e. as a prophet].'[12] The truth is that both these themes are bound up with each other, for the traditional genealogy of Muḥammad also includes a series of prophets, among whom are Abraham and Ishmael. However, another *ḥadīth*, which is absent from the canonical collections, and in which explicit reference is made to *Nūr muḥammadī*, was destined to play a major part in the meditation on the Prophet's primordiality. It is mentioned by one of the Companions, Jābir ibn ᶜAbdallāh, and runs as follows: 'O Jābir, God created the light of your Prophet out of His Light before he created things.'[13]

11. Ibn Saᶜd, *Ṭabaqāt*, Leiden 1909, I/1, p. 5.

12. Ibid., I/1, p.96. Ṭabarī, *Tafsīr*, Cairo 1323AH, XXI, p. 79. A wealth of information about the Muḥammadan Light may be found in the article by U. Rubin, 'Pre-existence and Light', *Israel Oriental Studies*, V, 1975, pp. 62-119. This almost exhaustive study is not, of course, rendered less indispensable by our own brief reference to the subject. Even though we are unable to accept Goldziher's thesis (of which more later), Rubin's charge that he twisted the meaning of the texts in order to make them confirm the idea of Neoplatonic influence, particularly in the case of Ibn ᶜAbbās' words quoted above, seems to us to go too far. Apart from the books and articles to which direct reference is made in this chapter, the *Nūr muḥammadī* is the subject of L. Massignon's article of that title in *EI*[1]. See also Henry Corbin, *En Islam iranien* (cf. index, s.v. *ḥaqīqa muḥammadiyya* and 'lumière muhammadienne').

13. Ismāᶜīl al-ᶜAjalūnī, *Kashf al-khafā'*, Beirut 1351 AH, I, pp. 265-266; Zurqānī, *Sharḥ al-mawāhib*, Cairo 1329AH, I, pp. 46-47. We must remember that several *aḥadīth* exist which are similar in form and differ only in the term used at the end: 'The first thing that God created was the Calamus' (Tirmidhī, *tafsīr*, s. 68; *qadar*, 17; Abū Dāwūd, *sunna*, 16; Ibn Ḥanbal, v/317); 'The first thing that Allāh

The Muḥammadan Light and later interpretations of it in the doctrine of the *ḥaqīqa muḥammadiyya* soon gave rise to an idea which appears in many texts prior to Islam, under various guises. There is the *Logos spermatikos* which enabled St Justin (died c. 165) to 'christianize' retrospectively the forms of truth which had existed prior to the coming of Christ;[14] there is, above all, the *verus propheta* mentioned above, who travels from prophet to prophet until his perfect and definitive manifestation as Jesus. The 'pseudo-Clementine romance' (attributed to the fourth Pope, Clement of Rome, who died in 97), which derives its subject-matter from Jewish and Judaeo-Christian sources strongly redolent of gnosticism, illustrates this doctrine, whence Islam, according to Oscar Culman, was to reap the heritage that orthodox Christianity rejected.[15] Goldziher was the first to look for traces of neo-platonic and gnostic influence in the texts relating to the *Nūr muḥammadī.*[16] There is evidence that analogies exist with Manichean beliefs as well as with the Hindu concept of *avatāra*. But without ruling out, here as elsewhere, the earlier or later borrowings by Islam of vocabulary and conceptual tools from various religious heritages that it took under its wing, we nevertheless find these historical explanations unacceptable, because they end by denying the specificity and coherence of the spiritual experience of believers. Similar attempts have been made to prove that *taṣawwuf* was merely a heterogenous collection of non-Islamic ideas and practices—a thesis of which Massignon, among others, has effectively demonstrated the inanity.

The Muḥammadan revelation is explicitly viewed as the confirmation and fulfilment of the revelations preceding it (*muṣaddiqan bi–ma*

---

created was the Intellect'. On Ibn Taymiyya's discussion of the Ṣūfī interpretation of these, see *Majmūʿ fatāwā* XI, p. 232, and XVIII, pp. 336-38.

14. *Patrologie grecque*, VI, 397, b, c.

15. O. Culman, *Le Problème littéraire et historique du roman pseudo-clémentin*, Paris 1930 (see p. 208 ff. and 230 ff. on the *verus propheta*). It is hardly necessary to say that, despite Henry Corbin's support of him, we are unable to accept the thesis of L. Cirillo, according to which the Gospel of Barnabas (cf. note 7) transmits, on this and other points, a genuinely Judaeo-Christian teaching. Cf. L. Cirillo and Michel Frémaux, *L'Évangile de Barnabe*, Paris 1977.

16. I. Goldziher, 'Neuplatonische und Gnostische Elemente im Hadīth' (*Zeitschrift fur Assyriologie*, 1909, XXII, pp. 317-44). Cf. also A. A. ʿAfīfī, *Naẓariyyāt al-islāmiyyīn fī 'l-kalima (Majallat kullīyat al-ādāb*, Fuad I University 1934, pp. 33-75), and *The Influence of Hermetic Literature in Muslim Thought, B.S.O.A.S.*, XIII, 1950, pp. 840-55.

bayna yadayhi, Qur'ān 46:30): according to the Qur'ān (2:4, 2:136, etc.), the true believers are those who believe in what was revealed to Muḥammad *and in what was revealed before him*. The concept of the *verus propheta*, symbolized by the long pilgrimage of the Muḥammadan Light through the aeons, is a logical consequence of this fundamental doctrine, according to which the successive prophetic messages, as multiple manifestations of the one Truth, are so many stages leading up to him who will bring the 'full sum of the Words' (*jawāmiᶜ al-kalim*),[17] simultaneously perfecting and abrogating the previous Laws. But the Qur'ān is not only a source of doctrine. The experience of the souls and tongues which express it is formed within it as within a matrix, and stamps its shape indelibly upon the burning metal of its visions and symbols.

Leaving aside the historical problem, which appears to us to lead nowhere, let us turn to some of the texts which, from century to century, bear witness to the unwearying attention given by the Muslim spiritual masters to the *Nūr muḥammadī*. Jaᶜfar al-Ṣādiq, commenting on verse 68:1 which starts with one of the fourteen 'luminous' (*nūrāniyya*) single letters that occur at the beginning of twenty-nine *sūras*, says: 'The *nūn* is the light of pre-eternity out of which God created all beings and which he bestowed on Muḥammad. This is why it was said [in verse 4 of the same *sūra*]: "You are endowed with a sublime nature"—endowed, that is, with this light which you were privileged to receive in pre-eternity.'[18] Sahl al–Tustarī, one of the teachers most frequently quoted by Ibn ᶜArabī,[19] relates how Khaḍir said to him, 'God

17. *Ūtītu jawāmiᶜ al-kalim*; this *ḥadīth* occurs in Bukhārī, *taᶜbīr*, 11; Muslim, *masājid*, 5, etc.

18. This text is an extract from Jaᶜfar al-Ṣādiq's *Tafsīr*, which has been preserved, albeit in an incomplete form, in Sulamī's *Ḥaqā'iq al-tafsīr* and edited by Nwyia in the *Mélanges* of the Saint-Joseph University, Beirut 1968, XLIII, with the title *Le Tafsir mystique attribue* à *Jaᶜfar Ṣādiq* (p. 226). Nwyia has a slightly different translation of it in *Exégèse coranique et langage mystique*, Beirut 1970, p. 167. It goes without saying that this remark of the sixth imām is closely related to the identification (legimate but restrictive) of the 'luminous letters' with the fourteen immaculate ones in Imāmic Shīᶜism. Nevertheless, it is quoted by Sunnī writers—along with other remarks of Jaᶜfar's—as the expression of a truth which is part of the undivided Islamic inheritance. We should note likewise that Corbin mentions a reference to the Muḥammadan Light made by the fifth imām, Muḥammad al-Bāqir (*En islam iranien*, I, pp. 99-100).

19. Cf. *Futūḥāt*, II, p. 60, 662; III, pp. 41, 86, 395; IV, pp. 249, 376; *Kitāb al-tajallīyāt*, ed. Osman Yahia, III, p. 304, etc.

created the Light of Muḥammad out of His own Light . . .. This Light dwelt before God for a hundred thousand years. He directed His gaze towards it seventy thousand times each day and each night, adding a new light to it with each glance. After it, He created all the creatures.'[20] Al-Ḥākim al-Tirmidhī, a contemporary of Sahl, also emphasizes Muḥammad's pre-existence: 'The first being to be mentioned by God was he. The first to appear within the divine Knowledge was he. The first to be desired by the divine Will was he. He was first in the divine Decrees, first in the well-guarded Tablet, first when the Covenant (*mīthāq*) was made.'[21]

In the *Kitāb al–ṭawāsīn*, al-Ḥallāj (died 309/922), referring to the 'Verse of the Light' (Qur'ān 24:35), identifies the 'tabernacle' (*mishkāt*) mentioned in this famous text with Muḥammad, and the 'torch' (*miṣbāḥ*) in the tabernacle with the *Nūr muḥammadī*. He also says of the Prophet's tribe that it is 'neither of the East nor of the West', thereby assimilating it to the 'blessed tree' whose oil, according to this verse, feeds the 'torch'. 'The light of prophethood', he writes, 'has sprung from his light; and his light issues from the Light of mystery . . .. The design [allotted to this light] precedes the [other] designs, the existence [prepared for him] precedes the void, the name destined for him precedes the Calamus . . .. All knowledge is but a drop of his knowledge, all maxims are a mouthful of his river, all epochs an hour of his time . . .. He is the first to have been included in the divine prescience, he is the last to have been sent as a prophet!'[22]

Furthermore, this extolling of the Prophet, which assigns him a cosmic function beyond his historical role, is not limited to a small circle, but occurs in popular texts such as the *Kitāb al-Shifā bi-taʿrīf al-Muṣṭafā*,[23] written by the famous Mālikī judge Qāḍī ʿIyāḍ (died

20. Louis Massignon, *Textes inédits concernant l'histoire de la mystique en pays d'Islam*, Paris 1929, p. 39. The importance of the Muḥammadan Light in the doctrine of Sahl al-Tustarī has been analysed by Gerhard Böwering, *The Mystical Vision of Existence in Classical Islam*, Berlin-New York 1980, p. 149 ff; particular attention should be paid, on p. 150, to Sahl's commentary on verses 13-18 of *sūra* 53.

21. Al-Ḥakīm al-Ṭirmidhī, *Khatm al-awliyā'* (section 8), p. 337.

22. *The Kitāb al-Ṭawāsīn* has been edited by L. Massignon, Paris 1913. On the subject of this work, which is a posthumous collection of texts dating from the end of Ḥallāj's life, see the second edition of *La Passion de Hallaj*, Paris 1975, III, p. 297 ff., from which (pp. 304-6) the following quotations are taken.

23. Qāḍī ʿIyāḍ, *Kitāb al-shifā*, Damascus 1392/1972.

544/1149). Seven centuries later, the emir ᶜAbd al-Qādir al–Jazā'irī, after writing a brief commentary on the first verse of the *sūra* of the 'Night Voyage', the audacity of which might alarm someone 'to whom the secret of the Muḥammadan Reality has not been unveiled', wonders whether 'Perhaps he might say to me, as did Ibn Taymiyya on looking at ᶜIyāḍ's *Shifā*: this little Maghribī is exaggerating!' ᶜAbd al-Qādir was reassured by a vision in which he was required instead to add to what he had already written.[24]

During the age of Ibn ᶜArabī, on the initiative of the Ayyubids or, rather, of the Ṣūfis who inspired them, the Prophet's *mawlid*, or birthday, began to be celebrated on a regular basis. In the poetical compositions, naïve or accomplished, that flourished in the same period, the themes of which we have been speaking were developed in terms that were sometimes allusive but more often perfectly explicit. This is so in the case of the *Tā'iyya* by Ibn al-Fāriḍ, in which he has the Prophet say, 'There is no living thing that does not derive its life from me, and all desiring souls are subject to my will'; 'Even though I am a son of Adam in form, in him I have an essence of my own which testifies that I am his father.'[25]

However, it is to Ibn ᶜArabī himself that we must turn for a more detailed explanation of the doctrine which is contained incipiently within the theme of the *Nūr muḥammadī*, and of its relationship with *walāya*. Chapter Six of the *Futūḥāt Makkiyya* is entitled 'On the knowledge of the start of spiritual creation' (*al-khalq al-rūḥānī*), and lists, under this heading, the questions to be discussed: 'Who was the first to be endowed with existence? Where was he endowed with existence? In accordance with what model? What is his aim?'

24. *Kitāb al-Mawāqif*, Damascus 1966-67, I, pp. 219-20.

25. Ibn al-Fāriḍ, *al-Tā'iyya al-Kubrā*, Cairo 1310 AH, together with Qāshānī's commentary in the margin of his *Dīwān*, verse 639 p. 189 and 631 p. 175. Examples of these poems in praise of the Prophet, which plainly convey the doctrine of the *ḥaqīqa muḥammadiyya*, can be found in ᶜAlī Ṣāfī Ḥusayn, *al-Adab al-ṣūfī fī Miṣr fī 'l-qarn al-sābiᶜ al-hijrī*, Cairo 1964, pp. 230 ff., which contains works by Aḥmad al-Badawī, Ibrāhīm al-Dasūqī, etc. We can mention only a few representative texts; but a systematic enquiry into prophetological doctrine would go beyond Ṣūfī literature to the 'professions of faith', especially those of the Ḥanbalites or of writers influenced by Ḥanbalism, such as Abū Bakr al-Ājurrī (died 360/970) in his *Kitāb al-Sharīᶜa*. A great deal of information about the different forms of venerating the Prophet in Islam is contained in Annemarie Schimmel's book *And Muhammad is His Messenger*, Chapel Hill, 1985.

The beginning of creation, replies the Shaykh al-Akbar, was *al-habā'*, the primordial 'dust'—a term which is the equivalent, in his writings, of *al-hayūlā*, what philosophers call the *materia prima*;[26] and the first thing in *al-habā'* to be endowed with existence was the *ḥaqīqa muḥammadiyya raḥmāniyya*, the Muḥammadan Reality which proceeds from the divine Name *al-Raḥmān*, the All-Merciful, 'which was not confined within any space because it was illimitable'.[27] God

epiphanized Himself by means of His Light to this dust, which is called by speculative thinkers the first universal matter and in which the entire universe existed *in potentia*, and each thing that was in this dust received this Light according to its capacity and predisposition, as the corners of a room receive the light of a torch, and are more fully and brightly lit up the nearer they are to the torch. Indeed, God said, 'The symbol of His Light is like a niche with a torch in it' (Qur'ān 24:35), thus comparing His Light to a torch. Now there was nothing in the dust that was closer to the light, or more disposed to receive it, than the Reality (*ḥaqīqa*) of Muḥammad, which is also called the Intellect.[28] He [i.e. Muḥammad] is thus the head of all the universe and the first being to come into existence . . .. And the universe proceeeds from his epiphany.[29]

Chapter Three Hundred and Seventy-one of the *Futūḥāt* (section 9: 'On the universe, that is to say on all that is other than God, and on its organization') contains a long account of the birth of the cosmos, in

26. Cf. *Futūḥāt*, III, p. 107.

27. Ibid., I, p. 118; O. Yahia's edition, II, p. 220.

28. This identification of the *ḥaqīqa muḥammadiyya* with the first Intellect (*al-ʿaql al-awwal*) is based on the equivalence established between them by the *aḥadīth* mentioned in note 13. Ibn ʿArabī uses both versions of these *aḥadīth* according to the context. See for example *Futūḥāt*, I, p. 125 ('The first thing that God created was the Calamus').

29. *Futūḥāt*, I, p. 119; O. Yahia's edition, II, pp. 226-27. The end of this sentence draws attention to the eminence of ʿAlī ibn Abī Ṭālib, the closest to him (i.e. Muḥammad) of all men. Cf. O. Yahia's note on line 6, p. 227, and his introduction on p. 36 of the same, pointing out the difference in this passage between the first and second drafts of the *Futūḥāt* (cf. the 1293 AH edition of it, I, p. 154). O. Yahia sees it as expressive of a 'tendency towards Shīʿism' which is more marked in the first draft. It should be noted, however, that, unlike the second draft, which was completed in 636 AH and of which we possess an autograph manuscript, the first is known to us only through a manuscript postdating Ibn ʿArabī (the copy was completed in 683 AH) and is thus not equally reliable. On the problem of the identification of the Seal of the Saints, of which we will speak later, this passage furnished Ḥaydar Āmolī (*Naṣṣ al-nuṣūṣ*, p. 195) with an argument for making Ibn ʿArabī contradict himself—and this in spite of the fact that he was unaware of the first draft.

which Ibn ʿArabī describes the successive appearance of the forms of beings in the original 'cloud' (*al-ʿamā'*), which is no other than the 'Breath of the Merciful One' (*nafas al-Raḥmān*). The first being to be endowed with existence in this 'sphere of the cloud' was the 'divine Calamus', the 'first Intellect' who is also the 'Muḥammadan Reality' or the 'Reality out of which all things were created', the 'universal Holy Spirit', the 'point of balance of the divine Names'.[30] In another work by Ibn ʿArabī, the *ʿAnqā' Mughrib*, whose main theme is actually the 'Seal of Sainthood', there is a series of highly significant observations: 'The Spirit attributed to God [in verse 32:8, where it is said that God breathed "His Spirit" into Adam] is the Muḥammadan Reality.'[31] The Prophet 'is the ultimate kind (*al-jins al-ʿālī*) who contains all kinds, the supreme father of all creatures and of all men, even though his clay (*ṭīnatuhu*, his physical nature) only appeared afterwards'.[32] 'The Muḥammadan Reality arises out of the Lights of Absolute Plenitude (*min al-anwār al-ṣamadiyya*) in the dwelling of Unity (*al-aḥadiyya*).[33] 'The Muḥammadan Reality was endowed with existence, and then out of it He drew the universe'.[34] The last chapter of the *Fuṣūṣ* is just as explicit: 'He is the most perfect creature of the human race. For this reason things begin with him and will be sealed by him: indeed, he was a prophet when Adam was between water and clay; and then [when he manifested himself] through his elemental form, he was the Seal of the Prophets.'[35]

30. *Futūḥāt*, III, pp. 443-44. We find here the equivalences referred to in note 28, in addition to other technical terms borrowed from previous Ṣūfis: Ibn ʿArabī explains (*Futūḥāt*, III, p. 77) that the expression 'the Reality out of which all things are created' (*al-ḥaqq al-makhlūq bihi kullu shay'*) goes back to Ibn Barrajān (died 536/1141) who derived it from verse 15:85, and that it corresponds to what Sahl al-Tustarī, for his part, calls *al-ʿadl*, Justice. A similar description of the levels of universal manifestation, in relation, this time, to the structure of the human being, and which assigns priority to the *ḥaqīqa muḥammadiyya*, can be found in the *Tadbīrāt Ilāhiyya*, ed. Nyberg, p. 211.

31. *ʿAnqā' Mughrib*, Cairo 1954, p. 40.

32. Ibid., p. 41.

33. Ibid., p. 36.

34. Ibid., p. 37. On the *ḥaqīqa muḥammadiyya*, see also pp. 50-51.

35. *Fuṣūṣ*, I, p. 214. See also *Profession de Foi (Tadhkira)*, edited and translated by R. Deladrière, Paris 1978, chapter 2 ('La Realite principielle de l'Envoyé'). In our opinion, this work cannot be attributed to Ibn ʿArabī, although it bears the stamp of his doctrine and contains extracts from his writings. On the problem of the attribution of the *Tadhkira*, see Denis Gril's review in the critical bulletin of the *Annales islamologiques*, XX, 1984, pp. 337-39.

Another concept, which forms a complement to the *ḥaqīqa muḥammadiyya*, is that of the 'Perfect Man' (*al-insān al-kāmil*).

It is through him that God looks at His creatures and dispenses His Mercy upon them; for he is the adventitious man, and yet he has no beginning; he is ephemeral and yet he is everlastingly eternal. He is also the Word which divides and unites. The world subsists in virtue of his existence. He is to the world what the setting of a seal is to the seal: that is to say the place where the imprint is engraved, the symbol with which the king seals his treasures. This is why he has been called *khalīfa* [lieutenant, vicar, deputy]: for through him God preserves His creation, as the seal preserves the treasures. As long as the king's seal remains unbroken, no one would dare to open the treasures without his permission. Thus Man has been charged to guard the kingdom, and the world will be preserved for as long as the Perfect Man subsists therein.[36]

Properly speaking, the term *insān kāmil* is applied to man insofar as he is *in actu* what he was intended and created to be, that is to say, insofar as he realizes in an effective manner his original theomorphism; for God created Adam 'according to His form'.[37] As such, he is 'the place where the two seas flow together' (*majmaᶜ al-baḥrayn*:an expression borrowed from verse 18:60), he in whom the two realities, higher and

36. *Fuṣūṣ*, I, p. 50. On the *insān kāmil*, see R. A. Nicholson, *Studies in Islamic Mysticism*, Cambridge 1921, chapter 2; A. A. ᶜAfifi, *The Mystical Philosophy of Muhyid-Din Ibnul Arabi*, Cambridge U.K. 1939, chapter 2; L. Massignon, *L'Homme parfait en Islam et son originalité eschatologique* (1948), in *Opera minora*, Beirut 1963, I, pp. 107-25; H. H. Schaeder, 'Die islamische Lehre vom Vollkommenen Menschen', *Zeitschrift des deustchen morgenländischen Gesellschafts'* LXXIX (1925), pp. 192-268; T. Izutsu, *Sufism and Taoism*, Berkeley and London 1984, chapters 15-17; cf. also the article by R. Arnaldez in *EI*², s.v., and by Suᶜād al-Ḥakīm in *al-Mawsūᶜa al-falsafiyya al-ᶜarabiyya*, Beirut 1986, I, pp. 134-48; and see Masataka Takeshita, *Ibn Arabī's Theory of the Perfect Man*, Tokyo 1987. Titus Burckhardt gives a slightly different translation of this passage from the *Fuṣūṣ* in his (incomplete) French version of the work (*La Sagesse des prophètes*, Paris 1955, p. 25). Chapter 60 of ᶜAbd al-Karīm al-Jīlī's *al-Insān al-kāmil* (Cairo 1949, pp. 44-48), where the author discusses the subject of the title, is not included among the excerpts from this work translated by Burckhardt in his *De l'Homme universel*, Lyon 1953.

37. Ibn Ḥanbal, II, p. 244, 315; Bukhārī, *isti'dhān*, 1. On the interpretation of this *ḥadīth*, quoted often by Ibn ᶜArabī, see among other texts *Futūḥāt*, I, p. 107. The idea of the Perfect Man as the mirror of God—another expression of his theomorphism—is also based on the *ḥadīth* (Tirmidhī, *birr*, 8) according to which 'the believer is the mirror of the Believer' (*al-mu'min*, a word which means the man who believes, and which is in addition one of the divine Names). Cf. *Futūḥāt*, I, p. 112; III, p. 134.'

lower, are united, the intermediary or 'isthmus' (*barzakh*) between the *ḥaqq* and the *khalq*, between God and creation.[38] He is also 'brother of the Qur'ān',[39] 'pillar of heaven',[40] 'the Word which totalizes' (*kalima jāmiʿa*)[41]—for all beings are Words of God[42] and He contains all of them synthetically within His perfect nature.

These various expressions can strictly be applied only to the *ḥaqīqa muḥammadiyya*, for it alone possesses these attributes *ab initio* and in full measure. In another sense, however, they are adequate to designate the *quṭb* and any beings who are able to assume his cosmic function. In any case, the terms *ḥaqīqa muḥammadiyya* and *insān kāmil* are not purely synonymous, but express differing views of man, the first seeing him in terms of his primordiality and the second in terms of his finality. The *kamāl* or perfection of the *insān kāmil* should not be understood in a 'moral' sense (so as to correspond with the 'heroic virtues'), but as meaning 'fulfilment' or 'completion'.[43] Properly speaking, this perfection is possessed only by Muḥammad, the ultimate and total manifestation of the *ḥaqīqa muḥammadiyya*. Yet, on the other hand, it is equally the goal of all spiritual life and the very definition of *walāya*. Hence, the *walāya* of the *walī* can only be participation in the *walāya* of the Prophet.

As we have seen, this participation or heritage (*wirātha*) can be either direct or indirect. 'Of the people on this Way, there are only two types of spiritual men who can be called *stricto sensu* Muḥammadans: those

38. *Inshā' al-dawā'ir*, ed. Nyberg, p. 22.

39. *Futūḥāt*, III, p. 94. That this term, properly speaking, can be applied only to the Prophet in terms of his *ḥaqīqa* is illustrated in another passage (*Futūḥāt*, IV, p. 21), where Ibn ʿArabī says: He who—among the members of his community who did not live during his epoch—wishes to see Muḥammad, let him look at the Qur'ān. There is no difference between looking at it and looking at God's Messenger. It is as though the Qur'ān had clothed itself in a form of flesh named Muḥammad ibn ʿAbdallāh ibn ʿAbd al-Muṭṭalib. This identification of the Prophet with the divine Word itself is corroborated in scripture by the words of ʿĀ'isha quoted above, who, when questioned about the Prophet's nature, answered: 'His nature was the Qur'ān'.

40. *Futūḥāt*, III, p. 418 (identified for this reason with the tree; cf. *Iṣṭ.*, s.v. *shajara*).

41. *Futūḥāt*, II, p. 446.

42. Ibid., I, p. 366; IV, pp. 5, 65.

43. The *ḥaqīqa muḥammadiyya*, the animal aspect of man, and the *insān kāmil* correspond respectively to the three stages (creation *fī aḥsani taqwīm*; fall *asfala sāfilīn*; restoration through faith and works) described in verses 4, 5, and 6 of *sūra* 95.

who have been privileged to inherit a knowledge relating to a legal provision which did not exist in any previously revealed Law or else those who, after having mastered all the stations (*maqāmāt*) have come to [the stage mentioned in the Qur'ān, 33:13] the "non-station",[44] such as Abū Yazīd [al-Bisṭāmī] and others like him. They also can be said to be Muḥammadans.'[45] In the first case, the word 'Muḥammadan' is used in a restricted sense: it applies to those favoured with a spiritual knowledge which results from the practice of one specific aspect of the Law brought by Muḥammad—that is to say, of a provision which belongs to this Law and does not merely confirm a previous one.[46] It refers, therefore, to the historical Prophet. In the second case, however, which concerns the *awliyā'* who have transcended all stations on the Way, the qualification of 'Muḥammadan' establishes a connection with the *ḥaqīqa muḥammadiyya* itself.

'As for all the rest' [those who cannot be called Muḥammadans in either of these senses], continues Ibn ʿArabī, 'each of them is linked to one of the [previous] prophets. That is why the Prophet said that "the wise are the heirs of the prophets",[47] not that they are all the heirs of one and the same prophet; and by "the wise" are meant the wise of this community. The Prophet is also reported to have

44. *Yā ahla Yathrib lā muqāma lakum*. Our translation takes into account the interpretation that Ibn ʿArabī gives of this verse in several passages of his work (*Futūḥāt*, III, pp. 177, 216, 500; IV, p. 28; *Mawāqiʿ*, p. 141, etc.). It is to this verse, also, that he alludes (although the editor is evidently not aware of it) in the *Risāla fī 'l-walāya*, p. 21, where he speaks of the 'station of the inexpressible' which is beyond all the others and says that it is mentioned 'in *sūra al-Aḥzāb*'.

45. *Futūḥāt*, I, p. 223; O. Yahia's edition, III, pp. 358 ff.

46. Indeed, as Ibn ʿArabī says in the passage immediately preceding this one, on a certain number of points the dispositions of Islamic Law coincide with previous rulings. He stresses, however, that the believer should accept and practise these inasmuch as they are part of the Muḥammadan Law, and not, for example, because they used to form part of the Torah. The idea of a spiritual knowledge that is generated through the practice of rules laid down by the law, and whose nature corresponds symbolically with the nature of the rules under consideration, occurs particularly in chapters 68 to 72 of the *Futūḥāt* as well as in the *Tannazulāt mawṣiliyya* (published in Cairo in 1961, under the title *Laṭā'if al-asrār*, by Aḥmad Zakī ʿAṭiyya and Ṭāhā ʿAbd al-Bāqī Surūr). The problem of the relationship between the Law and the Way is discussed later on.

47. Bukhārī, *ʿilm*, 10; Ibn Māja, *muqaddima*, 17. The *ḥadīth* which is quoted next in two different forms is absent from the canonical collections. As we saw (chapter 3, note 14), in the *Risāla fī 'l-walāya* the phrase 'The wise of this community are as the prophets of other communities' is attributed to ʿAbd al-ʿAzīz al-Mahdawī.

said, "The wise of this community are as the prophets of other communities", or, as one variant has it, "are like the prophets of the children of Israel".'

Do those who inherit directly from Muḥammad possess characteristics which distinguish them from the *awliyā'* who participate in the Prophet's heritage only through the intermediary of other prophets? Referring to two verses of *sūra al-Fatḥ* (48:4 and 48:18), Ibn ʿArabī concludes that, whereas the *sakīna*—the Hebrew *shakinah*—was manifested externally to the Children of Israel (in the Ark of the Covenant, or *tābūt*, Qur'ān 2:249), it descends 'upon' or 'into' the hearts of believers in the Muḥammadan community. This is the principle upon which the two types of *awliyā'* can be distinguished: 'The Signs (*āyāt*) given to the Children of Israel were visible; those which are given to us are in our hearts.[48] This is where the difference lies between the Muḥammadan heirs and the heirs of the other prophets: the latter are known to ordinary people by the suspension of natural laws (*kharq al-ʿawā'id*)[49] which is made manifest in their person. By contrast, the heir of Muḥammad is unknown to ordinary people and known only to the élite, for in him the suspension of natural laws is only manifested in his heart, as spiritual knowledge and spiritual state. At every moment he increases in knowledge of his Lord—and by that I mean a knowledge which has been realized and experienced.'[50] This initial distinction, however, is merely a starting-point for a typology of the *awliyā'*, about which Ibn ʿArabī, in the rest of this text and in other passages of his work, has a great deal more to say.

48. This distinction, together with the consequences that Ibn ʿArabī sees it as having for the typology of the Muḥammadan heir and the heir of another prophet, is connected with the distinction made in verse 41:53: 'We will cause them to see Our signs in the distance [i.e. in the macrocosm] and in themselves.'

49. Strictly speaking, *kharq al-ʿawā'id* should be translated as 'the breaking of habits', since, for Ibn ʿArabī as for most Muslim theologians, natural laws are simply statistical regularities, which man interprets in terms of the chain of cause and effect, but which cannot bind the Almighty. A miracle contravenes, not the nature of things, but our idea of them.

50. *Futūḥāt*, IV, p. 50.

CHAPTER

5

The Heirs of the Prophets

And it came to pass, when Moses came down from Mount Sinai with the two tablets of testimony in Moses' hand, when he came down from the mount, that Moses wist not that the skin of his face shone while he talked with him. And when Aaron and all the children of Israel saw Moses, behold, the skin of his face shone; and they were afraid to come nigh him . . .. And till Moses had done speaking with them, he put a veil on his face.

THIS biblical account (Exodus 34, 29-35) has its equivalent in Islamic tradition.[1] It is to the episode described in it that Ibn ʿArabī refers when he uses an example to illustrate the general considerations mentioned at the end of the last chapter:

When Moses returned from his Lord, God clothed his face in light as a sign of the authenticity of that which he declared; and so fierce was this light that no one could look on him without being blinded, so that he had to cover his face with a veil in order that those who looked in his face would not be taken ill when they saw him. Our teacher Abū Yaʿzā in the Maghrib was [a] Moses–like [type of saint] (*mūsawī al-wirth*), and God had bestowed on him the same miraculous sign. No one could look him in the face without losing their sight. He would then rub the man who had looked at him with one of the garments he was wearing and God would give him back his sight. Among those who saw him and were blinded in this fashion was our shaykh Abū Maydan, on an occasion when he paid him a visit. Abū Maydan rubbed his eyes with the garment that Abū Yaʿzā was wearing and recovered his sight. The miracles of Abū Yaʿzā are famous in the Maghrib. He lived at a time when I myself was there, but I was busy with other things and never saw him.[2] There were other

1. Thaʿlabī, *Qiṣaṣ al-anbiyā'*, Cairo 1371AH, pp.123-24.

2. On Abū Yaʿzā, who was one of Abū Madyan's teachers, see V. Loubignac, 'Un saint berbère, Moulay Bou Azza', *Hespéris* XXXI (1944); Al-Tādilī, *al-Tashawwuf ilā rijāl al-taṣawwuf*, ed. A. Faure, pp. 195-205, ed. A. Tawfiq, pp. 213-22; E. Dermenghem, *Le Culte des saints dans l'Islam maghrèbien*, 2nd edition, Paris 1982, pp. 59-70. A. Bel ('Sidi Bou Medyan et son maître Ed-Daqqāq à Fes', *Mélanges René Basset*, Paris 1923, I, pp. 31-68) mentions an unpublished work, devoted entirely to Abū Yaʿzā, by Abū 'l-ʿAbbās Aḥmad al-Tādilī (who died in 1013/1604 and is thus different from the Tādilī referred to above, who lived in the seventh/thirteenth century), the *Kitāb al-Ma'zā fī manāqib al-shaykh Abī Yaʿzā*.

saints then—among the Muslims—who were superior to him in knowledge, spiritual state and divine proximity, and who were known neither to Abū Yaᶜzā nor to anyone else.[3]

The quality of being heir to a prophet—and in another passage on the *wirātha mūsawiyya* Ibn ᶜArabī stresses that the heritage received in this way may sometimes be total, but may also be no more than partial[4]—essentially means conforming to the particular spiritual type represented by that prophet. Yet the relationship which is established between the saint and the prophet who is his model is not a vague 'patronage', but may rather be compared to the transmission of a genetic inheritance. It confers a precise and visible character on the behaviour, virtues and graces of the *walī*. An entire chapter of the *Futūḥāt* is devoted to the 'Christ-like' saints,[5] those who, whether fully or not, are the heirs of ᶜĪsā, or Jesus. Our analysis of it follows the sometimes disconcerting order in which Ibn ᶜArabī discusses the various aspects of the subject.

The description 'Christ-like' (*ᶜīsawī*) is applied first and foremost to the actual disciples of Jesus (*al-ḥawāriyyūn*; cf. Qur'ān 3:52, 5:12, etc.). But it is not simply a question of historical reminiscence, for some of them lived long enough to know and accept the revelation of

---

We have looked at two manuscripts of this work from the Abbey of Toumliline, thanks to the kindness of the librarian father at the Benedictine Abbey of En-Calcat. Also, there is now an excellent edition by A. Tawfiq (Rabat 1989) of the *Di'āmat al-yaqīn* by Abū 'l-ᶜAbbās al-ᶜAzfī (died 633). On the social and political context which explains the interest taken in this saint by the Alaouite dynasty, cf. Jacques Berque, *Ulémas, fondateurs, insurgés de Maghreb*, Paris 1982. Ibn ᶜArabī appears to intimate that he might have met Abū Yaᶜzā. But the date generally given for the death of Abū Yaᶜzā (572/1177) cannot be reconciled with the hypothesis that he was still alive when the author of the *Futūḥāt* was in the Maghreb: in 1177 Ibn ᶜArabī, who was then seventeen years of age, was living in Seville and had apparently never been away from his own country. This is doubtless a chronological error on his part—not the only one in the *Futūḥāt*. It seems unlikely that Abū Yaᶜzā has been confused with his son Abū ᶜAlī. On Abū Madyan (died 594/1197), see the article by G. Marçais in *EI*[2]. This shaykh, who, despite the fact that they never met in the flesh, was one of Ibn ᶜArabī's teachers, is very often mentioned in his writings (*Futūḥāt*, I, p. 221; III, pp. 65, 94, 117, 130, 136; IV, pp. 137, 141, 195; *Muḥāḍarat al-abrār*, Beirut 1968, I, p. 344; *Mawāqiᶜ al-nujūm*, p. 140, etc.)

3. *Futūḥāt*, IV, pp. 50-51.

4. Ibid., I, p. 482: The heir can inherit up to a half, a quarter, an eighth, a third, a sixth and so on.

5. Chapter 36 (*Futūḥāt*, I, pp. 222-26; O. Yahia's edition, III, pp. 356-89).

Muḥammad, and there are still some among us today (Ibn ʿArabī comes back later on to these cases of miraculous longevity). The former, who are obviously exceptions to the rule, therefore possess two inheritances, one received directly from Jesus and the other received indirectly from him through the intermediary of Muḥammad. As a result, they have the privilege of two *fatḥ*—illuminations—and of knowing two modes of spiritual experience (*dhawq*).

Furthermore, the Christ–like saints are the *awliyā'* who are born into Islam and who inherit only from Jesus, through the intermediary of Muḥammad. Their chief feature is the realisation of divine Unity through the elimination of all sensible representations (*mithāl*).

In fact, Jesus was not born of a male belonging to the human species, but of a Spirit who manifested himself (*tamaththul*) in a human form; that is why, in the community of Jesus the son of Mary more than in any other, the doctrine of the legitimacy of images predominates. Christians fashion representations of the divinity and turn towards them in order to worship, because the very existence of their prophet proceeded from a Spirit who clothed himself in a form; and so it is to this day in his community. But then came the Law of Muḥammad, which forbade symbolic representations. Now Muḥammad contains the essential reality of Jesus and the Law of Jesus is encompassed within his own. The Prophet thus tells us 'to worship God as though we were seeing Him', thereby causing Him to enter our imaginative faculty (*khayāl*). This is the only lawful mode of figurative representation for Muslims. But this representation, which is permissible and even commanded when it operates within the imagination, is prohibited in the sensible world, and it is forbidden to the Muḥammadan community to give God a sensible form.[6]

Thus, the worship of God as though we were seeing Him—by making use of the imaginative faculty—is a part of Christ's law which is ratified, in a way peculiar to Islam, by the Law of Muḥammad. It is also significant, observes Ibn ʿArabī, that this should have been prescribed by the Prophet in response to a question asked by the angel Gabriel, the Angel of Visitation, whom Islam identifies with the Spirit who assumed human form (Qur'ān 19:17) and whose breath engendered Jesus in the person of Mary.[7] The particular contribution of Muḥammadan Law is the remainder of the same *ḥadīth* ('. . . for if you do not see Him, He

6. This passage alludes to the well-known *ḥadīth* which says that perfection (*al-iḥsān*) is to worship God as though you were seeing Him (Bukhārī, *tafsīr*, s. 31, *īmān*, 37, etc.). This 'as though' is of major importance, since it sanctions the use of the *khayāl* in the spiritual life.

7. On Ibn ʿArabī's interpretation of this Qur'ānic verse concerning the conception of Jesus, see *Fuṣūṣ*, I, pp. 138-39.

sees you'). Insofar as he is a Muslim, the *ʿīsawī* saint could not of course be unaware of the second part of this *ḥadīth*. But insofar as he is a saint, it is the principle voiced in the first part which determines the specific modalities of his course.

A little later Ibn ʿArabī cites the example, quoted at the start of this book, of his teacher Abū 'l-ʿAbbās al-ʿUryabī,[8] who, he says, was an *ʿīsawī* at the end of his life. He also provides us with an important piece of autobiography when he adds that he himself, on the other hand, was an *ʿīsawī* to begin with, then *mūsawī* ('Moses-like'), then *hūdī* (derived from the name of the prophet Hūd; cf. Qur'ān 7:165ff., 11:50ff., 26:124ff.), after which he was the heir of all the prophets in turn, ending with Muḥammad himself. We will have occasion to speak further about the very special relationship between Ibn ʿArabī and Jesus. For the moment, let us say that the statement we have just quoted in this connection is explained in various passages in the *Futūḥāt*, in which the Shaykh al-Akbar says that at the time of his entry upon the Way, Jesus was his first teacher.[9]

We have already touched briefly on the question of the continued survival of witnesses of previous revelations in the midst of the Islamic community. Ibn ʿArabī returns to it here: 'In our age, and even today, there are some companions of Jesus and also of Jonah who live apart from men.' With regard to the companions of Jonah, the Shaykh al-Akbar tells us that he saw the tracks of one of them, who had been a little ahead of him, on the edge of the sea: the imprint of his foot was three and three quarters of a span long and two spans wide. A friend of Ibn ʿArabī's, Abū ʿAbdallāh ibn Khazar al-Ṭanjī, had spoken with this mysterious personage, who had foretold with faultless accuracy the events that were to take place in Andalusia in 585 (the year in which this meeting occurred) and 586.[10]

With regard to the existence of the immediate disciples of Jesus in the wake of the establishing of Islam, Ibn ʿArabī relates a story which goes

8. Ibn ʿArabī often mentions Abū 'l-ʿAbbās al-ʿUraybī (sometimes called Abū Jaʿfar). The first biographical note in the *Rūḥ al-quds* (Damascus 1964, pp. 46-48) is about him. See also *Futūḥāt*, I, p. 186; II, p. 177; III, pp. 208, 336, 539; IV, p. 123.

9. *Futūḥāt*, I, p. 155; III, pp. 43, 341; IV, p. 77.

10. The same story occurs in the *Futūḥāt*, II, p. 415. The years 585 and 586 of the Hegira correspond to the years 1189 and 1190 of the Christian calender. It was at this time that the Almohad sovereign Abū Yūsuf Yaʿqūb repulsed the Portuguese and Castilian attacks.

back to Ibn ᶜUmar,[11] adding that even if his chain of transmission is subject to dispute, this does not make it less valid 'for us and those like us', because it has been confirmed by an 'unveiling' (*kashf*). According to Ibn ᶜUmar, the caliph ᶜUmar, his father, wrote a letter to Nadla ibn Muᶜāwiya when the latter was in Iraq with his soldiers, ordering him to undertake a series of forays into the area surrounding the town of Ḥilwān. While carrying out this order, Nadla stopped at the foot of a mountain to say the afternoon prayer, and uttered the great call to prayer, or *adhān*. A mysterious voice echoed each formula of this ritual call, and shouted to him: 'O Nadla, I testify that Muḥammad is the Messenger of Allāh. Such is [the right] religion, which Jesus the son of Mary proclaimed to us. And the Hour will dawn over the community of Muḥammad!'

Suddenly the mountain split open and the head of the invisible person who had spoken these words appeared. He said that his name was Zurayb ibn Barthalmā. He had been commanded by Jesus, whose 'representative' (*waṣī*) he was, to remain in that place until the day at the end of time when the son of Mary would descend again to earth. A dialogue ensued in the course of which Ibn Barthalmā ('son of Bartholomew') charges Nadla to greet the caliph ᶜUmar for him and to give him a message in which he lists a certain number of signs which will herald the Day of Judgement.

When this message reached ᶜUmar, he remembered that the Prophet had mentioned that a *waṣī* of Jesus dwelt in this mountain on the edge of Iraq. He sent one of his companions to the spot in order to find Ibn Barthalmā and convey his greetings to him. On this occasion, Jesus' disciple did not reply to the call to prayer, even though the messenger repeated it five times a day for forty days, and no one was able to find out where he was hidden. But, says Ibn ᶜArabī, at the end of this story Ibn Barthalmā was still dwelling on this mountain, devoting himself in solitude to the worship of God.

In his commentary on this strange story, the Shaykh al-Akbar points out that this person and all those who, like him, are the still living 'representatives' or 'executors' (*awṣiyā*) of past prophets, are numbered among the saints of the Muḥammadan community, even though the content of the Revelation brought by the Prophet did not reach them in the ordinary way, but was received by them from Khaḍir in person, the

11. This account, which we have taken here from the *Futūḥāt*, I, p. 223 ff., also occurs in *Muḥāḍarat al-abrār*, II, p. 146 ff.

teacher of the 'solitary ones' (*afrād*). The existence of such beings is the reason why the Prophet forbade the killing of monks (*ruhbān*), who live apart from other created beings to be alone with their Lord, and ordered that they should be left to devote themselves in peace to their worship.[12] The duty of *tablīgh* or transmission of the faith, which is normally imposed on believers, does not need to be performed in their case, for they already possess 'evidence which comes from their Lord' (Qur'ān 6:57).

Ibn ʿArabī remarks that cases like these, in which God takes over the instruction of exceptional people (who are not necessarily *muʿammarūn* like Ibn Barthalmā, i.e. men from a pre–Islamic past endowed with supernatural longevity), resolve the apparent contradiction between the Qur'ānic affirmation that the Prophet is 'sent to all men' (7:158), and the indisputable fact that his message has not reached all of humanity. We can guess the significance that this elliptical statement has in relation to the esoteric status, in the Islamic economy, of the spiritual élites who by exoteric criteria belong to Revelations which have been abrogated. Such an interpretation is borne out by a reference to those who receive this divine assistance and who are also 'People of the Book', and as such have to pay the '*jizya*', the tribute levied on Jews and Christians; for, in paying this tribute, and thereby recognizing an obligation imposed by Muḥammadan Law, they are integrated into the Islamic order of things, and by this very fact their own Law, which theoretically has been invalidated by the coming of Islam, re-acquires for them a validity which is so to speak derivative. Nevertheless, as we may gather from the reference to the *jizya*, we are no longer speaking of anchorites, who by definition are outside the norms of a community, but of individuals who are, technically, 'infidels'.

As we can see, this excursus deviates only in appearance from the main theme, for it leads Ibn ʿArabī to depict *walāya* in a way which is far more inclusive than the definitions which confine it within the framework of a sociological Islam. The chapter continues with a description of the signs whereby one can distinguish the Christ-like type of saints: the graces they possess present an analogy with the miracles attributed to Jesus, and this is why they may be endowed, for example, with the ability to walk on water, but do not possess the ability to fly through the air. The latter is associated with the Muḥammad-type of saint, who

12. Bukhārī, *anbiyā*, 45; Muslim, *tawba*, 46-47, *zuhd*, 73.

inherits from Muḥammad a privilege of which the model and source is the nocturnal Ascension (*isrā', miʿrāj*).[13] They can also be distinguished by a spiritual energy (*himma*) which operates effectively on men and on things—a probable allusion to the power of Jesus (Qur'ān 3:49) to heal the blind and the lepers and to bring the dead back to life. Finally, their behaviour with regard to created beings, whatever religion they may profess, is remarkable for its compassion and gentleness. The *ʿīsawī* saint sees the best in all things. This is also true of Muḥammad, inasmuch as he is the sum of all the prophetic types and consequently integrates within himself the particular virtues of each: on passing by a decaying carcases, his companions said: 'How it stinks!', but the Prophet said: 'How white are its teeth!' But in the case of the Muḥammad-type of saint, the universal compassion that results from this perception of the positive quality of created beings, of the beauty or perfection which is inherent in them, is not made nakedly manifest as in the case of the Christ-like saint. God is compassion; but He is also Rigour, and the latter aspect may at times veil the former in the behaviour of the Prophet of Islam or of his heirs.

Is it possible to identify historic personages whose characters permit them to be identified as 'Christ-like' saints? As we saw, Ibn ʿArabī, in the example he gives of his teacher Abū 'l-ʿAbbās al-ʿUryabī, explains that the latter was *ʿīsawī* at the end of his life, whereas he himself was *ʿīsawī* when he entered upon the Way, after which he became successively *mūsawī, hūdī,* and so on. Leaving aside for the moment Ibn ʿArabī's personal situation, let us note that the same *walī* may, during the course of his existence, accumulate several prophetic heritages, which of necessity obscures the distinguishing features of each and effectively prevents us from mechanically employing the Shaykh al-Akbar's typology. It is none the less true that certain *awliyā'* possess features that enable an identification to be made, which is sometimes explicitly confirmed by Ibn ʿArabī himself. This is so in the case of Ḥallāj, who is mentioned several times in Chapter Twenty of the *Futūḥāt* where the Shaykh al-Akbar discusses 'the knowledge of Jesus',

13. It is none the less true that all the *awliyā'* experience a *miʿrāj* insofar as this symbolizes the stages of the spiritual journey which leads to perfect *walāya*: we will have occasion to discuss this point further when we analyse the *Risālat al-anwār* in the final chapter of this book. The restriction to the Muḥammadan saints alone of the privilege whose prototype is the Prophet's Ascension has reference only to the physical reality of moving 'through the air'.

and where he actually says, 'This knowledge was possessed by Ḥusayn ibn Manṣūr'—a remark which has particular reference to Ḥallāj's doctrine of *ṭūl* and *ᶜarḍ* ('height' and 'breadth'), terms which are plainly related to the symbolism of the cross.[14] The miracles traditionally associated with Ḥallāj, the sayings attributed to him, especially the famous verse: 'I will die in the religion of the cross' (*fa-fī dīn al-ṣalīb yakūnu mawtī*),[15] even his 'passion'—all these are a powerful confirmation of his connection with the Christ-like type of saint, which should be seen simply as the manifestation of one of the possibilities included in the sphere of Muḥammadan *walāya*.

Ibn ᶜArabī also warns his readers against the misunderstandings to which the behaviour of a *walī* may give rise: for example, his special relationship with a pre-Islamic prophet may cause him, on the point of death, to call on the name of Moses or Jesus, and thus make him wrongly suspected of having become a Jew or a Christian.[16] Another

14. *Futūḥāt*, I, p. 169. On the Islamic references to the symbol of the cross, see Michel Vâlsan's article of this title in *Études traditionelles*, March-June and November-December 1971, where he translates, analyses and comments on chapter 20 of the *Futūḥāt*.

15. L. Massignon and P. Kraus, *Akhbār al-Ḥallāj*, Paris 1936, Arabic text p. 82, French text p. 95. We will not elaborate on the case of Ḥallāj, concerning whom one need do no more than refer to the works by Massignon and above all to the posthumous edition of the *Passion*, as well as to R. Arnaldez' book *Hallaj ou la religion de la croix*, Paris 1964 (see in particular chapter 4). The fact that Massignon, even in the vocabulary of his translation (and his choice of the word Passion) was unable to resist the temptation to Christianize Ḥallāj, thereby arousing a somewhat suspect interest in certain sections of the Christian community, accompanied by a devaluation of other aspects of Islamic spirituality, undoubtedly justifies a cautious approach to his works. Yet the astonishingly Christian resonance of certain of Ḥallāj's words, particularly the famous *Anā 'l-ḥaqq*, which is difficult not to compare with 'I am the Way, the Truth and the Life' in St John's Gospel (14:6), was bound to create a confusion that only Ibn ᶜArabī's criteria can resolve.

16. *Risālat al-Anwār*, Hyderabad 1948, p. 16. Herman Landolt has drawn our attention to a curious story, to which this interpretation of Ibn ᶜArabī's might provide a clue. It concerns the Mughul prince Dārā Shikūh, whose spiritual teachers were Ṣūfīs who were profoundly influenced by the Shaykh al-Akbar, and who was executed for heresy at Delhi in 1069/1659. According to the Venetian traveller Niccolas Manucci (*Indian Text Series, Storia del Mogol*, translated by William Irvine, London 1907, I, p. 357 ff.), while he was in his cell he said several times over: 'Mahommet kills me, the Son of God gives me life.' It is obviously doubtful that these reported words were literally the words spoken, and the significance that Manucci attaches to them, as the indication of an unlikely conversion to Christianity, is more than suspect. If this story has any foundation, the concept of the 'ᶜ*īsawī*

easily recognized *ʿīsawī* saint, similar in many ways to Ḥallāj, is ʿAyn al-Quḍāt Hamadhānī,[17] a disciple of Aḥmad Ghazālī. He was accused of being a *zindīq* (heretic) and of laying claim to the dignity of a prophet, and was hanged at Hamadhān in 525/1131 at the age of thirty-three—the same age as Jesus, and the age, according to one *ḥadīth*, of all the chosen people in Paradise;[18] and later Ṣūfī writers have often said of him: *ʿīsawī 'l-mashrab wa manṣūrī 'l-maslak*, 'His source was Jesus, his way was the way of Manṣūr (al-Ḥallāj).'[19] Similarly, one of the most venerated teachers of the Naqshbandiyya *ṭarīqa*, ʿUbaydallāh Aḥrār, says explicitly of himself that he is *ʿīsawī*, and explains that in virtue of this fact he has inherited the ability to 'quicken hearts', as Jesus had the ability to bring the dead back to life.[20]

There are,[21] however, more recent examples to be found. Michel Vâlsan, who forty years ago led me to discover the importance of the idea of *wirātha* in Ibn ʿArabī's doctrine of *walāya*, wrote practically nothing on the subject. However, a few precious pages of his[22] describe the specifically *ʿīsawī* nature of a contemporary Muslim saint, Shaykh Aḥmad al-ʿAlawī, who died in 1934 and whose face, in some indefinable fashion, bore a Christ-like stamp which struck several of his European

---

type' might explain it. For other possible cases of *ʿīsawī* saints, see the article by M. Baliver, 'Chrétiens secrets et martyrs christiques en Islam', *Islamochristiana*, no. 16, Rome 1990.

17. On ʿAyn al-Quḍāt, cf. L. Massignon, *Passion*, index, s.v. Hamadhānī. His *Shakwa 'l-gharīb (The Complaint of the Exile)*, written in prison in the year of his death, has been edited and translated by M. b. Abd El-Jalil, *Journal asiatique*, 1930 (January–March).

18. Baghawī, *Maṣābīḥ al-sunna, ii*, p. 152.

19. Abd El-Jalil, op. cit., pp. 12-13; L. Massignon, *Passion*, II, p. 177. It is hardly necessary to point out that the use of these terms is later than Ibn ʿArabī and is evidence that his doctrine of *walāya*, and the distinctions established by him between the types of sainthood, were accepted in Ṣūfī circles. Characteristically, ʿAyn al-Quḍāt performed a 'Christ-like' miracle by restoring a dead man to life (cf. his *Tamhīdāt*, ed. A. Usayrān, Tehran 1962, pp. 250-51).

20. Cf. Muḥammad al-Rakhāwī, *al-Anwār al-qudsiyya fī manāqib al-sāda al-naqshbandiyya*, Cairo 1344 AH., pp. 157-58. (The sentence about the *maqām iḥyā' al-qulūb* refers to the Qur'ān, 3:49).

21. Cf. *Études traditionelles*, July-October 1962, p. 166, note 2 and p. 169, note 12.

22. 'Sur le cheikh Al-Alawī', *Études traditionelles*, January-February 1968. This note completes a review, already published in the same review, of Martin Lings' book, *A Moslem Saint of the Twentieth Century*, London 1961.

visitors. Michel Vâlsan bases himself for the most part on the recurrence of Jesus himself or of his name in a series of visions in which the shaykh appeared to the members of the *zāwiya* of Mostaghanem, at the time when their last teacher had died and they were having to find a successor. 'For us', he writes,

> this particular series of visions is indicative not only of Shaykh al-ᶜAlawī's spiritual condition, but also of his initiatic function . . .. [The *ṭarīqa* to which he belonged], apart from its normal role in the Islamic scheme of things, had also to demonstrate by its existence the effective presence of *taṣawwuf*, as a way of initiation, on the borders of the Western world and even within the sphere of European influence on the Muslim world . . . and it thus had to express itself in terms which were suited to an effective and efficient contact with Western intellectual sensibilities.

The very powerful attraction that the Shaykh al-ᶜAlawī exercised over certain Europeans who became his disciples, and the part played by his *ṭarīqa* in introducing *taṣawwuf* into France and other Western countries, are confirmation both of the suitability of the type of *walāya* he incarnated and of the nature of the milieu in which he was called upon to represent *taṣawwuf*.[23] A correspondence of this sort, no doubt, can explain both the fascination of Ḥallāj for the Christian world (in the wake of Massignon's writings on him), and enable us also to understand the strange fate of a thirteenth century Ṣūfī like Ibn Hūd, in whose house the Jews of Damascus used to gather to study, under his direction, Maimonides' *Guide of the Perplexed*.[24] In this case, the *walī* would be a *mūsawī* type or, more probably, *ibrāhīmī*, since Abraham represents

23. The *ᶜīsawī* character of Shaykh al-ᶜAlawī is further confirmed by certain details of his dying moments, to which Michel Vâlsan has chosen to make no more than a discreet reference at the end of his article. A similar interpretation would seem to apply to the case of the emir ᶜAbd al-Qādir, whose person, behaviour and virtue of character likewise mark him out as an *ᶜīsawī*-type, but who in addition played a part in the relations between Islamic esotericism and the West which we intend one day to explore. Some preliminary facts can be found in the introduction and the notes of our translation of extracts from his *Kitāb al-Mawāqif*, published under the title *Écrits spirituels*, Paris 1982.

24. Kutubī, *Fawāt al-wafāyāt*, Cairo 1951, I, pp. 123-25; Ṣafadī, *Wāfī*, Wiesbaden 1979, XIII, pp. 156-57. Ibn Hūd was born in Murcia in 633/1235, and died at Damascus in 697/1297. He was connected with the school of Ibn Sabᶜīn (who speaks of the *Guide of the Perplexed* in his *Risāla Nūriyya*: see *Rasā'il Ibn Sabᶜīn*, ed. Badawī, Cairo 1965, p. 157) and was therefore classed by Ibn Taymiyya among the *ittiḥādiyya*. On the Hūdid dynasty, see *EI*², s.v., (see the article by D. M. Dunlop. Ibn Hūd was the brother of Muḥammad ibn Yūsuf al-Mutawakkil, the Sultan of Granada).

the common trunk and the point of junction of Judaism and Islam. The details we possess, however, are neither sufficient nor sufficiently accurate to justify a definite pronouncement. Neither is it possible to decide, on the basis of information handed down by the hagiographers, that Aḥmad Badawī (died 675/1276), the famous saint of Tanta, was a *mūsawī* type, in spite of the similarities between him and Abū Yaᶜzā, about whom Ibn ᶜArabī speaks in the passage we cited earlier. Like Abū Yaᶜzā, Aḥmad al-Badawī used to veil his face, and although some writers, both Muslim and Western, have tried to explain this in a very prosaic fashion, others tell us that on the insistent request of one of his disciples, he agreed one day to lift his veil and the indiscreet disciple died on the spot.[25]

Just as there is no 'key to dreams' instantly available to anyone who happens to want one, there is no instant 'key to the saints' to unlock the doors of *walāya*: if conjecture is permissible—and in rare cases based on evidence which is beyond doubt—only the *ᶜārif*, the true gnostic, thanks either to his spiritual perspicacity (*firāsa*) or to an 'unveiling' (*kashf*), knows how to interpret unerringly and in all circumstances the evidence of the mark of the prophet present in the *walī* himself or in his reported acts and words. The same saint can 'inherit' from several prophets; alternatively, he may receive only part of the inheritance of one of them. In both cases, identification becomes a more delicate matter, since the distinguishing features are either too many or too few. Furthermore, we must not lose sight of the fact that the prophetic 'words' (*kalimāt*) which form the structure of *walāya* cannot be reduced to the twenty-seven prophets mentioned in the *Fuṣūṣ*: we referred in Chapter Three to a text in which it is stated that at any given moment there are one hundred and twenty-four thousand saints (or types of sainthood), corresponding to the one hundred and twenty-four thousand prophets who, according to a *ḥadīth*, have succeeded each other

25. Shaᶜrānī, *al-Ṭabaqāt al-Kubrā*, Cairo 1954, I, p. 184. On Aḥmad al-Badawī, see the article by K. Vollers and E. Litmann in *EI*[2], which contains a large number of references but the tone of which is deplorably contemptuous (Badawī is described in it as 'representing the lowest type of derwish', of having 'extremely feeble intellectual powers'). Veiled saints are not rare in the history of Sufism. In Nabhānī's *Jāmiᶜ karāmāt al-awliyā'* (Beirut, n. d., I, p. 308), for example, in the pages immediately preceding the section on Aḥmad al-Badawī, there is a brief mention of another saint of the seventh century of the Hegira, Shaykh Abū 'l-ᶜAbbās Aḥmad, who was actually named *al-mulaththam*, 'the veiled one', and who was considered a *muᶜammar*, being gifted with prodigious longevity.

since the start of human history. As the multiplicity of the divine Names can be reduced to a limited series of 'mother Names' (*ummahāt*),[26] in the same way the multiplicity of the prophets can be reduced to a restricted number of main types, from whom the others proceed by means of differentiation. These are the basic models who appear in chapter after chapter of the *Fuṣūṣ*. Even so, whether or not we take the figure of one hundred and twenty-four thousand at its face value, it is still a fact that from each of these models there derives a large family of lesser 'words' whom any thorough typology would have to take into account, and of whose very names we are ignorant.[27] On the other hand, even if we confine ourselves to the twenty-seven prophets in the *Fuṣūṣ*, and supplement the information, often allusive in character, contained in it with information from other texts (such as Ibn ᶜArabī's account of his meeting with the prophets of the seven planetary heavens, to be discussed later on, or the highly cryptic *Kitāb al-ᶜAbādila*),[28] it is still very difficult to discover criteria in the work of the Shaykh al-Akbar which everyone has the ability to grasp. The content of the chapters in the *Fuṣūṣ*, even their very titles, alert us to particular forms of spiritual knowledge which are the exclusive property of one or other of the prophets and which the *awliyā'* will inherit: the knowledge

26. Cf. *Fuṣūṣ*, I, p. 65. According to the point of view adopted, Ibn ᶜArabī gives different lists of these *ummahāt al-asmā'*. In *Futūḥāt*, I, p. 100, he lists seven: *al-Ḥayy, al-ᶜĀlim* (sic), *al-Murīd, al-Qādir, al-Qā'il, al-Jawwād* and *al-Muqsiṭ* (the corresponding passage of O. Yahia's edition omits the name *al-Qādir*), and explains that they are themselves engendered by the Name *al-Mudabbir* and *al-Mufaṣṣil*. In *Futūḥāt* II, p. 437, he reduces them to three: *Allāh, al-Rabb, al-Raḥmān*.

27. Islamic literature, particularly the *qiṣaṣ al-anbiyā'* genre, contains a number of facts, most often considered to be suspect *isrā'īlīyyāt*, and whose sources are either Jewish (the Bible or the Talmud) or Christian (the canonical or apocryphal Gospels, the Acts of the Apostles), about certain people whose stories come to be included among the accounts concerning the prophets mentioned in the Qur'ān. The inclusion—hotly disputed by the *ᶜulamā'*—of these people in the series of the *anbiyā'* does not noticeably modify the problem.

28. One edition exists of the *Kitāb al-ᶜAbādila*—very imperfect but which has the merit of being the first—which we owe to ᶜAbd al-Qādir Aḥmad ᶜAṭā (Cairo 1969). The emblematic names at the head of the maxims are variously constructed, but often include the name of a prophet. Twenty-three out of the twenty-seven prophets in the *Fuṣūṣ* appear (Luqmān, Shuᶜayb, ᶜUzayr and Nūḥ are missing), as well as several of the non-Qur'ānic figures mentioned in the *qiṣaṣ al-anbiyā'*, such as Shamwīl, Dānyāl, Yūḥannā, Jirjīs, Yūshaᶜ. In the final chapter of this book we will speak in more detail of the *Kitāb al-ᶜAbādila*.

of the divine Names in the case of Adam, of the divine gifts in the case of Seth, of divine transcendence in the case of Noah, of passionate love in the case of Abraham, of destiny in the case of ʿUzayr, of compassion in the case of Solomon, of 'divine lieutenancy' (*khilāfa*) in the case of David, and so on. Yet the information collected about each *nabī* from scripture or tradition, and the record of what has been either written or spoken of him, which we find in Ibn ʿArabī, leave large areas obscure. One central idea, however, is fully present: the Muḥammadan community, in the person of its saints and at any given moment in its history, *simultaneously* recapitulates the 'wisdoms' contained in the successive prophetic revelations which have taken place since the start of the human cycle,[29] and the modes of spiritual realisation which correspond to them. This idea finds expression in the equivalence between the number of the *anbiyā'*, both known and unknown, and the number of the *awliyā'*, even if the exact relationship between the people in the first category and the people in the second escapes profane perception.

The number twenty-seven, which is the number of the main prophetic types mentioned by the author of the *Fuṣūṣ*, is also the number of prophets' names mentioned in the Qur'ān 'from which God has left out nothing' (cf. Qur'ān 6:38). What this means, in effect, is that this number contains synthetically the sum of all the forms of *nubuwwa*, and hence of *walāya*, manifested by each prophet individually out of the one hundred and twenty-four thousand. If this were not so, God, who cannot not tell us everything we need to know, would have mentioned others, if not all, of the prophets. The replacement of two of the names in the Qur'ān by two others in the *Fuṣūṣ* is not explained, as far as we know, anywhere in the work of Ibn ʿArabī. But, in the perspective of his work, the substitution makes sense only if the two Qurʿānic prophets who are not in the *Fuṣūṣ*, Dhu 'l-Kifl and al-Yasaʿ, about whom the Qur'ān gives no precise information, are in fact identical (in terms of their cyclic function and as manifestations of a particular 'wisdom') with the two others whose names have been substituted for theirs (Shīth and Khālid ibn Sinān).[30] We should also

29. In all strictness, one should speak here of a human cycle, since for Ibn ʿArabī, innumerable 'Adams' have succeeded each other, each of whom is the starting point of one of these cycles (*Futūḥāt*, III, pp. 348, 549).

30. It is interesting to note that the two non-Qur'ānic persons who are named in the *Fuṣūṣ* are situated at the two extremes of the cycle of prophethood: Shīth

observe that the number twenty-seven, as we saw above, is the same as the number of *dajjālūn*, 'impostors' or powers of illusion, who obviously bear the same relation to the 'saints of Satan' as the 'major' prophets to the saints of God.[31]

Finally, it must be noted that the number twenty-seven has a very significant connection with the Qur'ān itself: for the 'descent' of the Book took place on the Night of Destiny (*laylat al-qadr*), which is traditionally celebrated on the 27th of the month of Ramaḍān (Qur'ān 97:1). As we saw in Chapter Four, for Ibn ʿArabī the 'Perfect Man' is the 'brother of the Qur'ān', for he, like it, is *kalima jāmiʿa*, the 'Word which totalizes'. Therefore, according to the Shaykh al-Akbar's interpretation, this 'Night' is none other than the Prophet Muḥammad himself, for during it the fulfilment is accomplished, at the end of history, of *nubuwwa* and *walāya* of which all the previous prophets were simply aspects. Thus, *laylat al-qadr* is both the symbolic date of the last divine message, and also, for man himself, the date of the second birth through which he becomes that which he was from all eternity. This correspondence between the Qur'ān and the *insān kāmil* is strengthened by the fact that the descent of one and the ascension of the other come under the sign of the same number. In fact, it is on the night of the 27th of the month of Rajab that Islam each year celebrates the ascension (*miʿrāj*) from heaven to heaven which took the Prophet to the threshold of the divine Presence, at a 'distance of two bow-lengths or nearer' (Qur'ān 53:9). These two bows, according to Ibn ʿArabī, are the two semicircles whose conjunction brings together the divine realities

---

(Seth) is the first prophet after Adam, and Khālid ibn Sinān the last prophet before Muḥammad. We should explain that, in order to bring the number of names to twenty-seven, the list of Qur'ānic prophets, like Ibn ʿArabī's list in the *Fuṣūṣ*, must include the name of Luqmān (who is normally counted among the sages rather than the prophets) and that of ʿUzayr (the Ezra of the Bible) mentioned in the Qur'ān, 9:30, to whom the commentators do not usually attribute the quality of *nabī*, even though he is the restorer of the Torah and his association with Jesus in the same verse emphasizes the exceptional nature of his office (Ṭabarī, *Tafsīr*, ed. Shākir, XIV, p. 202, speaks of him as an inspired *ʿālim*). Suyūṭī (*al-Itqān fī ʿulūm al-Qur'ān*, Cairo 1368 AH, II, pp. 137-41), who does not include these two names, thus lists only twenty-five Qur'ānic prophets.

31. See the *ḥadīth* mentioned in chapter 1, note 21. Let us repeat that the rendering of *dajjāl* as 'antichrist' must therefore be applied only to him who is the seal of the *dajjālūn*, and whose appearance is one of the traditional signs that the end of time is approaching.

(*ḥaqā'iq ḥaqqiyya*) and the created realities (*ḥaqā'iq khalqiyya*) and restores the original unity containing the total sum of possibilities, symbolically expressed, here again, by the number twenty-seven.[32]

32. On the identification of *laylat al-qadr* with the human nature of the Prophet, see *Futūḥāt*, IV, p. 44. (According to Ibn ʿArabī, the Night of Destiny, even though for the Muslim community its date is fixed as the 27th of the month of Ramaḍān, circulates during the course of the year, but it is given to the *ʿārifūn* alone to recognize it when it comes and to reap the full benefit of the grace which the periodical recurrence of this descent brings with it. Cf. *Futūḥāt*, III, pp. 94, 159; IV, p. 486). On the meaning of the two arcs (*qāb qawsayn*), see *Futūḥāt*, II, p. 558; III, p. 543; IV, pp. 39, 51; *Kitāb al-Isrā'*, p. 50. See also the *Tafsīr* by Qāshānī (published under the name of Ibn ʿArabī), Beirut 1968, II, p. 554, commentary to verse 53:9.

CHAPTER

6

The Four Pillars

THE types of sainthood defined by Ibn ʿArabī correspond in a way to a horizontal manifestation of the possibilities contained within the total *walāya*, of which Muḥammad is the source and fulfilment. On the other hand, the community of the saints is built upon a vertical axis, along which the various degrees and functions are distributed.

Fatḥ—a word that we have translated as 'illumination' but which strictly speaking means 'opening'—'tears open' time and space. It is the immediate and instantaneous relationship of man with God, and as such it annuls both the 'where' and the 'when': as Abū Yazīd al-Bisṭāmī said, for the saint there is, in a sense, 'neither morning nor evening'. From another point of view, however, sainthood, being an assumption of human nature in its fullest sense, must paradoxically manifest itself under the forms and conditions intrinsic to the latter. In a sense the saint is 'nobody's son': between him and God there exists a relationship with no intermediary, expressed in Ibn ʿArabi's terminology by the technical term *wajh khāṣṣ*, meaning both the 'particular face' which in each being is eternally turned towards God, and the particular face of God or particular divine aspect which corresponds to that being.*[1] Even so, the saint included within a framework of time, a fact which is demonstrated explicitly by his belonging to an initiatory lineage (*silsila*), and more discretely by his being the heir to a prophet. He is emancipated from the six directions which determine the perception of ordinary men.[2] His 'place' is the 'non-place' ('the "where" no longer has a place', writes Ḥallāj in a famous quatrain); but he none the less occupies a strictly defined place on a cosmic stage whose determining principle is the hierarchy of the saints. Here typology becomes topology.

The origin of this hierarchical configuration and the terminology in which it is expressed are a matter of dispute, but are certainly prior to Ibn ʿArabī. In Ibn Taymiyya's opinion, all the *ḥadīth* invoked to bear

* Due to the extensive nature of the footnotes belonging to this section they are placed at the end of the chapter, beginning on page 98.

out this doctrine are apocryphal.[3] Ibn Khaldūn views these beliefs as borrowings from the Shīᶜites.[4] Conversely, to call to witness a Ṣūfī who was also a *faqīh* and a specialist in *ḥadīth*, Suyūṭī devoted an entire treatise[5] to this problem, based on the prophetic traditions that he considered authentic. It contains an account which, being prototypal, is of especial interest, and which is as follows: Abū Hurayra recounts: 'I went in one day to the Prophet. He said to me:

'In a moment a man will come towards me through that door; he is one of the seven men by means of whom God protects the inhabitants of the earth.' And behold, an Ethiopian (*ḥabashī*) came through that door. He was bald and his nose had been cut off. On his head he carried a pitcher of water. Allāh's messenger said, 'This is he.' Now this man, explains Abū Hurayra, was the servant of al-Mughīra ibn Shuᶜba, and it was he who washed down and swept out the mosque.'[6]

An extensive literature very soon developed around the theme of the 'Council of the Saints' (*dīwān al-awliyā'*), and has continued to do so down to our day.[7] One of its main features is the recurring theme of the 'hidden saint', already known to us from the *ḥadīth* quoted in Chapter One ('He is obscure among men and no one points at him'), and who also comes into the story told by Abū Hurayra. A more detailed illustration of this aspect of *walāya* comes in the hagiographic texts relating to one of the great saints of the twelfth century, ᶜAbd al-Qādir al-Jīlānī. The episode has an interest which is more than merely anecdotal, and which is conferred on it by the importance of this saint, who is frequently mentioned by Ibn ᶜArabī[8] and of whom we will speak further, by the evident connection between these types of story, which are often held to be no more than folk tales, and by an essential element in Ibn ᶜArabī's doctrine of *walāya*. What follows is one version of the story:

Shaykh Abū 'l-Ḥasan al-Baghdādī, commonly known by the name of Ibn Satantana al-Baghdādī, recounts: I devoted myself to the pursuit of knowledge under the direction of our teacher, Shaykh ᶜAbd al-Qādir, and I was in the habit of spending most of the night awake in order to ensure that he wanted for nothing. One night in the month of Ṣafar 553,[9] he went out of his house. I held out a pitcher to him [thinking that he wanted to perform the ritual ablution] but he did not take it, and went towards the gate of the *madrasa*. The door opened before him of its own accord. He went out and I went out behind him, saying to myself, "He does not know that I am here." Then the gate closed again and the shaykh walked to the gate of Baghdad which opened before him. He went out and I went out after him, and the gate shut. He only went a short distance but suddenly we were in a country that was unknown to me.

He entered a place that resembled a *ribāṭ* ['convent']. There were six people there who greeted him with eagerness. I took refuge behind a pillar. Then I heard a groan nearby. After a second, the groaning ceased. A man came in and went towards the place where the groans had come from. He came out again carrying someone on his shoulders. Then another man came into the room. He was bare-headed and had a long moustache.[10] He sat down in front of Shaykh ᶜAbd al-Qādir, who made him say the two *shahādas*, cut his hair and moustache, made him cover his head with a skullcap and gave him the name Muḥammad. Then the shaykh said to the people who were present, 'I have been commanded that this man should replace him who is dead' (*umirtu an yakūna hādhā badalan ᶜan al-mayyit*).

They answered, 'So be it!' Then the shaykh went out and left them. I went out and walked behind him. We only went a short distance, and there we were in front of the gate of Baghdad which opened before us as before. Then the shaykh went to the *madrasa*, where the gate also opened, and entered his dwelling.

The next day, when I sat down before the shaykh to study with him, I begged him to explain to me what I had seen. He replied, 'As regards the place, it is Nihāwand.[11] As for the six people whom you saw there, they were the noble *abdāl*. The man who was groaning was the seventh of them, and when he was on the point of death I came there to be present for it. As for the man whom I made to say the two *shahādas*, he was a Christian, an inhabitant of Constantinople. God had ordered me to put him in the place of the *badal* who had died. He came to me, made a profession of Islam before me, and now is one of them. Finally, as regards the man who entered and who bore the dead man on his shoulders, it was Abū'l-ᶜAbbās al-Khādir; he took him away to see to his funeral.'

The shaykh then made me promise not to speak of all this to anyone during his lifetime.[12]

Although other hagiographic accounts tell of the sudden appointment to a position of importance in the invisible college of the saints of individuals who are of no particular note, and even of avowed sinners,[13] the paradox of divine election in this case is even more surprising. The man who is suddenly assigned a place among the *abdāl*—one of the highest ranks in the hierarchy of the saints, as we shall see[14]—is not simply an obscure Muslim: he is an infidel, a *rūmī*, and his investiture takes place immediately after his profession of faith.[15]

Islamic information in the first centuries about the Pole (*quṭb*), the *awtād* and the *abdāl* is, for the most part, difficult to interpret: the terminology is fluid, and the different sources vary and contradict each other as to the number of holders of each 'grade' and the nature of their functions in a way which the commentators do their utmost to resolve, without eliminating the confusion. Here again, Ibn ᶜArabī was the first to organize and explain these traditional facts, allusive and variable as they were, and to lend them coherence with an overall doctrine of *walāya*. But we would be gravely mistaken as to the nature of his undertaking if we were to see it merely as the systematic classification of already existing material and the establishment of a more rigorous vocabulary. It is with a description that we are concerned, and the person who records it claims over and over again to have been a witness: at Cordoba, he saw twenty-five Poles who preceded the Prophet Muḥammad;[16] at Fez, in 593AH, he met the Pole of his own time.[17] In the texts to be analyzed we will come across a great deal of this sort of thing. Thus, we are not dealing here with some sort of theoretical construct but—as we have said from the beginning—with the expression of a conviction based on direct vision and personal experience. Furthermore, we shall see that Ibn ᶜArabī does not speak in the sole capacity of a witness, but that he prides himself on the authority he possesses on a different account.[18]

The Shaykh al-Akbar wrote a good deal about the subject in hand.[19] However, the most comprehensive survey of it comes at the start of Volume Two of the *Futūḥāt*, in the very lengthy Chapter Seventy-Three which also contains the answers to Tirmidhī's questions. We will use this text as our guide. First of all, there are some general considerations about *risāla*—the status proper to the *rasūl* or Messenger—and *nubuwwa* or Prophethood. What is sealed by Muḥammad, Ibn ᶜArabī says, is legislative prophethood (*nubuwwat al-tashrīᶜ*), which is acquired only through divine election. On the other hand, there is 'general prophethood', which does not involve the establishment of a new sacred law and which can be acquired (*muktasaba*). There are four corner-stones of religion (*arkān al-dīn*): *risāla, nubuwwa, walāya* and *īmān* or faith. But *risāla* is the *rukn jāmiᶜ*: it contains the other three. This appears to contradict what was said earlier in Chapter Three, namely, that the most universal sphere is *walāya*. In fact, the problem is only one of vocabulary: to avoid all confusion, instead of *risāla* we should say *rasūl*; for each Messenger is by definition *rasūl, nabī, walī* and *mu'min*—messenger, prophet, saint and believer—whereas the reverse is not true because not every believer is a saint, not every saint a prophet, and not every prophet has the supreme status of a Messenger. The status of *rasūl*, then, is the most inclusive of all. Its disappearance would bring in its wake the disappearance of the human race. As a result, the world is never without a living *rasūl* who is its Pole (*quṭb*). By 'living', says Ibn ᶜArabī, we should understand: corporeally alive (*ḥayy bi-jismihi*). He explains that after Muḥammad's death, 'Allāh preserved three of the Messengers, corporeally alive in this world.' The first of these in the list that follows is Idrīs, who is generally identified in Muslim tradition with Enoch of the Bible, but of whom the Qur'ān (19:56-57—verses 21:85-86 merely mention his name) says only that he was 'lifted up [by God] to a sublime place'.[20] 'God preserved him alive in body', writes Ibn ʿArabī,

> and assigned him the fourth heaven to be his dwelling place. Now the seven heavens are part of this world; they exist for as long as it exists and their form vanishes when it vanishes . . .. God also preserved, living in this world, Elijah and Jesus . . .. These are the three whom everyone acknowledges to be *rusul*. Regarding Khaḍir, the fourth, there is some divergence of opinion, though not as far as we are concerned, about his being *rasūl*. These four beings exist in the flesh in this world below, and are its Pillars (*awtād*, singular *watad*). Two of them are the two Imāms and one of them is the Pole, who is the place of God's beholding on this earth. Messengers have not ceased and will not cease to be in this world until the Day of Resurrection, and this does not contradict the fact that [in spite of the status of *rasūl*, which usually involves legislative authority] they do not bring a religion which revokes the religion brought by Muḥammad and profess no religion but his. But most people are ignorant of this matter.
>
> Thus, one of these four Messengers, Jesus, Elijah, Idrīs and Khaḍir, is the Pole. The latter is one of the corner-stones of the House of Religion, and corresponds [in the Kaʿba] to the corner of the Black Stone. Two of the others are the Imāms, and the four of them make up the whole assembly of Pillars. Through one of them God protects faith, through another sainthood, through another prophecy, through the fourth the mission (*risāla*), and through all of them He protects the purity of religion. He among them who is the Pole will never die, that is to say, he will be preserved from the loss of consciousness [which will come upon all beings when the angel's trumpet sounds on the Day of Judgement, Qur'ān 39:68] . . .. Within this community, there corresponds at all times to each of these Messengers a being who is 'on the heart' of that Messenger and is his deputy (*nā'ib*). Among our companions on the way, most of the saints know the Pole, the two Imāms and the Pillar (*watad*, the fourth person of the group) only through these deputies; and that is why all seek to attain that station (*maqām*). But when they attain it, they discover that they are merely the vicars of the Pole, the Imām and so on, and that the true Imām is someone else; the same is true of the office of the Pillar . . .. Do not under-estimate the importance of what I have been saying, for you will find it said nowhere else among those whose words concerning the secrets of this way have come down to us.

Even though it is generally held in Islam that the four people mentioned by Ibn ʿArabī belong forever to the world of the living (two of them, Idrīs and Jesus, dwell in the celestial spheres, and the other two, Elijah and Khaḍir, dwell on this earth unseen by most mortals), this is the first time that they have been assigned the supreme offices in the esoteric hierarchy. All previous traditional teaching, in fact, seems to identify the rightful holders of these offices as being individuals who, according to Ibn ʿArabī, are really only the successive deputies of the true *awtād*. Thus the connection between prophethood and sainthood is confirmed and strengthened: the sphere of *walāya* is not autonomous, but is subject until the end of time to the perennial authority of the only prophets who are still living since the death of Muḥammad.

How are the roles divided between these four prophets? Chapter Seventy-Three of the *Futūḥāt* has nothing very specific to say on the subject, but other texts fill the gap.[21] Idrīs, dwelling in the fourth heaven of the Sun and occupying a middle position in the centre of the seven planetary spheres, has the office of *quṭb* or Pole of the universe. The two Imāms are Jesus and Elijah. Lastly, Khaḍir is the fourth *watad*.[22] The visible hierarchy described later on is in fact simply a reflection of this permanent structure, which in turn is itself no more than the refraction of the higher reality whence it derives its authority. Indeed, another passage from the *Futūḥāt*,[23] apparently contradicting what went before, states: 'As for the one and only Pole, it is the spirit of Muḥammad (*rūḥ Muḥammad*), by which all the Messengers and all the Prophets are sustained.' Idrīs, Elijah, Jesus and Khaḍir are, likewise, simply differentiated projections of the *ḥaqīqa muḥammadiyya*: in a certain sense, they too are only 'deputies'.

Next, Ibn ʿArabī embarks on a detailed description of the 'men of God' (*rijāl Allāh*). These are divided into many classes or categories (*ṭabaqāt*). Among these categories, whose definition sometimes involves a highly complex blend of criteria, a distinction is to be made between a first series of thirty-five *ṭabaqāt*, which maintain a constant number of individuals in every epoch and correspond to cosmic functions, and a second one which corresponds either to types or to degrees of sainthood. The first category of all is the category of the Poles (*aqṭāb*),

who are the sum of all the states and all the stations, in either an immediate or a derivative fashion by means of deputies, as we saw. However, the meaning of the word 'Pole' may be stretched to cover all those who are the pivots of a certain spiritual station and who alone are in full possession of it at any given moment. One may also say of a man dwelling in a certain place that he is its Pole. In the same way, the shaykh who presides over an assembly is the Pole of that assembly. But in the technical sense, and in the absence of any other definition, the Pole is a term which properly speaking can be applied only to one person in every epoch. He is also named *ghawth*, 'help'. He is one of the 'proximate' (*al-muqarrabūn*; cf. Qur'ān 56:11), and is the head of the community for his time.

Some of the Poles possess an authority which is manifested and hold the office of caliph in the external sense, just as they are caliphs in the inner sense in virtue of their spiritual rank. This was so in the case of Abū Bakr, ʿUmar, ʿUthmān and ʿAlī, Ḥasan and Muʿāwiya ibn Yazīd, ʿUmar ibn ʿAbd al-ʿAzīz[24] and al Mutawakkil.[25] Others are caliphs only in the inner sense and possess no apparent external authority, such as Aḥmad ibn Harūn al-Rashīd al-Sabtī[26] or Abū Yazīd al-Bisṭāmī and most of the Poles.

Next are the Imāms, of whom there are never more than two at any given time. One of them is called ʿAbd al-Rabb ('servant of the Lord') and the other ʿAbd al-Malik ('servant of the King'), while the Pole is called ʿAbd Allāh: for every man has a divine Name that corresponds to him, and the Pole is named ʿAbd Allāh, whatever his [profane] name may be. It is always so, just as the Imāms are always 'ʿAbd al-Rabb' and 'ʿAbd al-Malik'.[27]

The *Kitāb manzil al-quṭb*, or *Book of the Spiritual Dwelling of the Pole*, throws additional light on these three offices.[28] 'The Pole is both the centre of the circle of the universe, and its circumference. He is the Mirror of God, and the pivot of the world. He is bound by subtle links to the hearts of all created beings and brings them either good or evil, neither one predominating. But from the point of view of the Pole, these things in themselves are neither good nor evil: they *are* (*wa-huwa ʿindahu lā khayr wa-lā sharr wa-lākin wujūd*), and become good or bad as a result of the vessel that receives them . . ..[29] The Pole's dwelling place is the dwelling place of pure existentiation (*ījād*) . . .. He is the universal Veil within Existence.[30] He keeps the treasures of divine Generosity. God is perpetually epiphanized to him . . .. He is located in Mecca, whatever place he happens to be in bodily. When a Pole is enthroned at the level of the *quṭbiyya*, all beings, animal or vegetable, make a covenant with him other than men and *jinns* (with a few exceptions) . . .. This explains the story about the man who saw the huge snake that God has placed around Mount Qāf,[31] which encircles the world. The head and the tail of this snake meet. The man greeted the snake, who returned his greeting and then asked him about Shaykh Abū Madyan, who lived at Bijāya in the Maghrib. The man said to it, 'How do you come to know Abū Madyan?' The snake answered, 'Is there anyone on earth who does not know him?'[32] Chapter Three Hundred and Thirty-Six of the *Futūḥāt*[33] is entirely about this pact of allegiance with the Pole, and says that all the spirits (*arwāḥ*) participate in it; each of them asks the *quṭb* a question inspired by God and receives an answer it did not know.[34]

On the other hand, the distinctions which apply to the *awliyā'* in general apply to the *aqṭāb* as well:

The most perfect of the Poles is the Muḥammadan Pole. The ones below him are divided hierarchically according to the rank of the Prophets whose heirs they are; for there are the heirs of Jesus, of Abraham, of Joseph, of Noah, and so on; and the position of each pole is determined by the position of the prophet whose heir he is, but all of them proceed from the 'tabernacle' [*mishkāt*, which is of course the 'tabernacle of light', *mishkāt al-anwār*, so designated in verse 24:35] of Muḥammad. Thus, some are superior to others, but this superiority relates only to their spiritual knowledge, and there is no distinction to be made between them as regards their office (*quṭbiyya*) and the government of the universe (*tadbīr al-wujūd*).[35]

This Pole, who is a 'face without a nape' (*wajh bilā qafā*) because nothing escapes his eyes,[36] himself escapes the eyes of others. The earth does not fall back before him, he does not walk through the air or on water, he does not feed himself by emancipating himself from secondary causes. He makes use of supernatural powers only at rare moments, when divinely commanded to do so. If he hungers, it is of necessity and not through choice: he does not call attention to himself by excessive asceticism. He is patient in wedlock, for there is no state in which he can more perfectly realize absolute servitude (*al-ᶜubūdiyya*) than the state of marriage.[37]

The *Kitāb manzil al-quṭb*, in common with other texts, describes the nature and the respective roles of the two Imāms.[38] The Imām on the left, whose secret 'name' is ᶜAbd al-Rabb, watches over the equilibrium of the world (*ṣalāḥ al-ᶜālam*). He is the 'sword of the Pole' (*sayf al-quṭb*) and usually succeeds him. If he dies first, the Imām on the right becomes the Imām on the left and is himself replaced by the fourth 'pillar'. As regards Shaykh Abū Madyan, who as we saw above succeeded the previous Pole one or two hours before his death, Ibn ᶜArabī explains in this passage that from now on his esoteric name was ᶜAbd al-Ilāh (the equivalent of ᶜAbdallāh), and that his previous name, ᶜAbd al-Rabb, passed immediately to a man from Baghdad, previously the Imām on the right, whose esoteric name was ᶜAbd al-Wahhāb.[39] The Imām on the right, ᶜAbd al-Malik, has the task of watching over the world of the spirits (*ᶜālam al-arwāḥ*): 'His knowledge is knowledge of the things of heaven and he knows nothing about the earth.'[40]

Having been viewed in terms of their functions as such, the Pole and the two Imāms are considered insofar as they are elements of the next category, the category of the four Pillars or *awtād* which they constitute with the addition of a fourth person, the *watad*, who is Khaḍir's 'substitute'. 'Through one of them God protects the east, through another the west, through another the south and through another the north—all of this must be understood from the Kaᶜba. They are also called 'mountains' (*jibāl*) on account of Allāh's words (Qur'ān 78:6): 'Have we not made the earth into a cradle and the mountains into pillars (*awtādan*)? For He stabilized the movement of the earth by means of the mountains, and the authority (*ḥukm*) of those of whom we are speaking (over the world) is analogous to the authority of the mountains over the earth.

Allāh is also referring to their station when He repeats the words of Iblīs: 'We will approach them [i.e. men] from in front and from behind, from their right and from their left' (Qur'ān 7:17). It is by means of the *awtād* that God protects these four directions, and they themselves are guarded against all that might come from there. Thus the demon has no power over them because he can only come at the son of Adam from one of these sides. As for above and below [if these are added to the four directions already mentioned], perhaps they are the concern of the six [spiritual men] of whom, if God wills, we will speak later.[41]

At the start of this section, Ibn ᶜArabī claims to have known one of the *awtād* of his time, in Fez. His name was Ibn Jaᶜdūn, and he earned his living sifting henna. One of the notes in the *Rūḥ al-quds* is about him, and provides more information. There is one remark which merits particular attention, for it describes a characteristic which we have already come across both in the prophetic traditions and in the literature of Sufism: when Ibn Jaᶜdūn was absent, says Ibn ᶜArabī, no one noticed, and when he was present, no one asked him his opinion. When he arrived somewhere, no one thought to welcome him. When a subject was being debated in front of him, the speakers discussed it as though he were not present.[42] Here, the saint's transparency is complete.

Before going on to the next category, the Shaykh al-Akbar makes two further points. The first concerns the 'name' of the *awtād*, which in the case of three of them is added on to the name conferred on them in their capacity as Pole or Imām: they are ᶜAbd al-Ḥayy (servant of the Living One), ᶜAbd al-ᶜAlīm (servant of the Knower), ᶜAbd al-Qādir (servant of the Powerful), and ᶜAbd al-Murīd (servant of Him Who Wills). The second point is much more general and precludes the possibility of a serious misunderstanding: 'All that we say here', writes Ibn ᶜArabī, 'is said in connection with spiritual *men (rijāl)*, but it may apply equally to women.' This statement is further emphasized and clarified in other texts: 'Each category that we speak of contains both men and women.' 'There is no spiritual quality belonging to men to which women do not have equal access.' 'Men and women have a part to play at all levels, including the level of the Pole (*ḥattā fī 'l-quṭbiyya*)'.[43]

Notes to Chapter Six

1. On the *wajh khāṣṣ*, cf. *Futūḥāt*, I, pp. 319, 347; II, p. 294; III, pp. 23, 235, 248, 260; IV, p. 315; *Fuṣūṣ*, I, p. 174.

2. This spatial indeterminacy—for 'whichever way you turn, the Face of God is there', Qur'ān 2:115—is conveyed chiefly by the fact that, as regards his physical being, the saint becomes a face without a nape: like the Prophet who could see the faithful praying behind him, he sees in all directions at one glance. Ibn ᶜArabī describes his experiences of this charisma in *Futūḥāt*, I, p. 491, and II, p. 486. Part of the same order of phenomena is the fact that the body is freed from the specialization of its organs. Any sense can substitute for any of the others: the *walī* is able to 'see' scents or 'hear' visible things, and so on (*Futūḥāt*, I, p. 221). On this characteristic aspect of the experience of the *fatḥ*, see the autobiographical account by ᶜAbd al-ᶜAzīz al-Dabbāgh (*Kitāb al-Ibrīz*), Cairo 1961, pp. 14-16; cf. also p. 354), which is one of the most extraordinary documents known on this subject. All this should be compared to Ibn ᶜArabī's statement that the divine writings which, in certain exceptional circumstances, fall into the hands of man, are to be read in all senses (*Futūḥāt*, III, p. 605). On this subject, see also ibid., I, p. 320; *Taj.*, ed. O. Yahia, III, p. 462.

3. Ibn Taymiyya, *Majmūᶜat al-rasā'il*, I, pp. 21-26; see also M. U. Memon, *Ibn Taymiyya's Struggle Against Popular Religion*, The Hague 1976, p. 65.

4. *Discours sur l'histoire universelle (Muqaddima)*, trans. V. Monteil, Beirut 1967-1968, III, pp. 1022-23. On this vast and complicated theme, see the excellent article by F. de Jong in *EI*², s.v. *quṭb* (IV, p. 548 ff.), which, however, says nothing about an essential point of Ibn ᶜArabī's doctrine on this subject. Without embarking on a detailed analysis of the positions adopted by Orientalists, let us recall that for L. Massignon (*Essai sur les origines du lexique technique*, Paris 1954, pp. 132-34), we are dealing with 'a doctrine which is far more ancient in Islam than is generally believed', '. . . which is not necessarily Imāmite in origin, whatever Ibn Khaldūn may have said about it. In the tenth century it was already classic . . .. Indeed, it was specifically spoken about from the ninth century onwards'. Henry Corbin (*En islam iranien*, I, p. 229; II, p. 76; III, p.279 . . .) sees it as a crypto-Shīᶜite doctrine (in his opinion, the *quṭb* is a metamorphosis of the *imām*) and he suggests that the hierarchy of the *awliyā'* in Sufism was inspired by the hierarchy of the Ismaili secret societies.

5. This treatise occurs again in *al-Ḥāwī lī' l-fatāwī*, Cairo 1959, II, pp. 417-37. In the next century, Ibn Ḥajar al-Haytamī (*Fatāwā ḥadīthiyya*, Cairo 1970, p. 322) was to adopt a position similar to Suyūṭī.

6. Suyūṭī, ibid., p. 428.

7. One of the most interesting descriptions—for the topographical details it gives—of the *dīwān al-awliyā'* occurs in ᶜAbd al-ᶜAzīz al-Dabbāgh-'s, *Kitāb al-Ibrīz*, p. 326 ff.

8. Cf. for example *Futūḥāt*, I, p. 233; II, pp. 14, 19, 223, 308; III, pp. 34, 560. Ibn ᶜArabī further says, in his attestation of investiture which concludes his *Kitāb Nasab al-khirqa*, that he received the *khirqa* (the gown or mantle of initiation) in Mecca from the hands of Shaykh Jamāl al-Dīn Yūnus al-ᶜAbbāsī, who had it directly from ᶜAbd al-Qādir al-Jīlānī. Despite being invested with the *khirqa* in other ways, this investiture establishes a special relationship between him and ᶜAbd al-Qādir. On ᶜAbd al-Qādir al-Jīlānī (or al-Jīlī, or al-Kilānī, or al-Gīlānī), see the article by Margoliouth in *EI*[1] and by W. Braune in *EI*[2]; see also the thesis by Jacqueline Chabbi, 'ᶜAbd al-Qādir al-Jīlānī, idées sociales et politiques', Sorbonne 1971, and her article 'ᶜAbd al-Qādir al-Jīlānī, personnage historique', in *Studia islamica*, no. 38 (1973), pp. 75-106. The most interesting hagiographical source is the *Bahjat al-asrār wa maᶜdan al-anwār* by Shaṭṭanūfī (died 713/1314), Cairo 1330 AH (with Jīlānī's *Futūḥ al-ghayb* in the margin), of which the *Qalā'id al-jawāhir* by Muḥammad ibn Yaḥyā al-Tādhafī, Cairo 1956, is a plagiary. There are many editions of works attributed to ᶜAbd al-Qādir, in particular *al-Ghunya li ṭālibī ṭarīq al-ḥaqq* and *al-Fatḥ al-rabbānī*.

9. This event took place, therefore, eight years before the death of ᶜAbd al-Qādir, who is said to have died in 561 AH.

10. These two details enable us to identify the newcomer as a non-Muslim.

11. This town in the province of Hamadhān is several hundred kilometres away from Baghdad.

12. Tādhafī, *Qalā'id al-jawāhir*, p. 31.

13. The characteristic features of this type of account are found in the apologue of the sincere *murīd* and the false *shaykh*, related by ᶜAbd al-ᶜAzīz al-Dabbāgh, *Ibrīz*, pp. 371-72.

14. Unlike other terms which we will come across later in this chapter, the term *abdāl* (singular *badal*) comes into at least one *ḥadīth* (*Lā tasubbū ahl al-Shām fa-inna fīhim al-abdāl . . .*), mentioned by Suyūṭī in the treatise cited in note 5.

15. Some further points of interest in this account are: the presence of Khaḍir; the part played by ᶜAbd al-Qādir, who is obviously the Pole (*quṭb*)—although this means there is one too many, for, as we shall see, the Pole is one of the *Abdāl*; the presence of the 'indiscreet witness'—whose part is taken here by the narrator—which cannot be fortuitous, and which suggests that he himself will be called on one day to fill the office of *badal*; the departure from the rule according to which, at each level of the hierarchy, the replacement of the deceased titular is effected by a member of the category below 'going up a step'.

16. *Futūḥāt*, I, p. 151.

17. Ibid., IV, p. 76. This person, who is not named in the *Futūḥāt*, is identified in the *Durra Fākhira* (trans. Austin, *Sufis of Andalusia*, London 1971, p. 152, number 62) as going by the name of al-Ashall al-Qabā'ilī.

18. The definitions provided by Ibn ᶜArabī and the structure of the hierarchy of the saints as he describes it (see below) are found later, in outline at least and often in detail, in most of the works of Ṣūfī literature in which these problems are raised

or discussed. We cannot here undertake an analysis of this vast body of documents, where, besides the classics, consideration would also have to be given to the innumerable smaller works arising out of the literature of the *ṭuruq*, even to the literature produced by a movement as unorthodox as the *anṣār* of the Sudanese Mahdī. Later on, we will give several examples relating to the Seal of Sainthood. However, strict precision is not always uppermost in the use of traditional elements or of Ibn ʿArabī's formulation of them: there is no local saint who has not been proclaimed *ṣāḥıb al-zamān*, no shaykh who has not been credited with the power to make his followers into *awtād* or *abdāl*, no *ṭarīqa* which does not claim the exclusive privilege of supplying at every epoch the Pole of the time. When one is not just dealing with pious hyperbole, Ibn ʿArabī's explanations and his criteria usually make it possible to become aware of the underlying confusion of doctrine.

19. Apart from chapter 73 of the *Futūḥāt*, part of which we summarise below and in which this subject is discussed from page 3 to page 39 of volume II, the chapters of particular interest are: chapter 270 (II, pp. 571-74); chapter 336 (II, pp. 135-40); chapters 462 to 556 (IV, pp. 74-196). See also several short treatises: *Ḥilyat al-abdāl*, Hyderabad 1948, translated into French by M. Vâlsan with the title 'La parure des abdāl', in *Études traditionelles*, nos. 286-87, September-October and November 1950; *Kitāb Manzil al-quṭb, Risālat al-Anwār* (analysed below), *Kitāb al-Tarājim*, all three published in Hyderabad in 1948; *Mawāqiʿ al-nujūm*, Cairo 1956. The treatise on the *Mubāyaʿat al-quṭb*, of which Osman Yahia has not registered a single manuscript, is undoubtedly identical to chapter 336 of the *Futūḥāt*.

20. Cf. the article by G. Vajda, s.v. in *EI*[2]; the references it contains should, of course, be expanded to include—in addition to the passage from the *Futūḥāt* (I, p. 5) summarized here—chapter 4 of the *Fuṣūṣ* (ed. ʿAfīfī, I, pp. 75-80), and chapter 22 (I, pp. 181-87), in which Idrīs is assimilated to Ilyās (i.e. Elijah).

21. Cf. *Futūḥāt*, II, p. 455; *Kitāb al-Isfār*, Hyderabad 1948, p. 32; *Tarjumān al-ashwāq*, Beirut 1961, p. 24.

22. The fourfold nature of this structure, which corresponds explicitly with the four corners (*rukn*, plural *arkān*) of the Kaʿba, also bears a relation to the levels of universal Manifestation, as we shall see when we discuss Ibn ʿArabī's cosmology (see chapter 10, n. 70).

23. *Futūḥāt*, I, p. 151.

24. The Poles named here are, firstly, the four initial caliphs (the *rāshidūn* caliphs, meaning orthodox or well-guided), who successively took over the leadership of the community after the Prophet's death. Next is Ḥasan, son of ʿAlī, who, when elected caliph, abdicated in favour of Muʿāwiya, who founded the Umayyad dynasty. Muʿāwiya was the grandfather of the next-named Muʿāwiya ibn Yazīd, whose rule was brief in the extreme (forty days according to some, two or three months according to others; cf. Ibn ʿArabī's note on him in *Muḥāḍarat al-abrār*, Damascus 1968, I, p. 67—a work whose authenticity is beyond doubt, despite certain suspicions, on which see *GAL*, S1, 799—and Suyūṭī, *Ta'rīkh al-khulafā'*, Cairo 1969, pp. 210-11), and who died aged twenty-one. ʿUmar ibn ʿAbd al-ʿAzīz, eighth Umayyad caliph, famous for his piety, reigned from the month of Ṣafar 99 until the month of Rajab 101 (717-18).

25. Al-Mutawakkil (206/822-247/861), the twelfth Abbassid caliph, put an end to the persecution (*miḥna*)—started by the caliph al-Ma'mūn—of Muslims who, contrary to the Muʿtazilites, held that the Qur'ān was uncreated in nature.

26. Aḥmad ibn Hārūn al-Rashīd, son of the fifth Abbasid caliph, is mentioned several times by Ibn ʿArabī: *Tanazzulāt mawṣiliyya* (published in Cairo in 1961 under the title *Laṭā'if al-asrār*, p. 194); *Futūḥāt*, II, p. 15 (where Ibn ʿArabī relates how he met him one Friday in front of the Kaʿba in 599AH, i.e. several centuries after his death) and IV, p. 11.

27. *Futūḥāt*, II, p. 6.

28. *Kitāb manzil al-quṭb*, p. 2.

29. This means that his function is on a level which, ontologically speaking, precedes the level at which things endowed with existence become qualified as good or evil.

30. This perhaps surprising name derived from the fact that the Pole, his function being what it is, in a sense comes between God and created being.

31. On the theme of Mount Qāf in Islamic cosmology, see the article by M. Streck and A. Miquel in EI^2, s.v. *Ḳāf*.

32. *Kitāb manzil al-quṭb*, p. 4. Ibn ʿArabī explains (*Kitāb manzil al-quṭb*, p. 12; *Mawāqiʿ al-nujūm*, pp. 139-40) that Abū Madyan was the 'Imām of the left' and only acceded to the *quṭbiyya* 'one or two hours before his death' (in 595/1197). The same story, in expanded form, comes in the *Rūḥ al-quds*, where the man talking to the snake is identified as Mūsā Abū ʿImrān al-Ṣadrānī, of whom more later.

33. *Futūḥāt*, III, p. 135-40.

34. Those who are exempt from the obligation imposed by the pact are the 'sublime spirits' (*al-ʿālīn*; see Qur'ān 38:75)—that is to say, according to *Futūḥāt*, IV, p. 312, the *muhayyamūn*, the 'spirits overcome with love', who never cease their contemplation of the divine Beauty and Majesty and are unaware that the world even exists. The *muhayyamūn* are also called the *karūbiyyūn*, or Cherubim.

35. *Kitāb manzil al-quṭb*, p. 6.

36. Ibid., p. 2. On the expression 'a face without a nape', see above, note 2.

37. *Futūḥāt*, II, pp. 573-74.

38. Information about the two Imāms is contained in all the texts which have reference to the Pole, as indicated in note 19.

39. *Kitāb manzil al-quṭb*, p. 12.

40. In *Futūḥāt*, chapter 270 and in *Mawāqiʿ al-nujūm*, p. 139, Ibn ʿArabī alludes to the correspondence between the three functions of the Pole and the Imāms, and the three divine functions ('Lord of men', 'King of men', 'God of men') mentioned at the start of the last *sūra* of the Qur'ān (114:1-3), which is, as we know, a *sūra* of protection. This correspondence is not without significance with regard to the modes of operation of the protection invoked by the believer who recites these verses. Let us note, on the other hand, that a contradiction exists between most of Ibn ʿArabī's texts about the esoteric names of the two Imāms and *Futūḥāt*, II, p. 571, where it is the Imam of the right who is named ʿAbd al-Rabb. If this is not a mistake on the part of the author or a copyists's error, the most likely explanation is that there has been a reversal of perspective, with the Imām on the

left of the Pole appearing to an observer to be on his right, and the Imām of the right on his left.

41. *Futūḥāt*, II, p. 7. On the *awtād* and the next category, the *abdāl*, cf. *Futūḥāt*, I, pp. 152-61 (chapters 15 and 16).

42. *Rūḥ al-quds*, p. 72, number 17 (Austin, *Sufis of Andalusia*, pp. 114-16). Ibn Jaʿdūn died at Fez in 597/1200.

43. These three quotations are taken respectively from *Futūḥāt*, II, p. 26; II, p. 35; and III, p. 89.

CHAPTER

7

The Highest Degree of *Walāya*

CHAPTER Seventy-Three of the *Futūḥāt* lists eighty-four 'classes' of spiritual men, thirty-five of which have a constant number of occupants at any given moment. We cannot deal with all the categories here, so we will merely mention the most important of them, intending, in this chapter and the next, to concentrate in greater detail on the two which represent, respectively, what we might call the arch and the keystone of them all.

Having discussed the four 'pillars', Ibn ʿArabī goes on to speak of the seven *abdāl* (singular *badal*), so named because

> when they depart from a place and wish to leave a substitute (*badal*) in it, because they see that it will be of profit either to themselves or to others, they leave a 'person' (*shakhṣ*) who is so like them in seeming that whoever looks at him has no doubt that he has seen the being in question. In fact, it is not he, but a spiritual form that he leaves in place of himself, having in view the purpose that his knowledge has assigned [to this substitution].

It is through the *abdāl* that God preserves the seven climes.[1] The first among them is in the footsteps (literally, 'on the foot', *ʿalā qadam*) of Abraham and is in charge of the first clime, the second is in the footsteps of Moses, the third is in the footsteps of Aaron, the fourth is in the footsteps of Idrīs (this is the clime in the middle, corresponding to the heaven of the Sun in the hierarchy of the planetary spheres, and this *badal* is none other than the Pole himself), the fifth is in the footsteps of Joseph, the sixth is in the footsteps of Jesus and the seventh is in the footsteps of Adam. Once again, the connection between *nubuwwa* and *walāya* is plain. The symbolic names of the *abdāl* (among which are the names of the *awtād*, since each of these categories, as we saw, is included in the one below it) are the expression of a privileged relationship with one of the divine Names. Besides ʿAbd al-Ḥayy, ʿAbd al-ʿAlīm, ʿAbd al-Wadūd (servant of the Most Loving, similar to ʿAbd al-Murīd in the

1. On the *iqlīms* or 'climes', see André Miquel's article in *EI*², s.v. 'Iḳlīm'.

previous listing) and ʿAbd al-Qādir, there are ʿAbd al-Shakūr (servant of Him who is grateful), ʿAbd al-Samīʿ (servant of Him who hears), and ʿAbd al-Baṣīr (servant of Him who sees).

To each of these divine qualities there corresponds one of the *abdāl*. Allāh looks upon them through these qualities and each quality has a dominant influence on one of them.

Ibn ʿArabī saw the seven *abdāl* of his time at Mecca together, but says that he had met two of them before: Mūsā al-Ṣadrānī in Seville in 586[2] and Muḥammad ibn Ashraf al-Rundī, named *Shaykh al-Jabal*.[3]

Next come the *nuqabā'*, a word usually translated as 'leaders' (in the Qur'ān 5:12 it is applied, in the singular, to the twelve heads of the tribes of Israel), but which it would be better to render as 'seekers', a word which accords with its etymology and also corresponds more closely to the characteristics of these people as Ibn ʿArabī describes them. There are twelve of them, 'the number of the signs in the Zodiac', and they possess the knowledge of the revealed Laws. 'They have the power to see the evil hidden in men's souls and to know their deceits and their trickeries. As for Iblīs [the devil], they can see right through him . . .. When they see someone's footsteps in the sand, they know whether these are the tracks of one of the chosen or one of the damned.' The *nujabā'*, or Nobles, are eight in number. 'The signs of the divine approval are manifest in them because of their spiritual state, not through their own choice but because their states govern them.' Whereas the *nuqabā'* know the secrets of the ninth heaven—the heaven without stars—the *nujabā'* possess the secrets of the eight lower spheres: the heaven of the fixed stars and the seven planetary heavens.[4] The *ḥawāriyyūn*, a rather enigmatic name used in the Qur'ān to designate the apostles of Jesus (cf. Qur'ān 3:52, 5:112, 61:14, and so on), constitute a very small category, since there is never more than one

2. There is a number about Mūsā al-Ṣadrānī in the *Rūḥ al-quds* (pp. 74-76, number 19; Austin's translation, pp. 121-23), where it is explained that he visited Ibn ʿArabī to bring him a message from shaykh Abū Madyan.

3. Cf. *Rūḥ al-quds* (pp. 72-74, number 18; Austin's translation, pp. 116-21). The *Durra Fākhira* (trans. Austin, p. 151, number 60) also mentions the story of the meeting of one of Ibn ʿArabī's companions, ʿAbd al-Majīd ibn Salma, with another *badal*, Muʿādh ibn Ashras. This story also comes in *Ḥilyat al-abdāl*, p. 3 (French translation by M. Vâlsan, *La Parure des abdāl*, Paris 1951, pp. 11-13), and in *Futūḥāt*, I, p. 277. The passage from the *Futūḥāt* analysed here is from vol. II, p. 7.

4. Ibid., II, pp. 7-8.

of them at any given time. This one *ḥawārī* 'defends religion both by the sword and by convincing evidence, for he has been given the knowledge of how to express himself and present evidence, and also the knowledge of swordfighting, as well as bravery and the ability to answer the challenges made against the authenticity of revealed religion.' Since the Prophet's death, only this one *ḥawārī* has been permitted, as the 'inheritance' due to him, to perform *muʿjizāt*—that is to say, supernatural acts which, unlike the *karāmāt* granted to the saints, are the exclusive privilege of the prophets.[5]

The next category, the name and nature of which are somewhat surprising, is the category of the *rajabiyyūn* or 'men of Rajab', who number forty. They are so named because 'the spiritual state (*ḥāl*) which corresponds to their station (*maqām*) is manifest in them only during the month of Rajab, from the moment of the appearance of the new moon until the end of the lunar month. They then lose this state and do not regain it until the month of Rajab the following year . . .. In some of them there survives throughout the year something of what they perceived (through intuitive unveiling) in the month of Rajab, while in others nothing of it survives at all.' Ibn ʿArabī tells of the visit he paid to one of them at Dunaysir in Mesopotamia. This person, who is identified briefly in the *Durra fākhira* as al-Khaṭarī, had the singular gift, and not only in the month of Rajab, of being able to detect the

5. Ibid., II, p. 8. For a definition of the *muʿjizāt*, see Abū Ḥanīfa, *al-Fiqh al-akbar*, Cairo 1327 AH, p. 69; Bāqillānī, *Kitāb al-Bayān*, ed. McCarthy, Beirut 1958, pp. 37-49. Unlike the *karāmāt*, the *muʿjizāt* are preceded by a challenge (*taḥaddī*). In this passage from the *Futūḥāt*, Ibn ʿArabī criticizes the attitude adopted by Abū Isḥāq al-Isfarā'inī, an Ashʿarite theologian who died in 418/1027, according to whom the saints cannot perform supernatural acts similar to those performed by the Prophet. The difference between *muʿjizāt* and *karāmāt* lies not in the form taken by the supernatural act, but on the one hand in the intention (or absence thereof), of the agent of it, and on the other hand in the fact that *muʿjizāt* are the rightful property of the prophets, whereas *karāmāt* are inherited by the saints (and modelled in accordance with the prophetic type who predominates in the *walī's* heritage). Ibn ʿArabī also says, without further explanation, that he met the *ḥawārī* of his time in 586. He says further that during the time of the Prophet, this office was held by al-Zubayr ibn al-ʿAwwām. Al-Zubayr was one of the first to be converted (the fifth, apparently) and was one of the ten Companions who received the promise of paradise, and did in fact receive the name *al-Ḥawārī* from the Prophet himself.

extremist Shīʿites (*rawāfiḍ*) even when they were posing as Sunnīs, because they appeared to him metamorphosed into swine.[6]

Whereas the first thirty-five categories correspond to specific hierarchical functions connected with the government of the higher worlds (*ʿālam al-arwāḥ, malakūt*) and the lower worlds (*ʿālam al-ajsām, mulk*), this is no longer so in the case of most of the *ṭabaqāt*, described, one after another, in the rest of Chapter Seventy-Three of the *Futūḥāt*. The individuals who make up these groups possess knowledge and powers, and they all have some role to play in the divine economy of Manifestation, but this role does not define the category in question. These categories contain a variable number of beings whose common bond is the fact of their having attained to a certain *degree*, or realized a certain *modality*, of spiritual life. To add to the complexity, this means that, among other things, the same man can be present in several categories simultaneously. Several of the modalities, in fact, can be possessed concurrently, and the attainment of a certain degree implies that he who has attained it is eminently in possession of the levels below. If we add to these various parameters those which are furnished by the typology of the prophetic heritages described earlier, we arrive at a combination of inexhaustible richness. The example of the Pole is particularly revealing. From the point of view of function, he belongs to the category of the *quṭbiyya* (of which he is the sole representative), but he also belongs to the categories of the *awtād*, the *abdāl*, and so on (and in addition he may, or may not, hold the external office of *khilāfa*). On the other hand, like all saints he is part of a prophetic 'family': he is *mūsawī, ibrāhīmī, shuʿaybī*, and so on, and, ultimately, all of them at once. He is in possession of 'all the states (*aḥwāl*) and all the stations (*maqāmāt*)' concurrently, and by the same token occupies a place in the groups or sub-groups which correspond to this double series of distinctions. Finally, in a most logical fashion, he is also present in a last category which we are about to explore, and which represents the highest degree of *walāya*. This is the category of the *afrād* or solitaries.[7]

6. *Futūḥāt*, II, p. 8; *Durra fākhira*, trans. Austin (*Sufis of Andalusia*), p. 160; *Muḥāḍarat al-abrār*, Damascus 1968, I, p. 418 (where the animals are not swine but dogs). This anecdote, even though it concerns the *rawāfiḍ*, could not conceivably have been written by someone with a secret sympathy for Shīʿism. On the subject of Ibn ʿArabī's attitude towards Shīʿism, see *Futūḥāt*, I, p. 282 and III, p. 343.

7. Many passages in Ibn ʿArabī's writings concern the *afrād*. We are specifically referring here to *Futūḥāt*, chapter 73 (II, p. 19) and above all to chapters 30, 31,

The information contained in Chapter Seventy-Three on the subject of the *afrād* is relatively succinct, and will therefore be supplemented here by an analysis of the wealth of detail contained in Chapters Thirty to Thirty-Two of the *Futūḥāt*. In these chapters, moreover, in a way most unusual in the work of the Shaykh al-Akbar, the *afrād* are designated by the symbolic name of *al-rukbān*, the 'riders' or, more precisely, the 'camel-riders'. Unlike the *fursān*, who ride on horses (*rukkāb al-khayl*), the *rukbān* in question ride on camels (*rukkāb al-ibil*)—an essentially Arab mount, and as such one which possesses a symbolic character that is specifically Islamic and Muḥammadan. These *rukbān* (a term to be explained later), 'who are the solitaries' (*hum al-afrād*), are divided into two groups: those who travel 'on the camel of spiritual energy' (*nujub al-himam*; in the abundant camel vocabulary of Arabia, *nujub* means a pure-bred camel), and those who travel 'on the camel of action' (*nujub al-aʿmāl*). The Pole, the *awtād*, the *abdāl*, the *nuqabā'*, the *nujabā'*, and the *rajabiyyūn*, along with others, are all included among the *afrād*, the number of whom varies but is always an odd number and always greater than three.

The *afrād*, situated at the same spiritual level as the Pole, are not subject to his authority, except for those of them who are invested with a specific function (*imām*, *badal*, and so on) and who are thus equivalent to those in the initiatic hierarchy. In the human order they are equivalent to those in the angelic order who are the *muhayyamūn* or spirits overcome with love, also known as *al-karūbiyyūn*, the Cherubim. The divine Name which governs them is *al-Fard*, the Unique, which explains the fact that their spiritual level is unknown (*yujhal maqāmuhum*) and why they experience misunderstanding and reproach, for 'they have received a knowledge from God which is known to them alone'. This is illustrated by a reference to the story of Moses and Khaḍir (one of the *afrād*) in *Sūra* 18, in which Moses, in spite of repeated promises to keep silent, is astonished by his companion's strange and, legally speaking, aberrant behaviour. Reference is also made to the case of ʿAlī ibn Abī Ṭālib, who declared, pointing at his own breast, that innumerable forms of knowledge were stored in it, but that he could find no one capable of receiving them. Other past *afrād* are mentioned, including Ibn ʿAbbās and Zayn al-ʿĀbidīn, ʿUmar ibn al-Khaṭṭāb and Ibn Ḥanbal. Ibn ʿArabī, who says that in the course of a

32 (I, pp. 199-208). Cf. also I, p. 93; II, pp. 25, 675; III, p. 137; *Kitāb al-Tajalliyāt*, ed. O. Yahia, 1967, I, p. 39; *Kitāb al-Masā'il*, Hyderabad 1948, p. 28, etc.

single day at Mecca, on Mount Abū Qubays, he met seventy *afrād* (in a later passage he mentions the names of some whom he had visited in person), identifies as such several outstanding figures of twelfth century *taṣawwuf*: ʿAbd al-Qādir al-Jīlānī,[8] and two of his companions, Abū al-Suʿūd ibn al-Shibl[9] and Muḥammad ibn Qā'id al-Awānī.[10]

Leaving aside several paragraphs in which the *fuqahā'* or doctors of the Law are severely criticized for their attitude towards the gnostics (Ibn ʿArabī calls them the 'pharaohs of the saints' and the 'antichrists of the pious servants of God'), Chapter Thirty of the *Futūḥāt* furnishes us with some essential facts. To begin with, the *afrād* do not, normally, have disciples (the reservation is explained later): their task is not *tarbiya*, the initiatic instruction of novices, but is confined to *naṣīḥa* or counsel. They spread knowledge around them without claiming ultimate authority or imposing a discipline, as a gift which may be accepted or refused. In their 'spiritual ascensions' (*miʿrāj*), they see before them only the 'foot of the Prophet', whereas the other *awliyā'*, according to their different levels, see the foot of the Pole, of the *awtād*, of the *abdāl*, and so on. This proves the autonomy of the *afrād* in relation to all hierarchies. Finally, they have the right of sway over beings (*taṣarruf*), but those of them who belong to the first category (the *rukkāb al-himam*, who are mounted on the camels of spiritual energy) refuse to exercise it, as in the case of Abū al-Sūʿūd ibn al-Shibl. ʿAbd al-Qādir

8. On ʿAbd al-Qādir al-Jīlānī and the references to him in Ibn ʿArabī, see chapter 6, note 8.

9. On Abū Suʿūd ibn al-Shibl, see *Futūḥāt*, I, pp. 187, 201, 233, 248, 288; II, pp. 19, 49, 80, 131, 370, 522, 624; III, pp. 34, 223, 560. Ibn ʿArabī several times emphasizes the difference in status between ʿAbd al-Qādir and Abū Suʿūd: the former possessed the *ḥāl al-ṣidq* but not the corresponding *maqām*; the latter, however, possessed the *maqām* and not the *ḥāl*, and thus remained unknown to the world (II, p. 223); ʿAbd al-Qādir held the office of the *khilāfa*, whereas Abū Suʿūd, although equally able to hold it, had handed over to his Lord all authority over His servants (II, p. 308); ʿAbd al-Qādir sometimes succumbed to the temptation of *idlāl* (impudence, casualness), while Abū Suʿūd was exempt from this imperfection. However, for a critique of Abū Suʿūd, see *Futūḥāt*, II, p. 64.

10. The *Bahjat al-asrār* by Shaṭṭanūfī, Cairo 1330 AH, pp. 7-8, explains that Muḥammad ibn Qā'id al-Awānī was present when ʿAbd al-Qādir al-Jīlānī uttered the famous phrase that established him in his capacity as Pole of his time: 'This foot of mine is on the neck of every saint of God.' Nabhānī's note in *Jāmiʿ karāmāt al-awliyā'*, Beirut, n.d., I, p. 112, repeats, after Munāwī, the information given by Ibn ʿArabī (cf. *Futūḥāt*, I, p. 201; II, p. 130; III, p. 34), and says, wrongly, that al-Awānī was one of his teachers.

al-Jīlānī, on the other hand, exercised this power in obedience to a divine command. Muḥammad ibn Qā'id used it without being ordered to do so, which is a sign of imperfection. They have entered the Tents of Mystery (*surādiqāt al-ghayb*) and are hidden beneath the veils of ordinary behaviour (*ḥujub al-ʿawā'id*). They observe total servitude (*ʿubūda*), and their attitude towards Allāh is one of absolute dependence (*iftiqār*). They are the Heroes (*fityān*), the Hidden (*al-akhfiyā'*), 'those who draw blame upon themselves' (*al-malāmiyya*).[11] Ibn Jaʿdūn, who was mentioned at the end of the last chapter, is a striking example of the *malāmiyya* (Ibn ʿArabī prefers this form of the word to the more frequent but less correct *malāmatiyya*): when they are present, no one pays them any attention; when they withdraw, their absence goes unnoticed. They blend into the *ʿāmma*, the main body of believers: no apparent asceticism, no excessive visible devotions, no manifestly supernatural intervention in their very ordinary lives draws people's attention to them. The 'blame' is both what they inflict on themselves in a ceaseless effort to detect their own imperfections, and that to which they are subjected by the élite: the *fuqahā'* and the Ṣūfis (in this case Ṣūfis who are still far from the end of the Way) treat them with condescension, and, insofar as they notice their existence, are critical of their spiritual ordinariness. The motto of the *malāmiyya* could be the adage of which Ibn ʿArabī, in the *Futūḥāt*,[12] says: 'these words conceal immense knowledge', and according to which '[true] Sufism consists of the five prayers and the expectation of death'. The way of perfection ends, paradoxically, in pure and simple conformity with the Law.

Ibn ʿArabī comments repeatedly on the famous *ḥadīth qudsī*, in which God says: 'My servant does not cease to approach Me through supererogatory acts of obedience until I love him. And when I love him, I am the hearing with which he hears, the sight with which he

11. In Ibn ʿArabī's technical vocabulary, *malāmiyya* refers to a type of sainthood while *afrād* refers to the highest degree within this type. Therefore, all the *afrād* are *malāmiyya* but not the reverse. The passage which we summarize here (*Futūḥāt*, I, p. 201) might lead one to think that the last characteristics described apply exclusively to the *afrād* in the first category. Taken in full, the texts concerned with the *afrād* and particularly the two following chapters clearly prove that they apply equally to all of them. On the *futuwwa* and the *fityān* in the doctrine of Ibn ʿArabī, see *Futūḥāt* I, pp. 241-44, and II, pp. 231-34.

12. *Futūḥāt*, I, p. 188. Ibn ʿArabī attributes this phrase to Abū Suʿūd ibn al-Shibl.

sees, the hand with which he grasps, the feet with which he walks . . ..'[13]

Notwithstanding, this is not the most perfect proximity—and proximity, we must remember, is the true meaning of *walāya*. In the performing of supererogatory acts there is still the implicit affirmation of choice, of the servant's own will. But the pure servant—*al-ᶜabd al-maḥḍ*, a term which the Shaykh al-Akbar uses of himself[14]—is totally without *ikhtiyār*, free will. Thus, at the end of the path, it is only by practising the *farā'iḍ*, or legal obligations (epitomized by the five prayers in the saying quoted above) that he can realize fully his spiritual destiny. We are a long way from the *ibāḥa*, the laxness of fact or alleged antinomianism of principle that Ibn ᶜArabī's detractors so noisily condemn. He goes on to explain that when this point has been reached it is no longer God who becomes the hearing and the sight and the hand of the *ᶜabd*, but the *ᶜabd* who becomes the hearing with which God hears, the sight through which He sees, the hand with which He grasps. The *malāmiyya* 'in this world are the hidden, the pure, the trustworthy, those who are concealed among men . . .. For them alone is there a perpetual theophany.'[15] 'They are the princes and the imāms of the People of the Way; one of them is the supreme head of this world, and that is Muḥammad, God's Messenger. They are the wise men who put each thing in its rightful place. They affirm the secondary causes where necessary and deny them where they should be denied.'[16]

The ignorant man may say of the *malāmī* (singular of *malāmiyya*) what the infidels said of the Prophet: *ya'kulu 'l-ṭaᶜām wa-yamshī fī 'l-aswāq* (Qur'ān 25:7): he feeds like everyone else and attends to his business in the market place. The *malāmī*, as Ibn ᶜArabī describes him, knows at each moment that God acts *within* secondary causes and not through them (*ᶜinda 'l-asbāb la bi 'l-asbāb*), and that they are thus the Veil of the Peerless One. But He has chosen this veil and it is not up to the servant to tear it. So the *malāmī*, like the ordinary man—and he is

13. Bukhārī, *bāb al-tawāḍuᶜ*. This *ḥadīth qudsī* forms part of the *aḥādīth* collected by Ibn ᶜArabī in his *Mishkāt al-anwār*, Aleppo 1346 AH, no. 91. For the commentary on this *ḥadīth*, see *Futūḥāt*, I, p. 406; III, p. 68; IV, pp. 20, 24, 30, 449; *Naqsh al-Fuṣūṣ*, Hyderabad 1948, pp. 3-4; see also the anonymous commentary on the *Kitāb al-Tajalliyāt*, known by the title *Kashf al-ghāyāt* in the edition by O. Yahia, in the journal *al-Mashriq*, 1966, p. 679.

14. *Futūḥāt*, III, p. 41, 372.

15. Ibid., I, p. 181. See also III, p. 35.

16. Ibid., II, p. 16. On the *malāmiyya*, see also chapter 23 ibid., I, pp. 180-82.

ordinary in the fullest sense, through his conscious and voluntary conformity to the divine order of things—submits to the chain of secondary causes. He never makes use of exceptional powers and refrains from *shaṭaḥāt*, the ecstatic utterances which are considered by the vulgar to be proof of the highest sainthood. In the opinion of Ibn ʿArabī, who comes back often to this point, 'the ecstatic utterance (*shaṭḥ*) is an imperfection in man, for in the *shaṭḥ* he is raising himself to the level of divinity and thereby takes leave of his essential reality.'[17] This essential reality is *ʿubūdiyya*, absolute servitude. With reference to the doctrine of man as the microcosm joining within himself the four natural kingdoms, the Shaykh al-Akbar says, 'There is nothing higher in man than the mineral nature (*al-ṣifa al-jamādiyya*)', for it is the nature of stone, when left to itself, to fall, 'and this is true *ʿubūdiyya*.'[18] The *malāmī* is a pebble in the hand of God.[19]

We will now return to what Ibn ʿArabī has to say about the *afrād* who are the highest among the *malāmiyya*. Chapter Thirty-One of the *Futūḥāt* describes the principles (*uṣūl*) on which their special status is founded and explains the choice of the symbolic term *rukbān* as a name for them. The characteristic feature of the *afrād* is their renunciation of all personal movement (*al-tabarrī min al-ḥaraka*): the image of the stone which never stirs of its own accord is exactly appropriate here. The *afrād* have preferred repose (*sukūn*) to movement because the state of repose alone is in conformity with the original status, the ontological definition, of the true *ʿabd* (*al-iqāma ʿalā 'l-aṣl*). They are therefore 'carried' (Ibn ʿArabī had already used this expression in his early work, the *Risāla fi 'l-walāya*), and their 'mount' is the *ḥawqala*, the formula which is their perpetual invocation (*ḥijjīr*) and which runs: *lā ḥawla wa lā quwwata illā bi'Llāh*, 'There is no strength and no power save

17. Ibid., II, p. 232. Cf. ibid., II, pp. 387-88; *Iṣṭilāḥ al-ṣūfiyya*, p. 3. It is chiefly because of this imperfection that ʿAbd al-Qādir al-Jīlānī, even though he is one of the *malāmiyya* (*Futūḥāt*, III, p. 34), is situated on a less eminent level than Abū Suʿūd ibn al-Shibl (cf. note 9).

18. *Futūḥāt*, I, p. 710. Cf. also ibid., I, p. 529.

19. The fundamental text concerning the *malāmiyya* is Sulāmī's *Risālat al-malāmatiyya*, ed. A. A. ʿAfīfī in *al-Malāmiyya wa 'l-ṣūfiyya wa-ahl al-futuwwa*, Cairo 1945, pp. 86-120. The historical aspect of the problem—the emergence in Nīshāpūr in the ninth century of a *malāmī* movement and its consequences—does not concern us here, but forms the subject of Jacqueline Chabbi's article 'Remarques sur le développement historique des mouvements ascétiques et mystiques au Khorassan', *Studia islamica* XLVI, Paris 1977, pp. 5-72.

through God.' The response to this total giving up of their beings to God is that God takes them totally in charge. They are not those who desire (*al-murīdūn*) but those who are desired (*al-murādūn*), not those who move forward step by step under the illusion that they are walking of their own volition (*al-sālikūn*), but those whom God 'pulls' towards Him (*al-majdhūbūn*). During sleep they veil their faces and sleep on their backs, in a position of abandonment. Each of their nights, and better still every moment of their sleep, even in the daytime, is a *mi ͨrāj*, an effortless ascension like that of the Prophet who, similarly, did not travel but whom God caused to travel (*asrā bi- ͨabdihi*, Qur'ān 17:1). Secrecy (*kitmān*) is one of their principles: they conceal what they are and what they know until such time as they are commanded to reveal it to the outside world.

The next chapter deals with the *afrād* in the second category. These are invested with an *auctoritas* and, in order to perform the governing role (*tadbīr*) that God has assigned to them, are therefore obliged, at least in appearance, to take initiatives and exercise powers: a sacrificial renunciation of the *ͨubūdiyya* in the name of the *ͨubūdiyya*, since the servant must clothe himself with the attributes of the *rubūbiyya* or lordship. Ibn ͨArabī knew several *rukbān* of this type during his youth in Andalusia: Abū Yaḥyā al-Ṣinhājī, a blind man who lived in a mosque in Seville;[20] Ṣāliḥ al-Barbarī who, after travelling for forty years, spent the next forty years in another mosque in Seville, where he lived in the most abject poverty;[21] Abū ͨAbdallāh al-Sharafī who used to disappear each year at the moment of the Pilgrimage, having been transported miraculously to Mecca, and whose requests to God had so great a reputation for being granted that people would sidle up to him in the mosque and utter their own prayers aloud, thereby forcing him to say the 'Amen' which would ensure their fulfilment;[22] Abū 'l-Ḥajjāj al-Shuburbalī, who was so deeply absorbed in God that it took a visitor's comment to make him aware, in extreme old age, of the existence of a tree in front of the house he had lived in since childhood.[23]

Even though they do not benefit to the same degree from the sort of

20. *Futūḥāt*, I, p. 206; *Sufis of Andalusia*, p. 79, number 5.

21. *Futūḥāt*, I, p. 206; II, p. 15; III, p. 34. This character is discussed in the *Rūḥ al-quds*, pp. 51-52, under the name of Sāliḥ al-ͨAdawī; *Sufis of Andalusia*, pp. 73-76, number 3.

22. *Futūḥāt*, I, p.206; *Rūh al-quds*, p.52; *Sufis of Andalusia*, pp.76–79.

23. *Futūḥāt*, I, p. 206; *Rūḥ al-quds*, p. 53; *Sufis of Andalusia*, pp. 79-83.

invisibility which protects the inmost selves of the other *afrād*, the *afrād* who have a function to perform and whom Ibn ᶜArabī calls *al-mudabbirūn* (in the front rank of whom are the Pole, the *awtād* and the *abdāl*) are still *malāmiyya*. They know that they are themselves included in the secondary causes which are a veil before God; they act without acting, like the Prophet, who is told in a paradoxical verse which both affirms and denies that the act was performed by the seeming agent of it: 'It was not you who threw [the dust] when you threw, but God who threw' (Qur'ān 8:17).[24] Their *ḥijjīr*, their initiatic formula and constant invocation, is: 'He rules (*yudabbir*) all things and makes His signs visible' (Qur'ān 13:2): the *mudabbirūn* are *mudabbirūn* only in the eyes of others, the *tadbīr* or government (all these words have the same root) belongs to God alone. For them, the signs of God are visible in all things, or, rather, all things in their eyes are nothing other than the signs of God. Ibn ᶜArabī embarks on a rich and subtle exposition of this concept of signs, distinguishing finely between the many occurrences in the Qur'ān of the word *āyāt*; and, with reference to verse 30:23, he compares the decipherment of the meaning of the things of this world, which is the attribute of this category of *afrād*, with the interpretation of dreams. He ends the chapter by saying that one of the graces bestowed on these men who are among 'the greatest of the saints' is the knowledge of the secret and the meaning of *laylat al-qadr*, the night of descent discussed above. This constitutes a most illuminating reference to the chief feature of these *mudabbirūn*, which is precisely the fact that they descend toward the creatures after having achieved the ascension to the Creator—that, having arrived at Unity, they return to multiplicity. The word 'return' (*rujūᶜ*) is used by Ibn ᶜArabī in Chapter Forty-Five of the *Futūḥāt*[25] to designate the final stage of the Way for those who are the most perfect of the heirs, thereby contrasting 'those who return' with the saints who 'come to a stop' (*al-wāqifūn*) after

24. This verse refers to an episode during the battle of Badr. On the interpretation of it, see *Futūḥāt*, IV, pp. 41, 213; *Fuṣūṣ*, I, p. 185.

25. Chapter 45 (*Futūḥāt*, I, pp. 250-53) has been translated with a commentary by Michel Vâlsan in his article 'Un texte du Cheikh al-Akbar sur la "realisation descendante",' in *Études traditionelles*, no. 307, April-May 1953, pp. 120-39. The concept of a return toward the creatures, the importance of which will soon become clearer, is already evident in the *Risāla fī 'l-walāya*, pp. 25-27. We will leave aside the distinctions drawn by Ibn ᶜArabī between those who arrive (*al-wāṣilūn*), based on whether they have reached God through one of the Names of the Essence or through another of the divine Names.

reaching the summit. The latter, 'who know nothing but Him and whom He alone knows', may in fact be identified with the *muhayyamūn*, the Cherubim overcome with love. Their spiritual realization, however exceptional, does not have the same character of plenitude as that of the *rāji*ᶜ*ūn*, those who return; for the return to created being with the intention of teaching and guiding, whether spontaneous, as in the case of Abū Madyan, or divinely commanded, as in the case of Abū Yazīd al-Bisṭāmī, is the supreme mode of participation in the heritage of the prophets, who likewise had to 're-descend' from the highest station in order to carry out their mission. Such a descent is painful. Abū Yazīd, on receiving the divine command, 'took a step' in obedience to it and fainted, whereupon God said, 'Bring My beloved back to Me, for he cannot bear to be far from Me.' Nevertheless, it must not be thought of as a fall or regression, or even as a real absenting. The saint who is sent back to mankind does not lose what he has gained; his sacrificial exile is not a banishment. Thus the second category of *afrād* in the order of speaking is, in reality, the first.[26]

Finally, with regard to the level of the *afrād*, we must remember that the 'station of proximity' (*maqām al-qurba*) is situated between the *ṣiddīqiyya* (which other Ṣūfis, such as Ghazālī, take to be the highest point of *walāya*) and legislative prophethood, *nubuwwat al-tashrī*ᶜ.[27] Furthermore, as we saw, Ibn ᶜArabī has no hesitation in calling this supreme degree of sainthood—which, he says, was possessed by Muḥammad before the Revelation—by the name of 'general prophethood' (*nubuwwa* ᶜ*āmma*) or 'free prophethood' (*nubuwwa muṭlaqa*).[28] The line of demarcation between the *awliyā'* and the prophets in the

26. The difference between the state of the *wāqifūn*, those who come to a stop, and that of the *rāji*ᶜ*ūn*, those who return, clearly presents an analogy with the drunkenness (*sukr*) and the sobriety (*ṣaḥw*) which may predominate, according to the moment and the predisposition of one's being, at various stages of the spiritual life, even in the case of mere novices; but it cannot be reduced to this classic Ṣūfī opposition: as far as these *awliyā'* are concerned, it is no longer a question of simple states but of permanent status and objective realities.

27. *Futūḥāt*, II, p. 19. The *ṣiddīqiyya*, or station of 'Absolute Truth', is a term derived from the first caliph Abū Bakr, who was surnamed *al-ṣiddīq*. The notion that there may exist a level higher than the level which bears the name of Abū Bakr has often come under attack. These critiques are based on a misunderstanding which is possibly deliberate in some cases, for the notion does not call into question the eminence of Abū Bakr himself—indeed, Ibn ᶜArabī expressly considers him to belong to the category of the *afrād*. Cf. *Futūḥāt*, III, p. 78.

28. *Futūḥāt*, II, p. 19.

strict sense is clear (the former are no more than the heirs of the latter), but it becomes tenuous, and it is easy to understand how Ibn Taymiyya and many after him found it a cause for alarm.

In conclusion, we should remember that we can make two sorts of distinction between these 'solitaries' who have arrived at the extreme point beyond which, since the death of the Seal of the Prophets, there is no proceeding—distinctions which are necessary if we are to grasp Ibn ᶜArabī's doctrine in its entirety. Certain of the *afrād* have received in full the heritage of the Muḥammadan *walāya* and, as we shall see, this line of them has come to an end; others are the heirs of previous prophets, and their line remains open until the end of time. Also, there are some among the *afrād* who exercise no sway over another creature or over themselves; and there are others who 'return' to this world below from which they began their ascent, and they are the most perfect. All of them, however—in spite of the seeming distance between the two categories—are *par excellence* 'proximate' (*hum al-muqarrabūn*, as Ibn ᶜArabī writes at the beginning of the section devoted to them in Chapter Seventy-Three). In them the equivalence between *walāya* and *qurba*, sainthood and proximity, finds its definitive and unrivalled expression.

CHAPTER

8

The Three Seals

OF the spiritual functions listed at the beginning of Chapter Seventy-Three of the *Futūḥāt*, by far the most important is one which we have hitherto passed over in silence. This is the function of 'Seal of the Saints', which we alluded to briefly at the start of this book in connection with al-Ḥakīm al-Tirmidhī. The use of the singular, although doctrinally justified, does not take full account of what follows, for as we shall see, in its historical dimension sainthood is sealed three times.

Unlike many of the other terms we have encountered, the title of Seal of the Saints, or Seal of Sainthood (both these forms appear in the writings of the Shaykh al-Akbar), has no precedent in the vocabulary either of the Qur'ān or of the *ḥadīth*. It is, therefore, an 'innovation' (*bid*ʿ*a*), condemned as such even in our own day. The only scriptural backing it possesses, and which failed to convince the *fuqahā'*, is the prophetic tradition already mentioned, according to which the wise (*al-*ʿ*ulamā'*)—i.e. those who alone possess true knowledge, the *awliyā'*—are the heirs of the Prophets. Since there is a seal of the Prophets, who is Muḥammad (Qur'ān 33:40),[1] it follows that the saints must also have their Seal. Tirmidhī was the first to arrive at this conclusion in the third century of the Hegira. But the passages in his work in which reference is made to this novel idea are hardly very enlightening. In addition to those we have already quoted, there is the following:

Someone asked him, 'So what qualifies this saint, who has the caliphate of sainthood, and directs it and seals it?' He replied, 'He is close to the prophets and is almost on their level.' They asked him, 'Where is his station (*maqāmuhu*)?' He said, 'In the highest dwelling-places (*manāzil*) of the saints, in the kingdom of Singularity (*fardāniyya*), for he is alone in the contemplation of Unity. His private conversations [with God] take place face to face in the assemblies of Kings . . .. For

1. On the notion of the Seal of the Prophets and the doctrine that developed around it, see Y. Friedmann, 'Finality of Prophethood in Sunni Islam', *Jerusalem Studies in Arabic and Islam*, VII (1986), pp. 177-215.

him the veil has been lifted which covers the station of the saints, their degrees, the gifts and presents with which they have been favoured.'[2]

The expressions 'close to the Prophets' and 'Singularity' (a word that comes from the same root as *afrād*) refer to themes already encountered and which will be further elucidated in the doctrine of Ibn ʿArabī.

But who is the Seal of the Saints? On this subject Tirmidhī is silent. He confines himself to asking the question in his famous questionnaire, where it comes thirteenth and is phrased as follows: 'Who is he who is worthy to be the Seal of the Saints as Muḥammad is worthy to be the Seal of Prophethood?' Ibn ʿArabī answers this question on two occasions. In a first text written in 603AH, the *Jawāb mustaqīm* (the complete title is: 'The correct answer to the questions of Tirmidhī al-Ḥakīm'),[3] he says only, 'He who is worthy of this is a man who resembles his father. He is a non-Arab, of harmonious constitution . . .. The cycle of the Kingdom and of Sainthood will be sealed by him. He has a minister whose name is Yaḥyā [i.e. John]. His nature is spiritual as to its origin and human as to its place of manifestation.' The text of the *Futūḥāt* is more explicit and, above all, provides additional information of major importance:

There are in fact two Seals, one with which God seals sainthood in general and another with which He seals Muḥammadan sainthood. ʿĪsā [i.e. Jesus] is the Seal of Sainthood in an absolute sense. He is the saint who *par excellence* possesses the non-legislative prophetic function in the time of this Community [i.e. the Muslim community], for he is henceforth set apart from the function of legislative prophet and of Messenger (*rasūl*). When he descends at the end of time, it will be as the heir and the Seal, *and after him there will be no saint to be the holder of prophethood in general* . . ..

The office of the Seal of Muḥammadan Sainthood belongs to an Arab, one of the

2. Tirmidhī, *Khatm al-awliyā'*, p. 367. The section of this passage immediately following might lead one to think that the office of Seal of the Saints does not have one sole holder, and that it is maintained through history by successive holders. But Tirmidhī's reply to the question asked ('Do the saints in the category experience fear on their own account?') makes it clear that the theme of the dialogue has changed and that the conversations reported are concerned not with the Seal in particular, but more generally with the category of the *afrād* to which he effectively belongs.

3. We quote from the text of the *Jawāb Mustaqīm* edited by O. Yahia, following each of the questions asked by Tirmidhī (here, p. 161 of the *Khatm al-awliyā'*).

noblest in lineage and power. He is alive in our time. I met him in 595. I saw the sign which is exclusive to him and which God has hidden away in him from the eyes of His servants, but which He revealed to me in the town of Fez in order that I might perceive in him the presence of the Seal of Sainthood. He is thus the Seal of free [i.e. non-legislative] prophecy about which most men know nothing. God has tested him by exposing him to the criticism of people who dispute the knowledge of God which he, in his innermost being, has the absolute assurance of having received from God Himself. As God has sealed legislative prophethood through Muḥammad, *through the Muḥammadan Seal he has sealed the sainthood which comes from the Muḥammadan heritage*, not the sainthood which comes from the heritage of other prophets: among the saints, in fact, some, for example, inherit from Abraham, some from Moses, some from Jesus, and after this Muḥammadan Seal there will be others; whereas no other saint will ever be 'on the heart' of Muḥammad.

The Seal of Universal Sainthood, after which there will be no other saint [who will reach that level], is Jesus, and we have met a number of saints who were 'on the heart' (*ᶜalā qalb*) of Jesus or another of the Messengers. I took my companions ᶜAbdallāh [Badr al-Ḥabashī][4] and Ismāᶜīl ibn Sawdakīn[5] to see this Seal. He prayed to God on their behalf and they profited from it.[6]

There are thus *two* Seals, one of whom is unambiguously identified: he is Jesus 'who resembles his father', that is to say the Spirit (*rūḥ*) breathed by the angel into Mary, and who is associated with John in the exercise of this function as he was during his first mission as a *rasūl*. The second Seal is an Arab, living, like Ibn ᶜArabī, in the sixth century of the Hegira. In reply to Tirmidhī's fifteenth question, the *Futūḥāt* explains further that his name is the same as the Prophet's (i.e. Muḥammad), and that he does not belong to the latter's physical lineage but to his spiritual posterity. He cannot therefore be confused with the Mahdī, who is a descent of Muḥammad by blood.[7] This assurance is strengthened by a poem which comes in another passage, in which Ibn ᶜArabī says:

> Yes, surely, the Seal of the Saints is present
> When the Imām of the worlds is still absent, the rightly-guided lord (*al-sayyid al-mahdī*) of Aḥmad's line.[8]

Yet this still does not tell us *who* the Seal of Muḥammadan Sainthood

4. This much-loved friend of Ibn ᶜArabī's died at Malatiya around 618/1221. On his death, see *Futūḥāt*, I, p. 221, and the *Durra Fākhira*, p. 158, number 71, in Austin, *Sufis of Andalusia*.

5. Ismāᶜīl ibn Sawdakīn, another very close follower of Ibn ᶜArabī's (and who transcribed, among other things, his precious oral commentary on the *Tajalliyāt*), died in 646/1248.

6. *Futūḥāt*, II, p. 49. 7. Ibid., II, p. 50. 8. Ibid., III, p. 328.

is, nor does it enable us to distinguish clearly between the respective roles of the two Seals—of whom there will soon be three, which does not simplify matters. Before proceeding to the arguments aroused by the contradictions and obscurities of Ibn ᶜArabī's writings, and attempting to reply to the questions raised in his texts or in the commentaries on them, we must run the risk both of increasing the reader's confusion and of repeating ourselves, and bring together all the main facts that we possess on the subject. Some of these have already been made known through the work, in particular, of ᶜAfīfī, Corbin and Izutsu,[9] but they are almost always in the form of short extracts which represent only a part of the theme under consideration.

Among them [i.e. *al-rijāl*, spiritual men] there is the Seal who is unique not only in every epoch but unique in [all the history of] the universe. Through him God has sealed Muḥammadan sainthood and there is no one among the Muḥammadan saints who is above him. There is also another Seal with whom God seals universal sainthood from Adam to the last of the saints, and this is Jesus. He is the Seal of Sainthood as he is also the Seal of the cycle of the Kingdom (*ᶜālam al-mulk*, for his coming is a sign that the end of time is approaching).[10]

The Seal of Muḥammadan Sainthood is the most knowledgeable of created beings on the subject of God. There is not now, and after him there will not be, a being who knows more than him about God and the Sunsets of Wisdom (*mawāqiᶜ al-ḥikam*). He and the Qur'ān are brothers, as the Mahdī is brother to the sword.[11]

The 'Sunsets of Wisdom' are here the prophets *inasmuch as they are saints*, for in them—in the inmost part of themselves, their *walāya*—is concealed the divine Wisdom whose essential aspects were described, as we know, in the twenty-seven chapters of the *Fuṣūṣ*. On the other hand, the prophets as such, that is to say *inasmuch as they are the revealers of the sacred Laws*, are the 'Sunrises of Wisdom' (*maṭāliᶜ al-ḥikam*). They are 'oriental' in terms of *nubuwwa*, and occidental in terms of *walāya*. The reference to the brotherhood which unites the

9. A. A. ᶜAfīfī, *The Mystical Philosophy . . .*, pp. 98-101; Henry Corbin, introduction to Ḥaydar Āmolī's *Naṣṣ al-nuṣūṣ*; *En Islam iranien*, cf. index, s.v. 'Sceau'; T. Izutsu, *Sufism and Taoism*, chapter 16. Stephane Ruspoli, in his article 'Ibn Arabī et la prophétologie shiᶜite', *Cahiers de l'Herne*, issue dedicated to Henry Corbin, Paris 1981, pp. 224-39, gives a French translation—very inaccurate in places—of *Futūḥāt*, I, pp. 319-20, and *Futūḥāt*, II, p. 49. The texts from the *Fuṣūṣ* are evidently included in the various translations of this work, including the partial translation by Burckhardt.

10. *Futūḥāt*, II, p. 9.

11. Ibid., III, p. 329.

Qur'ān with the Seal is identical with a statement we came across in connection with the Perfect Man,[12] but it may also be compared to a famous verse at the beginning of the *Futūḥāt*[13] in which Ibn ᶜArabī says:

I am the Qur'ān and the Seven oft-repeated (*al-sabᶜ al-mathānī*).

The expression 'the Seven oft-repeated' is traditionally used to designate the introductory *sūra* of the Qur'ān, or *Fātiḥa*, 'the one that opens'.

The role of Jesus as the Seal of Universal Sainthood is affirmed several times, but in the various texts where it appears it is accompanied by explanations or nuances which oblige us to take them all into account. In Chapter Fourteen of the *Futūḥāt* ('On the knowledge of the Secrets of the Prophets—by which I mean those of the saints who are prophets'; the reference here is to the highest level of *walāya*, where it becomes non-legislative prophethood), Ibn ᶜArabī writes:

When Jesus descends at the end of time, he will judge only according to the Law revealed to Muḥammad. He is the Seal of the Saints. One of the favours accorded to Muḥammad was that the sainthood of his community and sainthood in general should be sealed by a noble Messenger Prophet . . . . On the day of the Resurrection, Jesus will be present in two groups simultaneously: with the Messengers in as much as he is one of them, and with us [i.e. with the Muḥammadan community] in as much as he is a saint. This is a station with which God has honoured only him and Elijah, and no other prophet.[14]

The following are two more passages which provide us with apparently contradictory information about the relationship between the Seal of Universal Sainthood and the Seal of Muḥammadan Sainthood:

Muḥammadan Sainthood, that is to say the sainthood of the Law revealed to Muḥammad, has a particular Seal *who is inferior in rank to Jesus* because the latter is a Messenger. This Seal of Muḥammadan Sainthood is born into our times. I too have seen him;[15] I met with him and I saw in him the sign of his office. There will be no saint after him who is not subordinate to him, as there will be no prophet after

12. See chapter 4 of this book, and note 39 of the same chapter.
13. *Futūḥāt*, I, p. 9. This verse is taken from the *Kitāb al-isrā'*, p. 4.
14. *Futūḥāt*, I, p. 150.
15. The implication here is 'as I saw Jesus'. On Ibn ᶜArabī's meetings with the prophets, see chapter 1 and its note 3; on his special relationship with Jesus, see chapter 5, and note 9 of the same.

Muḥammad who is not subordinate to him. In this community, for example, it will be so in the case of Elijah, Jesus and Khaḍir.[16]

When Jesus descends to earth at the end of time, it will be granted to him by God to seal the Great Sainthood (*al-walāya al-kubrā*) which extends from Adam to the last of the prophets. This will be an honour for Muḥammad, since the universal sainthood—the sainthood of all communities—will be sealed only by a Messenger who is a follower of the Law. So Jesus will seal both the cycle of the Kingdom, and universal sainthood. He is thus one of the Seals in this world. As for the Seal of Muḥammadan Sainthood, who is the special Seal of the sainthood of the community which is visibly that of Muḥammad,[17] *Jesus himself will be placed under the authority of his office* along with Elijah, Khaḍir and all the saints of God who belong to this community. In this way, Jesus, although a Seal, will himself be sealed by the Muḥammadan Seal.[18]

A work written by Ibn ʿArabī before his final departure for the East has the *khatm* as its central theme. The work in question is the *ʿAnqā' mughrib*,[19] whose full title means: 'The astonishing Phoenix: on the Seal of the Saints and the Sun of the West.' The expression 'Sun of the West' draws attention to the apocalyptic nature of this book, and in this case is a reference to the Mahdī.[20] However, the information contained in it, which is frequently cryptic, is essentially concerned with the Seal of Universal Sainthood. Ibn ʿArabī singles out twenty-nine (unspecified) verses from the Qur'ān, occurring in fourteen (named) *sūras*,

16. *Futūḥāt*, I, p. 185. It may be noted that the last sentence of this text seems to imply the possibility of the existence, in other communities, of similar cases or, rather, of specific manifestations of the universal functions which in the language of the Muḥammadan community are represented by the figures of Elijah, Jesus and al-Khaḍir.

17. That is, the Muslim community in the historical sense of the term. This must be specified, since *fī 'l-bāṭin*, all the communities founded on the successive Revelations are Muḥammadan, in accordance with the doctrine of the *ḥaqīqa muḥammadiyya*.

18. *Futūḥāt*, III, p. 514; IV, p. 195.

19. We refer here to the commercial edition of the *ʿAnqā' Mughrib*, published in Cairo in 1954. We have also consulted the MS Rağib Paşa 1453 (fos. 133-180b), and, in particular MS Berlin Mo 3266, which is dated 597 AH and which was read in the presence of the author. The work was probably written in 595 AH (see pp. 15-17 of the Cairo edition). Ibn ʿArabī discloses that he intended initially to write about the Seal and the Mahdī in the *Tadbīrāt Ilāhiyya*, but eventually decided against it (pp. 5-6).

20. This expression echoes the *ḥadīth* on the 'signs of the Hour', in connection with which Ibn ʿArabī was questioned (cf. p. 10) by 'a man from Tabriz'. He refused to answer, because the questioner was prompted only by speculative motives, and showed no aptitude for genuine spiritual knowledge.

which speak of the Seal; a series of cross-checks establishes that these are passages in the Qur'ān which are either about Jesus or else contain an allusion to him.[21] In any case, we should observe that in this treatise the author is emphatic about the need to avoid confusing the office of the Seal with that of the Mahdī, and also to avoid interpreting the concept of the Seal in chronological terms. 'The Seal', he writes, 'is not called the Seal because of the moment in which he appears, but because he is the person who most completely realizes the station of direct vision (*maqām al-ᶜiyān*).'[22] Finally—and this is a precaution to be observed whenever Ibn ᶜArabī mentions the cosmic functions or touches on problems of eschatology—we should note that the reader is asked not to lose sight of the fact that everything said about the macrocosm has its correspondence in the microcosm. Within each being there is a Mahdī, a Seal and so on: 'When I speak in this book, or in another, of an event in the external world, my intention is simply to establish it firmly in the hearing of the listener and then to set him face to face with that which corresponds to it within man . . .. Turn your eyes towards your inner kingdom!'[23]

The following extract from the *Fuṣūṣ* takes us back to the Seal of Muḥammadan Sainthood and gives us some clues about the relationship between his office and the office of the Seal of the Prophets—that is to say, Muḥammad himself or, rather, the *ḥaqīqa muḥammadiyya*:[24]

He to whom God is epiphanised sees nothing but his own form in the mirror of absolute Reality (*al-Ḥaqq*): he does not and cannot see absolute Reality, even though he knows that in it he has perceived his own form. It is like a mirror in the sensible world: when you see a form in it, you do not see the mirror itself, even though you know that you only perceived the forms, or your own form, in that mirror. God has made this a symbol of the epiphany of His Essence, in order that he to whom He is epiphanized may know that he does not truly see Him . . .. We have already explained these things in the *Futūḥāt Makkiyya*.[25] When you have experienced this you have experienced the *nec plus ultra* of what it is given to created

21. *ᶜAnqā' Mughrib*, pp. 72-74. Note that the numbers mentioned coincide: the first 'fourteen' with the fourteen 'single Letters' or 'luminous Letters', and the 'twenty-nine' with the twenty-nine *sūra*s where the letters occur.

22. Ibid., p. 71.

23. Ibid., p. 7. This insistence on the correspondence between the microcosm and the structure of the macrocosm occurs equally in the *Tadbīrāt*, which was written during the same period of Ibn ᶜArabī's life (but before the *ᶜAnqā' Mughrib*).

24. *Fuṣūṣ*, I, pp. 61-64 (*faṣṣ Shīth*).

25. Cf. among other texts *Futūḥāt*, I, p. 163.

beings to experience. Do not aspire to anything more and do not exhaust yourself in a vain attempt to reach a higher level: there is none; beyond it there is only pure nothingness.

He is thus your mirror in which you look at yourself; and you are His mirror, in which He contemplates His Names and the manifestation of the powers which belong to each of them—and all this is nothing but Him!

This is a source of confusion. Among us, there is he who professes ignorance in spite of his knowledge and who says, like Abū Bakr, 'To recognize that one is powerless to reach Him is a form of reaching Him.' There is also he who knows yet does not say this (even though these words [Abū Bakr's] are excellent), but whose knowledge leads him to keep silent and not profess the impossibility of reaching Him. Such a man has the highest knowledge of God.

Properly speaking, this knowledge is possessed only by the Seal of the Messengers and the Seal of the Saints. No one among the prophets or Messengers may acquire it save from the Tabernacle of the Seal of the Messengers. No one among the saints may acquire it save from the Tabernacle of the Seal of the Saints, to the extent that the Messengers themselves only acquire it, when they do acquire it, from the Tabernacle of the Seal of the Saints. You must know, indeed, that the Mission (*risāla*) and Prophecy (*nubuwwa*)—I am speaking here of legislative Prophecy and the legislative Mission—come to an end, whereas sainthood does not. *That is why the Messengers themselves, inasmuch as they are saints, may acquire that of which we are speaking only from the Tabernacle of the Seal of the Saints*; and this is *a fortiori* true of the saints who are below them in rank. The fact that the Seal of the Saints obeys the Law which was brought by the Seal of the Messengers in no way diminishes his spiritual station, neither does it contradict what we were saying: *from one point of view he is below* [the Seal of the Messengers], and *from another point of view he is above him*. Exoteric teaching confirms this when it speaks of the superiority of ʿUmar [over the Prophet] in connection with the fate of the prisoners of Badr,[26] or in the story of the fertilization of the palm trees.[27] Perfection does not imply the pre-eminence of the perfect in all things and at all levels. Spiritual men attach importance only to a higher degree of knowledge of God. That is all they seek. Their thoughts take no account of what happens in the phenomenal world. Test the truth of what we say!

When God's Messenger compared prophethood to a wall of bricks, finished except for the placing of one more brick,[28] [he added that] he was that brick. Whereas as far as he is concerned there is only one brick missing, the Seal of the Saints of necessity enjoys the same vision and sees the same thing as the Messenger

26. After the battle of Badr, the Prophet asked his Companions what should be done with the prisoners. The opinion expressed by ʿUmar, which the Prophet was inclined not to follow, was confirmed by a revelation (Qur'ān 8:67).

27. This is an allusion to an episode in the Prophet's life during which he said to his Companions, 'When it comes to the things of this world below, you are the ones who know most about them' (Suyūṭī, *al-Fatḥ al-Kabīr*, I, p. 147).

28. Bukhārī, *manāqib*, 18.

of God, but there are two bricks missing from the wall, one of gold and the other of silver. They are not in the wall and it will not be finished until they are in place. He must then himself be put into the place reserved for these two bricks, for the Seal of the Saints is these two bricks and it is through him that the wall is completed. The reason why he sees two bricks is, on the one hand, because outwardly he obeys the Law brought by the Seal of the Messengers: this corresponds to the silver brick, which is symbolic of his outward form and also symbolizes that to which, in this form, he submits in matters of legal status. On the other hand, he derives directly from God, within his inmost self, the very thing of which outwardly speaking he is merely a follower. This is so because he perceives the true nature of the divine order of things and it cannot be otherwise. This is symbolized esoterically by the laying of the golden brick. For he draws from the same source that the angel draws from who brings the revelation to the Messenger. If you understand what it is that I am referring to, you have acquired a knowledge that will be of benefit to you in all things.

Every prophet, from Adam down to the last of them, draws from the Tabernacle of the Seal of the Prophets, even though this Seal, in his corporeal manifestation, comes after them; for in terms of his essential reality he was already in existence. This is what the Prophet meant when he said, 'I was a prophet when Adam was still between water and mud.'[29] But each of the other prophets only became a prophet at the moment when he was sent [to his community]. Similarly, the Seal of the Saints was a saint when Adam was still between water and mud, whereas the other saints only became saints when they fulfilled the conditions of sainthood by qualifying themselves with the divine characters—God named himself a saint when He said He is *al-Walī al-Ḥamīd* [the Saint, He who is praised, Qur'ān 42:28].

Inasmuch as he is a saint, the relationship between the Seal of the Messengers and the Seal of the Saints is the same as the relationship between himself and the prophets and messengers, for he is simultaneously saint, messenger and prophet. The Seal of the Saints is the saint, the heir, he who draws from the original source and contemplates all levels. He is one of the perfections of the Seal of the Messengers, Muḥammad, who will be the head of the assembly of prophets and the master of the sons of Adam when the gate of intercession is opened.

The last paragraph of this long passage is of major importance in establishing a perspective. To say that the messengers and the prophets themselves are dependent on the Seal of Muḥammadan Sainthood—to say, above all, that from one point of view this Seal is superior to the Seal of the Prophets—does certainly appear not only to be scandalous from the point of view of Muslim exotericism, but to contradict other texts where it is categorically stated that the prophets are superior to the saints. But as we have just seen, the Seal of Muḥammadan Sainthood is 'one of the perfections of the Seal of the Messengers'. A few lines in

29. On this *ḥadīth*, see chapter 4 and ibid., note 3.

the *Futūḥāt* throw light on this fundamental point.[30] 'This Muḥammadan Spirit'—another of Ibn ᶜArabī's names for the Muḥammadan Reality—'has places in the universe where it manifests itself. The most perfect [of these places] are the Pole of Time, the *afrād*, the Muḥammadan Seal of Sainthood and the Seal of Universal Sainthood, Jesus.' In other words, like the Pole and the other functionaries in the initiatic hierarchy, the Seal of Muḥammadan Sainthood, as a specific individual in history, is no more than a deputy, the support of the sensible manifestation of the *khatmiyya* or office of the Seal, which belongs always and forever to the Muḥammadan Reality alone. Outwardly, Muḥammad is the Seal of Sainthood, both universal and Muḥammadan; and so the somewhat surprising statements made in the *Fuṣūṣ* have reference not to his dependence with regard to another being but to the subordination within himself of the visible aspect to the hidden aspect, of the *nubuwwa*, which is an attribute of created being and comes to an end, to the *walāya*, which is a divine attribute and exists to eternity. The paradoxical relationship between the Seal of Universal Sainthood, Jesus, and the Seal of Muḥammadan Sainthood is to be understood in a similar fashion: as an individual, the visible holder of the latter office, being neither *rasūl* nor *nabī*, is inferior to Jesus, who is both. But as the outward manifestation in historical terms of the most inward and most fundamental aspect of the Muḥammadan Reality which is the source of all *walāya*, 'Jesus himself will come under the authority of his office' and will be 'sealed by this Muḥammadan Seal'.

Many other points need to be clarified. But before we approach the question of the identity of the Muḥammadan Seal, and define what is respectively 'sealed' by each Seal, mention must be made of a third person who is thus designated.[31] If we are not mistaken, Ibn ᶜArabī speaks only once of this person, in the last lines of the chapter in the *Fuṣūṣ* from which the preceding quotation was taken:

> The last-born of the human race will be in the footsteps of Seth (*ᶜalā qadam Shīth*) and will possess his secrets. No child will be born after him in the human race. He is

30. *Futūḥāt*, I, p. 151. See also ibid., III, p. 514, where Ibn ᶜArabī says, in connection with the Seal of Muḥammadan Sainthood: His rank in relation to the rank of God's Messenger is no more than that of a hair of his body in relation to the whole body. Cf. also *Futūḥāt*, I, p. 3.

31. It should be added that for Ibn ᶜArabī there is also a 'Seal of the Divine Names': the Name *Huwa* or 'He', which designates the absolutely unconditioned Essence (*Futūḥāt*, III, p. 514).

the Seal of Children (*khatm al-awlād*). He will have a sister born at the same time as him but she will emerge before him [from her mother's womb] and he after her. The head of this Seal will be near the feet of his sister. The place of his birth will be China and his language will be the language of the people of his country. Sterility will spread among men and women and there will be more and more marriages with no children.

He will call people to God and they will not respond to his call. When God takes his soul and the soul of the believers of his time, those who live after him will be like beasts. They will take no account either of the lawfulness of what is lawful, nor of the unlawfulness of what is not lawful. They will obey only the authority of their animal natures, and will follow only their passions, deprived of all reason and all sacred Law. And over them the Hour will dawn.[32]

This 'Seal of Children' does more than merely herald by his appearance the end of the human race, which becomes infertile. The expression 'in the footsteps of Seth' tells us clearly in the language of Ibn ᶜArabī that we have to do with a *walī*, and specifically a *walī* of the *shīthī* type. No man, and consequently no saint, will be born after him. How then is he situated in relation to Jesus who, at the coming of the Last Day, will seal the 'cycle of the Kingdom and of sainthood?' Before going more deeply into this, we must approach the problem of the identity of the Seal of Muḥammadan Sainthood. In a passage quoted above, Ibn ᶜArabī claims to have known him at Fez in 595AH. In another passage of the *Futūḥāt*[33] he says, 'I was informed about him at Fez, in the Maghrib, in 594AH'. Let us say at once that the date 595 is probably a *lapsus calami*, and that we should adhere to 594. The *Kitāb al-Isrā'*, completed, the author says *in fine*, at Fez in the month of *Jumādā* 594/1198, actually contains an allusion which in our opinion can only be explained with reference to a major spiritual event: the meeting, that is to say, with the Seal.[34] We

32. *Fuṣūṣ*, I, p. 67. The symbolic meaning of China as the ultimate place of spiritual Knowledge is suggested in the *ḥadīth* (absent from the canonical collections but which occurs in Bayhaqī and also in Suyūṭī's *al-Fatḥ al-Kabīr*, I, p. 193): 'Seek for knowledge, even if you have to go as far as China'. Some commentators have also seen an allusion to China in the enigmatic observation which comes in the apocryphal *Shajara Nuᶜmāniyya* (cf. O. Yahia, R.G., no. 665): 'When the *shīn* enters the *sīn* . . ..'

33. *Futūḥāt*, III, p. 514.

34. *Kitāb al-Isrā'*, p. 14. The date when the text was completed is given on p. 92. The date 594 is likewise explicitly confirmed in a poem in the *Dīwān*, Būlāq 1271 AH, pp. 332-33. However, we should also note that a somewhat unclear passage in the *ᶜAnqā' Mughrib* (pp. 15-16) seems to put the date at 595, and it is therefore difficult to be categorical on this question of chronology.

will suggest that it may be necessary to envisage an even earlier date as the start of the process of identifying the Seal. But first we must go back to the vision of the two gold and silver bricks, which we have already encountered in the *Fuṣūṣ al-ḥikam* and which occurs again in the *Futūḥāt* in the form of a highly personal narrative.

CHAPTER

9

The Seal of Muḥammadan Sainthood

IN a chapter devoted to Paradise, its 'dwelling places' (*manāzil*) and its 'levels' (*darajāt*), Ibn ʿArabī speaks of the possibility for man of perceiving his own Heavenly nature here and now, and thus of being 'in several places at once'—of occupying, that is, simultaneously and with full awareness, all states of Being, and not merely the human condition as it is commonly experienced. At this point, the theme of the two bricks makes an abrupt reappearance:

I had a vision of myself which was of this type, and I received it as good news (*bushrā*) from God, for it corresponded to something the Prophet said when he used a parable to describe his position in relation to the other prophets. He said, 'My place among the prophets is as when a man builds a wall and completes it except for one brick. I am that brick, and after me there is neither Messenger nor Prophet.'*[1] He compared the prophetic function, therefore, to a wall, and the prophets to the bricks which enable the wall to remain standing. This parable is perfect. Truly, that which the 'wall' signifies and which is being alluded to here can be made manifest only through the 'bricks' [i.e. the prophets], and the Messenger of God is the Seal of the Prophets [and thus corresponds to what is symbolized by the last brick].

While I was in Mecca in 599, I had a dream in which I saw the Kaʿba built of alternate gold and silver bricks. The building was complete; nothing remained to be done. I looked at it and admired its beauty. But then I turned to face the side between the Yemeni corner and the Syrian corner, and I saw, nearer the Syrian corner, a gap where two bricks, one gold and one silver, had not been laid in two of the rows of the wall. In the top row a gold brick was missing, and in the row beneath a silver one. Then I saw myself placed in the gap made by these two missing bricks. I myself was these two bricks, by means of which the wall was completed and the Kaʿba made perfect. I was standing, looking, and I was conscious of standing; and at the same time I knew without a shadow of a doubt that I was these two bricks and that they were me. Then I awoke and gave thanks to God.

When I was interpreting this vision, I said to myself: my place among the 'followers', in my own category [i.e. the category of the *awliyā'*], is like that of the Messenger of God among the prophets, and perhaps it is through me that God has sealed sainthood. 'And that is not difficult for God!' (Qur'ān 35:17). Indeed, I

* Due to the extensive nature of the footnotes belonging to this section they are placed at the end of the chapter, beginning on page 141.

recalled the Prophet's *ḥadīth* in which he used the parable of the wall, and the fact that he himself was the missing brick. I told this vision to someone who was an expert on these matters, a man who came originally from Tozeur and who was in Mecca at that time.[2] He interpreted what had happened to me, but I did not tell him the name of the person who had seen this vision.[3]

The word *ᶜasā*, which we have translated here as 'perhaps', can have an optative meaning in Ibn ᶜArabī. In that case, the same phrase would run: 'May I be he through whom God has sealed sainthood!'[4] Yet, even though this text suggests that Ibn ᶜArabī himself is, or hopes that he is, the Seal of Muḥammadan Sainthood, it does not clearly affirm that this is so. Moreover, the author leaves us in ignorance of the interpretation of his vision given by the 'man from Tozeur' whom he consulted. The texts we quoted previously make the matter even more ambiguous, since in them Ibn ᶜArabī speaks of the Seal as a person whom he has met, and who must therefore be other than himself. However, it would be most imprudent to deduce from his turn of phrase, which is ambiguous enough in itself, that Ibn ᶜArabī is definitely *not* the Seal: it is often the case, with him as with other Ṣūfis, that an event is recounted in which the main character is defined vaguely and in the third person, and that a subsequent cross-checking of various passages of his work establishes that this *fulān* or unspecified person or 'man of our Way' is no other than himself. Only a regard for discretion or prudence has dictated the grammatical dissociation.

That this is so in the case under discussion is evidenced by other passages in which Ibn ᶜArabī states directly that he himself is indeed the Seal. For example, a poem at the beginning of Chapter Forty–Three of the *Futūḥāt* reads:

> I am, without any doubt, the Seal of Sainthood
> In that I am the heir of the Hāshimite and of the Messiah.[5]

The 'Hāshimite' obviously means the Prophet Muḥammad, and the Messiah is one of the Qur'ānic names for Jesus, who was, as we saw, Ibn ᶜArabī's 'first teacher'.[6] It is important, chronologically, to note that this poem, in which Ibn ᶜArabī formally states that he is the Seal, was written before the account of his vision of the two bricks, in which he seems to be less categorical. It figures in the first draft of the *Futūḥāt*, which was composed between 599AH and 629AH, and was most probably written at the beginning of this long period.[7] Another, later text may appear to be less specific. Speaking of the 'station of Abraham' (*maqām*

Ibrāhīm), a term which can apply both to a place in Mecca opposite the Kaᶜba and to the spiritual 'station' of that prophet, Ibn ᶜArabī says, 'We hope to receive a portion of the divine Friendship [*al-khulla*, in allusion to the name *khalīl Allāh*, 'God's intimate friend', given to Abraham, Qur'ān 4:125] bestowed on Abraham, as on us was bestowed, in accordance with good news (*bushrā*) from God, a generous portion of the degree of the perfection and office of Seal.'[8] It could be concluded that at the time of writing these lines, Ibn ᶜArabī was not in full possession of the office of Seal. But the reservation he expresses in the words 'a portion' is sufficiently explained by the fact that the office of Seal is twofold and even threefold. The *khatmiyya* is common to Jesus, the last of the saints, and to the Seal of Muḥammadan Sainthood: the latter, therefore, possesses only part of it. This interpretation is confirmed by another poem (to which we have been unable to assign a date) in which Jesus is explicitly referred to along with Ibn ᶜArabī himself as holding the title of Seal:

I was created to assist the religion of God—
But the assistance comes from Him, as it is laid down in the Books—
For I come of Ḥātimī's lineage, and so I am generous
And of Ṭā'ī and of ᶜArabī—ancestor after ancestor.
. . . I am the Seal of all who follow him [i.e. the Prophet Muḥammad]
. . . Jesus, I say this without lying, is the Seal of those who went before.[9]

When it is remembered that Ibn ᶜArabī's full name is Abū ᶜAbdallāh ibn ᶜAlī *al-Ḥātimī al-Ṭā'ī*, there can be no confusion about the identity of the 'I' in the poem. Moreover, the verse contains a reference to a very famous figure of pre-Islamic Arabia, the poet Ḥātim al-Ṭā'ī, whose generosity was legendary and who was an ancestor of Ibn ᶜArabī's.[10]

But there is another text which is even more important, both because of the nature of it—it describes what Michel Vâlsan has rightly termed 'the appointment of the Shaykh al-Akbar to the supreme Centre'—and because of its position in the work. This is the opening account with which the prologue to the *Futūḥāt* begins, and in which the relationship between Jesus and Ibn ᶜArabī, inasmuch as they are both, in different ways, the Seals of Sainthood, is solemnly expressed by the Prophet himself or, rather, by the Muḥammadan Reality:

He [i.e. the Prophet] saw me behind the Seal [i.e. Jesus], *a place where I was standing because of the community of status that exists between him and me*, and he said to him, 'This man is your equal, your son and your friend. Set up for him before me the Throne of tamarisk.'[11] Then he made a sign to me, 'Rise, oh Muḥammad, and ascend to the throne, and celebrate the worship of Him who sent me, and my worship also, for in you there is a fragment of me which can no longer bear to be away from me, and that fragment governs your innermost reality.' . . . Then the Seal set up the Throne in that solemn place. On its front was written in blue light: "This is the most pure Muḥammadan station! He who ascends into it is its heir, and God sends him to watch over the respect for the divine Law!" At that moment the Gifts of Wisdom were bestowed on me: and it was as though I had been granted the Sum of the Words (*jawāmiʿ al-kalim*).[12]

'Finally', writes Ibn ʿArabī at the end of this account, 'I was sent back from this sublime vision to the world below, and I used the holy praise that I had just celebrated as the prologue to this book.'[13]

It is to be noted that although Ibn ʿArabī stands behind Jesus—a fact which indicates the *personal* superiority of the latter, inasmuch as he is a *rasūl*, over a mere *walī* who is his 'son'—the relationship is then reversed, since Jesus receives the order from the Prophet to set up the *minbar* from which the Shaykh al-Akbar will pronounce the divine praises—a fact which testifies to the *functional* supremacy of the Seal of Muḥammadan Sainthood.

The event described in the first pages of the *Futūḥāt Makkiyya*, which initiates the series of 'openings' or 'revelations'[14] recorded in the book and reflected in its title, took place in Mecca at the start of Ibn ʿArabī's first sojourn there. He arrived in Mecca in 598AH and the account was written in 599AH.[15] We are thus in possession of texts which, from the date of their composition and that of the events described in them, would seem to testify that the Meccan period following Ibn ʿArabī's emigration to the East was when he acquired the certainty that he was indeed the Seal of Muḥammadan Sainthood. Yet we are informed elsewhere that it was in Fez in 594 that he learned the identity of this Seal and saw 'the sign which distinguishes him'. We are thus confronted with a chronological enigma; but the problem is even more complex than it appears.

At the start of this book, we referred to the 'vision of Cordoba'. In the *Fuṣūṣ*, Ibn ʿArabī says of this vision, 'Know that when God caused me to see and made me a witness of the meeting of all the messengers and prophets of the human race from Adam to Muḥammad, in a place in Cordoba where I was taken in the year 586, Hūd was the only one among them who spoke to me. He told me the reason for their meeting together.'[16] This reason is not given in the *Futūḥāt*, where several references are made to the event.[17] The biographical note in the *Rūḥ al-quds* about Shaykh Abū Muḥammad Makhlūf al-Qabā'ilī, who lived in Cordoba, seems to furnish an answer, as follows:

One day, I left the shaykh in good health and returned home. When night fell, I went to bed. And behold, in my sleep I saw myself on an enormous plain covered in clouds, in which I was suddenly aware of a neighing of horses and a noise of hooves. I saw a troop of men, some on horseback and others on foot, who descended into this vast space until it was filled. I have never seen faces so beautiful, such brilliant garments, or more magnificent steeds. Among him I saw a tall man with a full beard, whose hand was on his cheek. He was the one I spoke to among all the members of this gathering. I said to him, 'Tell me the nature of this gathering.' He answered, 'They are all the prophets from Adam to Muḥammad. Not one is missing.' I said to him, 'And which one of them are you?' He answered, 'I am Hūd, the prophet of the people of ᶜĀd.' I asked him, 'Why have you come here?' He said to me, 'We have come to visit Abū Muḥammad [al-Qabā'ilī] in his sickness.' Then I awoke and enquired about Abū Muḥammad Makhlūf, and learned that he had fallen ill that same night. He lived for a few days, and then died. May God have mercy on him![18]

Even though this account tells us nothing about place or date, the nature of the gathering ('all the prophets'), the presence of Hūd, the fact that Shaykh Abū Muḥammad, whom Ibn ᶜArabī had just left when he had this vision, lived in Cordoba, must serve to convince us that this event is the same as the one recounted in the passages of the *Fuṣūṣ* and the *Futūḥāt* quoted above. The *Rūḥ al-quds*, then, seems to provide the explanation for the mysterious meeting of *anbiyā'* and *rusul* which Ibn ᶜArabī was privileged to behold.

But there are more complications to come. In his great commentary on the Qur'ān, the *Rūḥ al-bayān*, the Turkish Ṣūfī Ismāᶜīl Ḥaqqī (died 1137/1725) cites a text of Ibn ᶜArabī's which sounds authentic but which does not appear anywhere else, as far as we know,[19] and in which another motive is given for the gathering at Cordoba: the messengers and prophets are supposed to have met together in order to intercede with the Prophet Muḥammad for Ḥallāj, who had been insolent about him.[20] This second interpretation fits in with other writings of the Shaykh al-Akbar relative to Ḥallāj. But the last words of Ḥaqqī (or of Ibn ᶜArabī: the use of inverted commas is unknown in classical Arabic and we cannot tell where the quotation ends) casts doubt on it again: 'Between the moment when Ḥallāj left this world below and the time the aforementioned gathering took place, more than three hundred years had elapsed.' Since Ḥallāj died in 309AH, the vision must have occurred sometime after 609. But by 598, Ibn ᶜArabī had left Andalusia, never to return. If Ismāᶜīl Ḥaqqī's account is authentic, it must be admitted either that the event took place somewhere other than Cordoba, or that it happened much earlier than 609. Another consideration, too, is cause for concern: at the beginning of the *Rūḥ al-bayān*, this same Ismāᶜīl Ḥaqqī recounts a similar story in which the chief character is not Ibn ᶜArabī but Abū 'l-Ḥasan al-Shādhilī, a much younger contemporary of his, and the setting Jerusalem.[21]

There exists another interpretation of the vision of Cordoba which brings us back to our main theme, and the source of which is, in this case, very close to Ibn ᶜArabī. In his commentary on the *Fuṣūṣ*, Jandī (died c. 700/1300), a direct disciple of Ṣadr al-Dīn Qūnawī who was both the Shaykh al-Akbar's stepson and his pupil, says with regard to this vision that the messengers and prophets had met together in honour of Ibn ᶜArabī himself, in order to celebrate his accession to the office of Seal of the Saints and heir to the Seal of the Prophets. This, without any doubt, was an oral tradition that in Ibn ᶜArabī's circle was considered reliable because it originated from the Master himself.[22] The same interpretation is given by Qāshānī (died 730/1330), one of Jandī's followers,[23] and then by Dāwūd Qayṣarī (died 751/1350), who was a follower of Qāshānī.[24]

Nor is this all. In another passage of his commentary on the *Fuṣūṣ*,[25] Jandī, using the formula 'according to the reports that we have of the Shaykh's own words', which in his works introduces information received from Qūnawī, says that it was in Seville, in the course of a nine-month fast, that Ibn ᶜArabī was notified about his office as Seal. We know that the Shaykh al-Akbar did actually stay in Seville during the same year (586) in which the vision of Cordoba took place.[26] A chapter of the *Futūḥāt* which speaks of the Seal of Universal Sainthood and the Seal of Muḥammadan Sainthood also refers to an 'unveiling' (*kashf*) that occurred at Seville.[27] Jandī's information is thus quite likely, at least, to be true. But he adduces a third fact which he expressly says that Qūnāwī told him, who in turn claims that he is repeating Ibn ᶜArabī's own words. According to the latter, when he was preparing to sail from Andalusia to the Maghrib, he decided not to put to sea until all the future events of his life, both inner and outer, had been revealed to him in detail. God granted his request and showed him all his future situations ('including' he said to Qūnawī, 'the fact that one day your father was to be my companion') up to his death. 'Then,' he adds, 'furnished with this intuitive perception and this certainty, I embarked.'[28] The date of this departure for the Maghrib is undoubtedly in 589. This subtle showing of his destiny, therefore, must of necessity have included prefigurations of the visionary experiences he was to undergo in the East, most notably the solemn 'appointment' related in the prologue to the *Futūḥāt*.

What conclusions are to be drawn from all this? Firstly, Ibn ᶜArabī, in spite of some ambiguous statements, identified himself categorically with the Seal of Muḥammadan Sainthood. He wrote it; he said it. His immediate followers transmitted it from one to the other and never questioned it. On the other hand, although we cannot establish a precise chronology, the news that the office of *khatm* was to be his was announced very early in the spiritual life of the Shaykh al-Akbar—at all events, it preceded both his arrival in Mecca and the 'meeting' in Fez in 594AH by several years. If this is so, how are the apparent contradictions to be reconciled? If Ibn ᶜArabī knew that he was the Seal from his youth onwards (he was twenty-six lunar years old in 586AH), what is the meaning of the visions which came later and which would seem *a priori* to be redundant? The answer, it seems to us, is that we must distinguish the announcement itself from the signs which were later to confirm and explain it, and above all from the effective realisation of what had been announced. The prophetic mission of Muḥammad, which is the archetypal point of reference for the 'Muḥammadan heir' that Ibn ᶜArabī considered himself to be, only commenced, strictly speaking, with the appearance of the angel who brought the initial revelation to the cave of Jabal al-Nūr. But, as a famous *ḥadīth* says,[29] the Prophet was prepared for the descent of the divine Word upon him by a series of visions over a period of several months. Similarly, the 'unveilings' and dreams which punctuate Ibn ᶜArabī's career should be viewed not as merely repeating each other but as successive stages in it. Seen in this light, his appointment by the Prophet himself in the presence of all the messengers represents the culminating point of his ascent, and consecrates, as Michel Vâlsan points out, the universal character of the office of Seal of Muḥammadan Sainthood.[30]

Before attempting to describe the nature of this office and the relation it bears to that of the other Seals, we must go further into the question of the identity of their respective titulars. We have seen that the first disciples in direct succession agreed on Ibn ᶜArabī's being the Seal of Muḥammadan Sainthood.[31] The identity of the Seal of Universal

Sainthood, Jesus, is clearly stated by the Shaykh al-Akbar and does not generally give rise to argument, except, as we shall see, among Shiiᶜite authors. The 'Seal of Children' is not named, and—in the writings at any rate of Qūnawī, Jandī and Qāshānī—is clearly distinguished from the other two. This is not so in the case of Qayṣarī,[32] according to whom the title of 'Seal of Children' is another name for the Seal of Universal Sainthood: a curious mistake to make, considering that the *Fuṣūṣ* describes him as having quite different characteristics from those of Jesus. Jīlī (died 826/1423) confirms the identifications made by the first commentators,[33] and so does Bālī Effendī (died 960/1553), who stresses, like his predecessors, that the Seal of Muḥammadan Sainthood is he after whom no saint will again be 'on the heart of the Seal of the Prophets', although this does not mean that there will not be saints who are the heirs of other prophets. It is only the Muḥammadan heritage that has come to a full stop.[34]

In his summary of the *Futūḥāt*,[35] Shaᶜrānī (died 973/1565) quotes Ibn ᶜArabī briefly on the subject, without comment. In his long hagiographic work, *al-Ṭabaqāt al-kubrā*, however, he introduces a new element. Speaking of the great Egyptian saint Muḥammad Wafā (died 801/1398), he says that the latter's son, ᶜAlī Wafā, stated that his father was the Seal of the Saints.[36] Shaᶜrānī, with customary prudence, adds: 'Many men of sincere spirituality have claimed to occupy this office of Seal. It seems to me that at every epoch there is a Seal, just as—in accordance with Muḥammad Wafā's words quoted above—there is a Khaḍir for every saint.' What is certain is that as we get further away from the age of Ibn ᶜArabī, the concept of the oneness of the Seal—which is explicit in his writings and which seems moreover logically inseparable from the finality of the role of Seal, as the name itself implies—is gradually lost sight of, even by those whom one cannot accuse of not reading his works properly.

The eminent Naqshbandī spiritual master Aḥmad Sirhindī (died 1034/1624), who is often represented (wrongly, as Y. Friedmann has pointed out) as an adversary of Ibn ᶜArabī's, claims to be in possession of the knowledge that the Shaykh al-Akbar says is reserved for the Seal of the Saints, and even appears to attribute to himself a rank superior to that of the Seal.[37] Ṣafī al-Dīn Qushāshī (died 1071/1661), who had received the *khirqa akbariyya* and is a link in one of its still 'living' chains of transmission, apparently claimed the *khatmiyya* for himself. The author of the biography which comes at the end of his *Simṭ al-majīd*[38] tells us that in the margin of Aḥmad Shaykhān Bāᶜalawī's *Shaqq al-jayb*, beside a passage saying that there is only one Seal (of Muḥammadan Sainthood) and that this seal is Ibn ᶜArabī, Qushāshī has a note which says that this refers to a 'divine level' (*martaba ilāhiyya*) to which all beings may hope to attain, and that this office is secure until the end of time. 'We have achieved this', adds Qushāshī, who says that he had five teachers before attaining to this level, 'and we have lived [in that dwelling-place].'

Also curious is the case of ᶜAbd al-Ghanī al-Nābulusī (died 1143/1731), one of Ibn ᶜArabī's great commentators and defenders in the Ottoman world. In one of his poems he says, 'He [i.e. Ibn ᶜArabī] is the Seal of the Saints in his time/You will find this to be true if you read his *Fuṣūṣ*.'[39] In his *al-Radd al-matīn*, an unpublished work in which he refutes the anti-Akbarian polemicists, he identified the Seal with the 'inheritor in full of Muḥammad sainthood' and explains that there have been many Seals, the last to date being Ibn ᶜArabī.[40] But Nābulusī's grandson, Kamal al-Dīn al-Ghazzī, tells us something which contradicts the above and is even more disconcerting when he says that his grandfather considered himself to be one of the Seals of Muḥammadan Sainthood (*lahu rutbat al-khatm al-khāṣṣ*).[41]

The examples are not limited to these. Among the classics of the *ṭarīqa tijāniyya*, a similar claim is said to have been made by Shaykh Aḥmad Tijānī (died 1230/1815), who apparently even maintained that when he had claimed the office of Seal for himself, Ibn ᶜArabī renounced his own claim to it.[42] On the other hand, there exists a Shīᶜite solution to the problem of the identity of the Seal, or rather Seals, which seems to have found its first expression in a fundamental work to which Henry Corbin drew attention. This is the *Naṣṣ al-nuṣūṣ*, written by Ḥaydar Āmolī, who died at the end of the eighth/fourteenth century, and the massive prolegomena to which have been edited by Corbin and Osman Yahia. It constitutes a vast and penetrating commentary on the *Fuṣūṣ al-ḥikam*, a work for which Ḥaydar Āmolī professes an admiration and even a veneration which are profound and moving.[43] Nevertheless, the Shīᶜite writer differs from Ibn ᶜArabī in one essential: for him, the Seal of Universal Sainthood is not Jesus but ᶜAlī ibn Abī Ṭālib; and the Seal of Muḥammadan Sainthood is the Mahdī.[44] This interpretation, although perfectly respectable, is none the less in direct contradiction to Ibn ᶜArabī's view of the economy of the cycle initiated by the Prophet, in which the functions of ᶜAlī and the Mahdī are eminent, indeed, but totally different. According to this view, ʿAlī is one of the Poles of Islam—a role, says Ibn ʿArabī, which none of the Seals may assume[45]—and the Mahdī's task, at the end of time, is to secure, *by the sword*, the submission of the universe to the sacred Law whose inspired interpreter he is.[46] Āmolī, then, exhibits typically Shīʿite characteristics: an obsessional regard for the purely blood lineage of the Prophet (ʿAlī is his cousin and son-in-law; the Mahdī is descended from him by blood), and, consequently, a highly exclusive personalisation of spiritual functions, in accordance with what is ultimately a literalistic conception of the traditional idea of *ahl al-bayt*. However this may be, and leaving aside any value judgement, it can still be acknowledged that Āmolī's interpretation is a dissident version of the Shaykh al-Akbar's doctrine; and it is, to say the least, surprising to see Henry Corbin or one of his students reverse the situation and represent Ibn ʿArabī's teaching as an errant Imāmology.[47]

We have already drawn attention to the exceptional importance of the emir ʿAbd al-Qādir al-Jazā'irī, as representing Akbarian tradition in its purest form.[48] After being released by Napoleon III, he retired to Damascus and wrote his *Kitāb al-Mawāqif* (*The Book of Stopping Places*), a work which arises entirely out of his meditations on Ibn ʿArabī's writings and his visionary conversations with the Andalusian Master, close to whom he had himself buried. Over and over again, ʿAbd al-Qādir calls the Shaykh al-Akbar the 'Seal of Muḥammadan Sainthood':[49] as far as he is concerned, there is no question of argument. But he is not content simply to affirm it, and there is a chapter where, with a clarity which is often lacking in the disciples of Ibn ʿArabī who preceded him, he summarises and puts in order all the facts relating to the three Seals and their respective offices.[50] This short chapter, which on every point conforms to the scattered information provided by Ibn ʿArabī himself, will guide us here in presenting the reader with an overall picture of the problem.

The Emir's exposition results in the following conclusions:

—Every *walī*, *nabī* or *rasūl* 'draws' from the 'Muḥammadan ocean' (*al-baḥr al-muḥammadī*)—a symbolic term for the concept known to us already as the *ḥaqīqa muḥammadiyya*.

—'General prophethood' (*al-nubuwwa al-ʿāmma*) corresponds to the highest degree of *walāya*, also called the 'Station of Proximity' (*maqām al-qurba*)—a term presenting an obvious connection with the primary meaning of the root *w.l.y.*, which should always be borne in mind. This proximity, evoked by the Qur'ānic image 'of two bow-lengths or even nearer', expresses, in language which accords with the Islamic perspective, the restoration of the primordial Unity.[51]

—Those who attain this level are the *afrād*. They are 'the prophets among the saints'. Here, of course, we are concerned with a prophethood which is non-legislative, since legislative prophethood has been definitively sealed by Muḥammad.

—'General prophethood' may be *muṭlaqa*—free, undetermined—when inherited from a prophet other than Muḥammad, or *muqayyada*—restricted—when inherited from Muḥammad.

—The general prophethood which is restricted is sealed by the Seal of Muḥammadan Sainthood, who is Ibn ᶜArabī. After him, the saints who attain to the *maqām al-qurba*, the rank of the *afrād*, are the heirs of prophets other than Muḥammad, and are thus in receipt of the Muḥammadan heritage in an indirect and partial manner.

—The general prophethood which is undetermined is sealed by Jesus when he returns at the end of time, after which no saint will ever be able to attain to the level of the *afrād*.

—The other degrees of *walāya* will remain open, however, until the coming of the Seal of Children, who is both the last-born of the human race and the last of the saints, and will be the last guardian of the heritage of Seth. The destiny of this third Seal, at the outer extremity of history, of necessity falls within the period within which Jesus, according to traditional eschatology, will cause peace to reign on earth. It is doubtless this concomitance which explains the apparent confusion we observed in Qayṣarī of Jesus with the Seal of Children.

We thus have a series of closures, beginning with the closing-off by Ibn ᶜArabī of the chief form of the highest degree of *walāya*, containing the fulness of the Muḥammadan heritage. Next, Jesus closes off its lesser degrees; and finally sainthood itself, in all its forms and all its degrees, is closed off by the last man to be born into this world. But it must be understood that the different Seals are never anything other than manifestations, more or less complete, of Muḥammadan Sainthood, which is veiled in the historical person of Muḥammad by his prophetic office, as Qāshānī tells us.[52] Thus, despite what some of Ibn ᶜArabī's texts might lead us to suppose, there is no question of any superiority of the Seal of Muḥammadan Sainthood over the Seal of the Prophets, since in fact these two offices belong to one and the same person. In his commentary on the *Fuṣūṣ*, Qayṣarī describes the relationship between the Muḥammadan Seal (who for him is Ibn ʿArabī) and the Prophet himself, employing an image which Āmolī is very mistaken in criticizing: this relationship, he says, is like the relationship of a king with the guardian of his treasure. Everyone who takes any of the treasure, including the king himself, has to go through the guardian of it. This does not mean, of course, that the king is subordinate to him.[53]

The reference to a 'treasure' is not accidental, but is directly related to the symbolism of the Seal. In the language derived by Islam from its Qur'ānic sources, the Seal is that which completes and fulfils: the Seal of the Prophets (Qur'ān 33:40) is he with whom the cycle of prophethood comes to a final end. But the Seal is also, and primarily, that which preserves the thing sealed and guarantees its inviolability. Ibn ʿArabī actually refers to it in this sense in a poem from his *ʿAnqā' mughrib*:[54]

> If the house were without a seal
> The thief would come unexpectedly and kill the child.
> Verify this, oh my brother, by considering him who protects the house of sainthood
> If he were not already present in the father of us all [Adam]
> The angels would not have been commanded to bow down before him [cf. Qur'ān 2:34].

'Guardian of the Treasure', 'Protector of the House of Sainthood' (*bayt al-walāya*): for Ibn ʿArabī, the Seal is not only the holder of an office of high dignity, but has a mission to accomplish. When the author of the *Futūḥāt* writes (and this is only one such comment among many): 'I was created to assist the religion of Allāh',[55] he is referring to this mission. His role, as he conceived it and as he has in fact fulfilled it, openly or secretly, for more than seven hundred years, is perceived by Ṣūfis as twofold: it both possesses a doctrinal aspect, and is a source of grace. Through his work, and especially through that mighty synthesis, the *Futūḥāt*, he has preserved the spiritual deposit (*amāna*) intact when it was being imperilled both by the internal rifts in the Muslim world and by the dangers that threatened from outside. Solitary watcher in the night of the century,[56] he keeps, for whoever is worthy of it, the 'treasure' which can no longer be fully transmitted by the teaching of masters; and this is the sense in which he is the Shaykh al-Akbar, the supreme teacher, the teacher of teachers. Through him, the spiritual knowledge contained in the *bayt al-walāya* remains living and accessible to those who possess the necessary qualifications, until the day comes when men will be 'like beasts'.

But Ibn ᶜArabī is not only the archivist and interpreter *par excellence* of sacred knowledge. Through his invisible presence, beyond death itself, he maintains and transmits a spiritual impulse or *baraka* which, when the circumstances require it, comes to quicken individuals and groups, to re-establish the ways of sainthood, and to restore what can be restored of the traditional Islamic order. Hence the importance of the *khirqa akbariyya*, whose course, like that of an underground river, may suddenly surface for a while into the light of day, and leave the imprint of Ibn ᶜArabī on one of the branches of an existing *ṭarīqa*.[57] Hence too the importance of the appearance of the Shaykh al-Akbar's *rūḥāniyya* in the visions of Ṣūfīs down to our time: from Qūnawī to the emir ᶜAbd al-Qādir, a long succession of people, known and unknown, was guided, aided and instructed by a teacher whom the grave did not divide from those who were still alive.[58]

However important the role, at a certain time or place, of those who, like Muḥammad Wafā, Qushāshī, or Aḥmad Tijānī, appear to have identified themselves—or whom their disciples have identified—as the Seal of Muḥammadan Sainthood, it is as nothing compared with the role that Ibn ᶜArabī has played and still plays, in a fashion discreet but observable, in the collective history of Sufism and above all in the personal history of many Ṣūfīs. No less evident is another fact: namely, the sincerity of the men who claim for themselves an office which is of necessity reserved for one being alone, since a Seal is, by definition, final. Their conviction can only derive from an inner, irrefutable awareness of a particular connection with this office: if error exists, it lies in the interpretation of the elements of this awareness, not in these elements themselves. Akbarian doctrine, especially the idea of the 'deputy' (*nā'ib*) that we encountered in the case of the Pole, furnishes us with an explanation. According to a formula employed by Qāshānī in his commentary on the *Fuṣūṣ*, the Seal possesses the *walāya shamsiyya* or 'solar' sainthood, whereas the other *awliyā'* possess only a *walāya qamariyya* or 'lunar' sainthood, whose light is therefore only reflected. In this perspective, the people mentioned can be viewed as a series of mirrors which receive and give back the rays of the *walāya shamsiyya*, or, if one prefers, as the known intermediaries (for there are unknown and less known ones) through whom the grace operates of which the one Seal is both guardian and dispenser.

Notes to Chapter Nine

1. Cf. note 28, chapter 8.

2. This could be a figure whom Ibn ʿArabī mentions on several occasions, namely Abū 'l-ʿAbbās ibn ʿAlī ibn Maymūn ibn Āb al-Tawzarī, called al-Qasṭallānī, who died in Mecca in 636/1238. It was in answer to a question of his that Ibn ʿArabī wrote the *Kitāb al-Khalwa al-Muṭlaqa* (*Futūḥāt*, I, pp. 391-92). For more about this person, see also *Futūḥāt*, IV, pp. 123 and 474. He must not be confused with Taqī al-Dīn Abū' l-Qāsim ʿAbd al-Raḥmān ibn ʿAlī ibn Maymūn ibn Āb, named in the *Kitāb Nasab al-khirqa* and in *Futūḥāt*, I, p. 187, as the man who passed on the *khirqa khaḍiriyya* to Ibn ʿArabī.

3. *Futūḥāt*, I, pp. 318-19 (V, pp. 68-70 in O. Yahia's edition). It should be remembered that this vision, which occurred in 599AH is considerably earlier than the passage from the *Fuṣūṣ* that we quoted in the last chapter. The *Fuṣūṣ* was not written until 627AH.

4. In connection with *ʿasā and laʿalla*, see for example *Futūḥāt*, II, p. 276, and III, p. 264. In general, the commentators (see for example Jandī, op. cit., p. 113) are of the opinion that whenever Ibn ʿArabī, speaking of his own function, uses an expression which conveys hope rather than certainty, he does so out of regard for the proprieties (*ādāb*) to be observed with respect to God.

5. *Futūḥāt*, I, p. 244. In accordance with O. Yahia's critical edition (IV, p. 71) *li-wirth* should be corrected to read *li-wirthī*.

6. Cf. note 9, chapter 5.

7. Cf. note 15 below. A second draft of the *Futūḥāt*, of which we possess the autograph manuscript, was written by Ibn ʿArabī between 632 and 636AH. See O. Yahia's critical edition for a comparison between the two drafts. The vision of the two bricks also took place in 599, but was not recorded in writing until much later.

8. *Futūḥāt*, I, p. 722 (at the time of writing, O. Yahia's edition stops just short of the chapter containing this passage).

9. *Dīwān*, Būlāq, 1271AH, p. 259.

10. On Ḥātim al-Ṭā'ī, cf. *EI*², s.v., the article by C. Van Arendonk. See also the *Cambridge History of Arabic Literature*, Cambridge 1983, I, pp. 382-83.

11. The Prophet's pulpit (*minbar*) at Medina was made out of tamarisk wood (Bukhārī, *jumʿa*, 26), so in this text—as confirmed a few lines further on—the reference is indeed to the Muḥammadan throne itself, in which Ibn ʿArabī will be seated by virtue of being the heir of Muḥammad in the fullest sense. The special relationship between the Prophet and the Shaykh al-Akbar is further emphasized by the fact that the latter's name is also Muḥammad, and that in addressing him the Prophet uses the name that they possess in common.

12. *Futūḥāt*, I, p. 3; O. Yahia's edition I, pp. 44-45. The translation used here is, with a few minor modifications, Michel Vâlsan's in his article 'L'investiture du

Cheikh al-Akbar au Centre Suprême', *Études traditionelles*, no. 311 (1953), pp. 300-11. On the *ḥadīth* of the *Jawāmiᶜ al-kalim*, cf. Bukhārī, *taᶜbīr*, 11, and Muslim, *masājid*, 5-8, etc. The Wisdom is the content or meaning of the Words, while the word 'sum' expresses the total and final nature of the Muḥammadan Revelation. As Michel Vâlsan observes (ibid., p. 304, note 5), the last sentence is specifically about the Shaykh al-Akbar's appointment to the status of heir to the Muḥammadan station from the point of view of universal Tradition.

13. *Futūḥāt*, I, p. 6; O. Yahia's edition , I, p. 58. The epistle in verse form addressed by Ibn ᶜArabī to his friend ᶜAbd al-ᶜAzīz al-Mahdawī, which follows immediately after the text just quoted (*Futūḥāt*, I, pp. 6-9; O. Yahia's edition, I, pp. 59-68) likewise contains several allusions to Ibn ᶜArabī's office as Seal. One of the last lines ('When I, the Imām, depart, I will be unable to appoint a successor in my place') stresses the strictly unique nature of this office, which for Ibn ᶜArabī has, as we saw, only one holder, unlike the office of Pole, of *watad*, etc. The term *Imām* in this line should be understood in its more general sense, and not in the more limited technical sense (*Imām* of the right, *Imām* of the left) which we mentioned in chapter 6, and which can in fact be applied to a whole succession of individuals.

14. The word 'revelation' used here to translate the Arabic term *Futūḥāt* is, obviously, merely an approximation, and should normally be used as a translation of the term *waḥy*.

15. On the date of commencement of the *Futūḥāt*, see O. Yahia's introduction to his edition, I, p. 28 of the Arabic text.

16. *Fuṣūṣ*, I, p. 110.

17. Cf. *Futūḥāt*, III, pp. 208 and 323, and iv, p. 77.

18. *Rūḥ al-quds*, Damascus 1964, p. 76, trans. Austin, pp. 123-24 (no. 20).

19. No mention of this story appears—as far as we know—in any work of Ibn ᶜArabī's in which al-Ḥallāj figures and in which one might logically, therefore, expect to find this account (*Kitāb al-Intiṣār*, pp. 14 ff; *Futūḥāt*, I, p. 169; II, pp. 122, 126, 337, 364, 370; III, pp. 17, 40, 104 (reference), 117; IV, pp. 84, 156, 194, 241, 328, 332; *Tajalliyāt*, p. 31). But Ibn ᶜArabī also wrote a treatise about al-Ḥallāj entitled *al-Sirāj al-Wahhāj fī sharḥ kalām al-Ḥallāj* (cf. O. Yahya, R.G., no. 651), of which no manuscript is known to exist, and from which Ḥaqqī may have been quoting.

20. *Rūḥ al-bayān*, Istanbul 1330AH, X, p. 456. This account comes in the commentary on *sūra* 93. Ḥallāj's insolence consists in his having reproached the Prophet for not having asked God for permission to intercede for all creatures without exception on the Day of Judgement, but only for the gravest sinners in his community. Cf. L. Massignon, *La Passion de Hallāj*, II, pp. 257, 332, 418. Jalāl al-Dīn al-Rūmī has a commentary on this episode in Ḥallāj's life, which he sees as the true reason for his condemnation (Aflākī, *Les Saints des Derviches tourneurs*, trans. into French by Cl. Huart, 2nd edition, Paris 1978, I, p. 254).

21. *Rūḥ al-bayān*, I, p. 248. We should add that Ḥaqqī refers in this connection to the *Muḥāḍarāt al-udabā'* by al-Rāghib al-Iṣfahānī, who died in 1108, well before the birth of Abū 'l-Ḥasan al-Shādhilī. There must of necessity be a mistake as regards either the source or the person. Since Shādhilī arrived in the East

at the end of the first half of the seventh Hegira century, the gap of more than three hundred years between the death of al-Ḥallāj and the vision is more plausible in his case.

22. Jandī, *Sharḥ Fuṣūṣ al-ḥikam*, p. 431.

23. Qāshānī, *Sharḥ Fuṣūṣ al-ḥikam*, Cairo 1321AH, p. 130.

24. Qayṣarī, *Sharḥ Fuṣūṣ al-ḥikam*, lithograph edition, Bombay 1300AH, p. 200.

25. Jandī, op. cit., p. 109.

26. On Ibn ᶜArabī's presence in Seville in 586AH, cf. *Futūḥāt*, II, pp. 7-8, 167, and IV, p. 156.

27. Ibid., IV, p. 77.

28. Jandī, op. cit., pp. 219-20, 263.

29. Bukhārī, *taᶜbīr*, 1, *tafsīr*, s. 96, 1-3, etc. The *ḥadīth* according to which the vision of good augury (*ru'yā ḥasana*) is the forty-sixth part of prophethood (Bukhārī, *taᶜbīr*, 3) alludes to the relationship between the period of time preceding the Revelation and the total duration of Muḥammad's prophetic mission.

30. Michel Vâlsan, op. cit., p. 301. We will see later on why this character of universality is not incompatible with the separate existence of a Seal of Universal Sainthood.

31. Besides the texts already indicated, cf. Jandī (op. cit. pp. 234-37), who explains that one of the signs marking Ibn ᶜArabī out as a Seal was a hollow between his shoulder blades the size of a partridge egg, corresponding to the analogous sign, in the form of a lump, that the Prophet has in the same part of his body. This makes the relationship between the *bāṭin (walāya)* and the *ẓāhir (nubuwwa)* very clear. See also Qāshānī, op. cit., pp. 34 ff.

32. Qayṣarī, op. cit., p. 78.

33. See his commentary on the *Risālat al-anwār*, Damascus 1929, especially pp. 5, 45, 54, 294. In his *al-Insān al-Kāmil* (Cairo 1963, p. 97) he makes the *khitām* (the 'affixing of the Seal') the highest of the three levels of the 'station of Proximity' (the other two are Friendship, *al-khulla*, and Love, *al-maḥabba*). This station in Jīlī corresponds to what Ibn ᶜArabī generally terms non-legislative prophecy.

34. Bālī Effendī, *Sharḥ al-Fuṣūṣ*, Istanbul 1309AH, pp. 52-56.

35. *al-Yawāqīt wa' l-jawāhir*, Cairo 1369AH, II, p. 89.

36. *al-Ṭabaqāt al-kubrā*, Cairo 1954, II, pp. 21, 30, 31. A previous case in which such a claim was made deserves mention. H. Landolt, in his article in the *Encyclopedia Iranica* about Abū 'l-Ḥasan Kharaqānī (died 425/1033), refers to an Istanbul manuscript (Murād Mollā 1796, fos. 337 f-352 f) in which, in a text written at the end of the twelfth century, this famous *walī* is called the Seal of the Saints.

37. Sirhindī, *Maktūbāt-e Emām-e Rabbānī*, Lucknow 1889 (see for example letter no. 31). Cf. Y. Friedmann, *Shaykh Ahmad Sirhindī*, Montreal/London 1971, pp. 33 ff.

38. Qushāshī, *al-Simṭ al-Majīd*, Hyderabad 1327AH, p. 183. The note by Nabhānī, *Jāmiᶜ karāmāt al-awliyā'*, 1, pp. 335-37, is merely a repeat of this biography.

39. Quoted by Kāmil Muṣṭafā al-Shaybī, *al-Ṣila bayna 'l-taṣawwuf wa 'l-tashayyuᶜ*, Cairo 1969, p. 474.

40. Ms Ẓāhiriyya 9872, fo. 45b. Strangely, this text, in spite of the clear distinctions made by Ibn ʿArabī in works which Nābulusī read and often commented on judiciously, states that the Seal of Universal Sainthood is . . . the Mahdī!

41. Kamāl al-Dīn al-Ghazzī (died 1214/1799), *al-Wird al-unsī wa 'l-warīd al-qudsī fī tarjamat al-ʿārif al-shaykh ʿAbd al-Ghanī al-Nābulusī.* This manuscript is in the possession of a descendant of Nābulusī, Muḥammad Rātib al-Nābulusī, and we owe our information about it to Mr. Bakrī ʿAlā' al-Dīn. The passage in question comes at the end of chapter 11.

42. Cf. the *Bughyat al-mustafīd* by Muḥammad al-ʿArabī al-ʿUmarī al-Tijānī, Cairo 1959, pp. 192 ff., which tells us that Shaykh Aḥmad Tijānī had received the news of his appointment to this office from the Prophet himself in the course of a waking vision. See also al-Ḥājj ʿUmar al-Fūtī, *Kitāb Rimāḥ ḥizb al-raḥīm*, in the margin of ʿAlī al-Ḥarāzim's *Jawāhir al-maʿānī*, Beirut 1383AH, II, p. 4 (section 36), and *al-Fatḥ al-Rabbānī* by Shaykh Muḥammad ibn ʿAbdallāh ibn Ḥusayn, Beirut, n.d., pp. 15 ff. There is also an unpublished work, which we have not been able to consult, by Shaykh Tijānī Aḥmad ibn al-ʿAyyāshī Sukaraj al-Anṣārī (died 1363/1944), entitled *Qurrat al-ʿayn fī 'l-jawāb ʿan al-as'ila al-muwādaʿa fī khabīʾat al-kawn*, which is a reply to Tirmidhī's questionnaire. The idea of the *khatmiyya* as a level which is in theory accessible to all, and not as an office unique in history, has been taken up again in our day by Dr. Abū 'l-Wafā al-Taftāzānī in his article in *Kitāb tadhkārī: Ibn ʿArabī*, Cairo 1969, p. 312. More recently, in his book *al-Jawāb al-Shāfi ʿalā as'ilat al-Ḥakim al-Tirmidhī*, Cairo 1988, Muḥammad ʿAlī Salāma claimed the office of seal for an Egyptian shaykh, Muḥammad ibn ʿAbdallāh Abū' l-ʿAzā'im (died 1356/1938).

43. Ḥaydar Āmolī, *Kitāb Naṣṣ al-nuṣūṣ fī sharḥ al-fuṣūṣ*, Paris and Tehran 1975. See the passages in praise of the *Fuṣūṣ* and their author, particularly pp. 64-154.

44. Ibid., pp. 173, 175 (where Āmolī says that he bases himself on *ʿaql, naql* and *kashf*: reason, tradition and intuitive unveiling), pp. 182 ff. Āmolī is strongly criticical of Ibn ʿArabī's Sunnī commentators—and especially of Qayṣarī, cf. p. 233 ff.—or else interprets them in a most curious way, saying (p. 231) that Qāshānī states that the Seal of Muḥammadan Sainthood is the Mahdī, or that Jandī says that ʿAlī is the Seal of Universal Sainthood. It is true that Qāshānī, in a passage of his commentary on the Qur'ān (*Ta'wīlāt*, I, p. 728, in connection with verse 17:79) makes an ambiguous statement which could justify this interpretation. But in his commentary on the *Fuṣūṣ* (p. 35) he makes a clear distinction between the Mahdī and the Seal, and (p. 130) is unequivocal about the office of Seal being Ibn ʿArabī's.

45. *Futūḥāt*, IV, p. 77. This incompatibility between the function of the Seal and that of the Pole (which is made too clearly for argument, even though some passages which allude to it, such as *Futūḥāt*, I, p. 160, could lend themselves to a contrary interpretation) must have been familiar to Qūnawī. Nwyia's interpretation of the meeting between Qūnawī and Abū 'l-Ḥasan al-Shādhilī (*Ibn ʿAṭā Allāh et la naissance de la Confrérie shādilite*, Beirut 1972, p. 26), which is based on a passage in Ibn ʿAṭā' Allāh's *Laṭā'if al-minan* (written in the margin of the work of the same title by Shaʿrānī, Cairo 1357AH, I, p. 95), is undoubtedly wrong, as we had occasion to point out to him shortly before his death.

46. On the Mahdī's function, see *Futūḥāt*, III, pp. 327-40, chapter 366, which deals with the Mahdī's ministers (*wuzarā'*).

47. Cf. chapter 3 of the present book, with note 4. Corbin's thesis with regard to the doctrine of the Seal is taken up again by Stephane Ruspoli in his article 'Ibn Arabī et la prophétologie shīʿite' (cf. note 9, chapter 8), where he accuses Ibn ʿArabī of gravely distorting Shīʿite doctrine—an accusation which is *a priori* absurd, seeing that it is addressed to a Sunnī; but for Ruspoli, the account of the vision described in *Futūḥāt*, I, pp. 319-20 is 'the spiritual testament of a Sunnī who is a Shīʿite at heart'. Ruspoli's evidence would be more convincing if he were not unaware of many of Ibn ʿArabī's writings on the Seal (to the extent where he states—p. 232—that Ibn ʿArabī never said, 'I am the Seal of *walāya*'), and if his reading of the texts that he has read were correct. Cf. p. 231 where he reads: *wa-qultu muta'awwalānī (sic)*, when what is actually written is: *wa-qultu muta'awwilan: Innī*, etc. Cf. also p. 234, where instead of *ḥashran maʿnan* (sic) he has read *ḥashran maʿanā*. The passage in Ibn ʿArabī's *Futūḥāt*, II, p. 49 about Jesus is not a reference to the Paraclete 'as clear as could possibly be': Ibn ʿArabī does not speak of 'a man like Jesus' but of 'a being such as Jesus'. It is true that Suhrawardī (died 587/1199), in his *Hayākil al-nūr* (ed. Muḥammad ʿAlī Abū Rayyān, 2nd edition, Cairo 1957, p. 88), referring to Jesus' words in John 14: 15-17, says that while the *tanzīl* is entrusted to the prophets, the *ta'wīl* and the *bayān* belong to *al-maẓhar al-aʿẓam al-fāraqlīṭī*, the supreme manifestation of the Paraclete, which for his commentator Ghiyāth al-Dīn al-Dawwānī (died 907/1501), who became a Shīʿite as the result of a dream, is the place of manifestation of *walāya* (ibid., p. 104). Ḥaydar Āmolī (op. cit., p. 212), likewise in a reference to the words of Jesus, identifies the Paraclete with the Mahdī. But in Sunnī tradition (see for example Ibn Hishām, *al-Sīra al-nabawiyya*, Cairo 1955, I, pp. 232-33), the Paraclete (*Baraqlītus*) is none other than the Prophet himself, in accordance with a well-known interpretation of verse 61:6.

48. Cf. my translation of extracts from his *Kitāb al-Mawāqif*, published under the title *Écrits spirituels*, Paris 1982, especially the introduction, pp. 20 ff.

49. Cf. *Kitāb al-Mawāqif*, 2nd edition, Damascus 1966-1967 (3 volumes successively paginated), pp. 742, 826, 861, 872, 1277, 1285, etc.

50. Ibid., pp. 1157-58 (*mawqif* 353).

51. Cf. the end of chapter 5, with note 32.

52. Qāshānī, op. cit., p. 34.

53. Qayṣarī, op. cit., p. 60.

54. *ʿAnqā' Mughrib*, pp. 62-63; *Dīwān*, p. 32.

55. *Dīwān*, p. 259. See, among other references made by Ibn ʿArabī to his own mission, *Futūḥāt*, I, p. 658; III, p. 323; *Kitāb al-Isrā'*, pp. 21-26; *Taj.* (ed. O. Yahia), pp. 300-1.

56. 'The entire universe fell asleep when the Messenger of God died . . .. We are presently living through the last third of this night of the universe' (*Futūḥāt*, III, p. 188).

57. In connection with the second half of the nineteenth century, we have drawn attention to one phase of this Akbarian renaissance (which is sometimes indicated by the addition of the *nisba 'al-akbarī'* to the name of a spiritual teacher) in our introduction to the *Écrits spirituels* of the emir ʿAbd al-Qādir (pp. 35-36),

where we point out that the *ṭarīqa shādhiliyya* and the *ṭarīqa naqshbandiyya* seem to have been particularly, although not exclusively, centres for this posthumous form of Ibn ʿArabī's influence.

58. This type of spiritual realisation, in which the *murīd* is attached in other respects to a living *shaykh* and through him to a regular *silsila*, yet whose true teacher is in fact a *walī* who is deceased, is well known in *taṣawwuf*, where it comes into the category of the *Uwaysiyya*. We may mention, among other famous cases of *Uwaysiyya*, Abū Yazīd al-Bisṭāmī, a posthumous disciple of Jaʿfar al-Ṣādiq; Abū 'l-Ḥasan Kharaqānī, posthumous disciple of Bisṭāmī; Bahā' al-Dīn Naqshband, posthumous disciple of ʿAbd al-Khāliq Ghujdawānī. On the visions of Ibn ʿArabī in Qūnāwī, cf. his *Nafaḥāt Ilāhiyya* (Ms BN 1354, fos. 70a, 70b, 110b, 111a). Another important example, this time in Jīlī, is the account of a vision that took place at Yanbūʿ in 789AH, and which he reports in his commentary on the *Risālat al-anwār*, p. 6 (the date of 889AH found in the Damascus edition is obviously a copyist's error or a printing mistake: Jīlī died at the beginning of the ninth century).

CHAPTER

10

The Double Ladder

AKBARIAN hagiology is ultimately arranged around three fundamental notions: *wirātha, niyāba, qurba. Wirātha*—the heritage of a spiritual knowledge or, if one prefers, of a mode of knowledge of God peculiar to one of the prophetic models—explains the forms taken by sainthood. *Niyāba*—the substitution of the *walī* in a role which, in the last analysis, actually belongs to the Muḥammadan Reality alone—forms the basis of the functions of sainthood. *Qurba*—proximity—defines its nature. We have already mentioned *qurba* in connection with the highest level of *walāya*. Its full significance will now become apparent.

How does one become a saint? Although sainthood of necessity forms part of a spiritual economy which regulates its forms and allocates its functions, none the less it is first and foremost the fruit of a quest which is personal and always without precedent: 'To each one of you We have assigned a road and a way' (Qur'ān 5:48). Ibn ᶜArabī always insists on the unrepeatability in an absolute sense of theophanies, and hence of beings, things and actions.*[1] Two 'travellers' (*sālik*) will never travel the same road. The fate that befalls one will never befall the other.

It is none the less true that all initiatic journeys, whatever their particulars, encounter stages and dangers whose nature and distribution conform to a model in the absence of which the notion itself of a 'spiritual teacher' would make no sense. This type of journey, enriched with innumerable variations, is one of the *topoi* of Ṣūfī literature. As elsewhere, but to a greater extent because in Islam the Prophet's *miᶜrāj* is a major point of reference, it is often described in symbolic form as an ascent.[2] We turn now to Ibn ᶜArabī's use of this theme of ascent, considered as a symbol of the journey leading to *walāya*.

The Epistle of the Lights (Risālat al-Anwār), to which we will refer for

* Due to the extensive nature of the footnotes belonging to this chapter they are placed at the end of the chapter, beginning on page 174.

guidance, was written at Konya in 602AH, and thus at the start of Ibn ʿArabī's life in the East, when he was forty-two lunar years old.[3] There are at least three editions of it in existence, all very inaccurate;[4] so our analysis is based on one of the oldest manuscripts, whose quality is excellent and which carries the guarantee of having been read in Qūnawī's presence.[5] The subtitle of this short work, 'On the secrets bestowed on him who practises retreat in a cell', gives the impression that it is a treatise on *khalwa*, a subject to which Ibn ʿArabī devoted Chapters Seventy-Eight and Seventy-Nine of the *Futūḥāt* and a separate opuscule, the *Kitāb al-Khalwa* (or *Kitāb al-Khalwa al-muṭlaqa*), written after the *Risālat al-Anwār*, to which it refers, but which is often confused with it.[6] In fact, although the practices of isolation (*ʿuzla*) and retreat (*khalwa*) are mentioned at the very beginning of the text as prerequisites to the quest, the intention of this *risāla*, as the author explains in his introduction, is to describe 'the modes of the journey towards the Almighty Master': a vertical journey, an ascent of the spirit which leads the *sālik* from heaven to heaven in the footsteps of the Messenger of God, whose *miʿrāj* has traced the map of the journey to be accomplished. The ascent to God is first and foremost an *imitatio Prophetae*.[7]

The *Risālat al-Anwār*, the extracts from which are given in italics, and which discusses the *miʿrāj* of the *awliyā'* with succinctness, is not the only work by Ibn ʿArabī on the subject. He speaks of it elsewhere, under various guises: allegorically in Chapter One Hundred and Sixty-Seven of the *Futūḥāt*, more autobiographically in Chapter Three Hundred and Sixty-Seven of the same work, in the *Kitāb al-Isrā'* (*the Book of the Night Voyage*). We will therefore refer to these whenever it becomes necessary to clarify the often very elliptical statements in the *Epistle*, thereby adopting—though adapting—the method followed by ʿAbd al-Karīm al-Jīlī, whose commentary is essentially a collection of quotations from Ibn ʿArabī, and will assist us on a number of important points.

The person to whom the *Epistle of the Lights* is addressed is not a novice. The author, therefore, does not linger on the preliminaries of the Way, analysed in detail in the classic manuals of *taṣawwuf*, or as he himself explains them in other passages of his works. This (unknown) person has already arrived, through the appropriate disciplines, at the central point at which the ascent begins. After uttering the traditional doxology, the first paragraphs are simply a reminder of the conditions to be fulfilled and the disposition required of him who embarks on this perilous enterprise:

I am replying, oh my dearest friend and most close companion, to the question you asked me about the modes of the journey (*sulūk*)[8] to the Almighty Master, the arrival in His presence, and the return,[9] from and through Him, to His creatures—a return which yet involves no separation, for nothing exists other than God, His attributes and His acts. Everything is He, is through Him, proceeds from Him, returns to Him; and were He to veil Himself from the universe even for the space of the blinking of an eye, the universe would straightaway cease to exist, for it survives only through His protection and His care. Yet of Him whose appearance in His Light is so brilliant that the eye cannot see Him (Qur'ān 6:103), it must be said that His appearance is a concealment.

It is scarcely necessary to call attention to the density of these few lines, in which so many of Ibn ʿArabī's fundamental ideas are summed up. 'Oneness of Being' (*waḥdat al-wujūd*) is posited from the start. The idea that it is God's very conspicuousness that hides Him from our view is a constantly recurring theme in his doctrine.[10] The necessity for the perfect *walī* to return to created being, to follow his 'ascent' with a 'descent' (this is discussed again at the end of the treatise) is affirmed at once.

I will first of all explain to you—may God assist you by His Grace!—how one makes one's way to Him, then how the arrival happens and how one stands still before Him, how one sits down on the carpet of contemplation of His Face and what He then says to you. Next I will explain how one returns from Him to the level of His acts, through Him and towards Him, and also how one is annihilated in Him—but this spiritual station is inferior to that of the return.

Know, oh my dearest brother, that although there are roads without number, there is only one that leads to God; and solitary (*afrād*) are those who travel it! Nevertheless, although this road is unique, it takes different forms, in accordance with the different states of being of the travellers. Indeed, these forms vary according to whether the travellers' constitution is or is not harmonious, according to whether their motivation is constant or subject to eclipse, according to the intensity or the feebleness of their spiritual energy, according to the uprightness or the obliquity of their resolution, according to whether their orientation is pure or tainted . . ..

The first thing about which we must enlighten you is knowledge of the 'dwelling places' (*al-mawāṭin*), of their number and of what is imposed upon you by the 'dwelling place' I have in view here.

These 'dwelling places', which are innumerable, are reduced by Ibn ʿArabī to six. The first is the dwelling place of '*Alastu bi-Rabbikum?*' ('Am I not your Lord?', Qur'ān 7:172)—that is, of the primordial

Covenant through which created beings solemnly acknowledged the divine suzerainty.[11] The second is the dwelling place of this world below. The third is the intermediate world (*barzakh*) to which we go 'after the lesser and the greater death'. This *barzakh*, says Ibn ᶜArabī elsewhere, is 'neither existent nor non-existent; it can be neither affirmed nor denied. And it is no other than the *khayāl*, the imaginal.' It encompasses all that is and all that is not, or all that contains within itself a contradiction (the 'possible-impossible', a square circle). What is formless assumes a form there, and it is this fact which, in the dreams of the ordinary man or the visions of the gnostic, makes it possible for knowledge to appear as milk, or wine, or a pearl, Islam as a dome or a pillar, the Qur'ān as honey or butter and God in the guise of a man.[12] The 'lesser death' is initiatic death (*al-mawt al-ikhtiyārī*), which is voluntary, while the greater death is the common fate of all.[13] The fourth dwelling place is that of the 'gathering on the earth of awakening' (a reference to Qur'ān 79:14), where men will assemble to await the Judgement.[14] The fifth is that of Paradise and Hell.[15] Finally, the sixth is the 'Dune of Vision' (a reference to Qur'ān 73:14) which is 'a hill of white musk where created beings will be when the vision of God takes place [in the future life].'[16]

The reference to these six fundamental states of total being is in the nature of a warning:

> Everyone who is endowed with intellect should know that the journey necessarily involves suffering, discomfort, trials and tribulations, confrontations with danger and terrifying fears. It rules out happiness, security and pleasure. The water [that the traveller finds on the way] tastes different every time, the winds do not blow in the same direction; the people he meets at one stage are different from the people at the next stage . . .: all this is by way of warning to those who wish prematurely to taste the joys of contemplation[17] somewhere other than in the dwelling place assigned to them.

The water and its different tastes represent spiritual knowledge, and the winds are the *nafaḥāt ilāhiyya*, the breath of divine Grace. Their diversity and the diversity of the people whom he meets on the way are the result of the nature of the journey, which in reality is a journey from divine Name to divine Name: at every step the *sālik* must conform to the implication of the particular Name under whose authority he is placed. Moreover, this world below (the 'second dwelling place'), to which he still belongs, is the world of effort and struggle (*mujāhada*). It is the 'prison' in which God for a time shuts up His creatures:

He who directs his spiritual energy and invocation to the end of bringing Him here, does in fact do so: but this contravenes the laws of spiritual propriety which apply to Him and must be obeyed . . . .. You should defer the obtaining of what you have thus obtained and reserve it for the appropriate dwelling place, that is to say the future world in which works will no longer have a place . . . .. The subtle part of the human being will indeed be restored to life according to the form of knowledge that it has acquired, and the bodies will be restored to life according to the form, whether ugly or beautiful, of the acts performed by them until their last breath. It is only when you have left the world of legal obligations and the realm of levels and ascensions that you will reap the fruit of what you have sown.

The goal of the *sālik* must not be *fatḥ* (opening, illumination), nor the vision of God: if the case arises, he will receive these as additional gifts. The time that he spends in this world must be devoted first and foremost to the acquisition of spiritual knowledge, in the understanding that this does not mean mere theoretical know-how. This priority is explained in a passage from the *Fuṣūṣ*: 'On the Day of the Resurrection, men will see God according to the degrees of the knowledge they had about Him [here below] . . .. Take care, then, not to lock yourself into one particular concept and accuse everything outside it of lack of faith. If you do so, a great good will pass you by! Apply yourself to becoming the *materia prima* of all the representations of God!'[18]

At the end of this preamble, Ibn ʿArabī explains some practical rules. The manner in which they are formulated, and the reference to the gifts which accompany their practice, are clear proof that the *Epistle* is intended for those whose spiritual aptitude is exceptional:

You must withdraw yourself (*ʿuzla*) from men and you must choose retreat (*khalwa*) rather than company.[19] You will be nearer to God in proportion to your retreating, both inwardly and outwardly, from created beings. It is demanded of you that you should have acquired beforehand the knowledge needful for you to discharge your responsibilities in respect of legal honourableness, prayer, fasting, piety, and all that has been prescribed you, no more. This is the first gateway of the journey. Next comes the performing of these acts, the practice of scruples,[20] ascesis,[21] and confident abandonment to God (*tawakkul*).[22] In the first of the successive states that you will experience, this abandonment to God will confer upon you the benefit of four supernatural favours (*karāmāt*)[23] which are the signs and the proof that you have reached the first level: the earth will fold up under your feet, you will walk on water, you will travel through the air, and all created beings will provide you with food [without any effort on your part]. In this matter, abandonment to God is the fundamental reality. After that, the stations (*maqāmāt*), the states (*aḥwāl*), the supernatural favours (*karāmāt*) and the divine descents (*tanazzulāt*) will succeed each other until death. But I adjure you in the name of God, do not enter your cell until you are aware of your station and of the extent to which you are able to oppose the power of the imagination. If your imagination has power over you, you must go into retreat only under the guidance of a teacher who is trained in discerning spirits and familiar with the Way. If, on the other hand, your imagination is under your control, do not fear to go into retreat.

This retreat, which is viewed here in its technical sense as a method of preparing one for the ascent to God, assumes its full significance when we turn to Chapter Seventy-Eight of the *Futūḥāt*, in which, as we said above, Ibn ᶜArabī discusses it from a metaphysical point of view. According to him, the *khalwa*, properly speaking, is the return to the original Void (*al-khalā'*, a word which comes from the same root)—that is to say, to the cloud (*al-ᶜamā'*) where, according to one *ḥadīth*,[24] God was 'before creating creation'. What is in question, therefore, is a de-creation, an idea which occurs in Jīlī's introduction to his commentary where he compares the phases of the journey to the successive removal of 'tunics' (*thiyāb*, sing. *thawb*) corresponding to each of the levels of universal manifestation: a progressive laying bare which is followed, during the return journey, by a reverse process of re–creation in which the traveller, from stage to stage, puts on again the coverings that he had left behind him. With regard to the word *tanazzulāt* in the passage from the *Epistle* just quoted, Jīlī says, 'When the traveller divests himself of his sensible form, which he is able to cast off thanks to spiritual discipline, to retreat and to continual invocation, and passes through the heavens and the spheres, through the stations of the pure spirits and the levels of the Names, God comes down to meet him in each of the mansions that he occupies in turn, and gives to him according to His good will. These gifts are called *munāzalāt*—a word that for Ibn ᶜArabī means a 'halfway meeting' between God and the *sālik*.[25]

The text of the *Epistle* continues with more advice:

It is incumbent upon you, before you go into retreat, to submit yourself to the discipline of initiation, that is to say, to purify your character, renounce heedlessness, and become able to bear what does you harm. He in whom illumination (*fatḥ*) precedes the practice of this discipline will not, save in exceptional cases, attain spiritual virility.

Let us note in passing that on his own admission, Ibn ᶜArabī is one of these very rare exceptions.[26]

Dietary precautions are also recommended when the person in retreat breaks his fast: both 'satiety and excessive hunger' must be avoided. 'Excessive dryness in the system leads to fantasies and prolonged delirium.' The ability to discern spirits is absolutely necessary:

You must distinguish between the inspirations (*wāridāt*) which are angelic in nature and those whose nature is fiery and satanic, by the effects you observe in yourself after they have passed. An angelic inspiration is followed by a sensation of freshness and joy, you experience no suffering, you are not altered in form; and it leaves in its wake a knowledge [which is new]. A satanic inspiration, on the other hand, leaves you with a sense of exhaustion in your limbs, you experience pain, sorrow and humiliation, you are in a state of bewilderment and mental derangement. Be on your guard, therefore, and persevere in your invocation until the moment when God empties your heart [of these suggestions]: for that is your goal.[27]

Neither must the *sālik* allow himself to fall into the trap of theophanies:

When you enter your cell, let your resolution be, if it pleases God: 'Truly, nothing is like God' (Qur'ān 42:11). Consequently, if any form manifests itself to you in your retreat and says to you: 'I am God!', you must reply: 'Glory be to God! You are *through* God!'[28] Keep in mind the form which appeared to you, but turn away from it and absorb yourself in perpetual invocation. This is the first resolution you must take. The second is to ask for nothing save from Him alone, and to assign no object to your aspirations other than Him. Even supposing that the whole universe were offered to you, you would have to accept it out of respect for the spiritual proprieties, but pay no attention to it and continue your quest: for He wished to test you. Each time you pay attention to it, He eludes you. But when you attain to Him, nothing eludes you.

There will be many tests. For example, from the beginning of this motionless journey in the solitude of his cell, the *sālik* will see 'what is normally invisible in the sensible world: neither walls nor darkness will prevent you from seeing what people do in their homes.' But the secrets perceived in this way must be silenced by the *sālik's* identifying himself with the divine Name *al-Sattār*, 'He who veils'. One must also distinguish between perceptions of this kind and mere hallucinations: if they are genuine, they disappear as soon as one shuts one's eyes, whereas if they are not, they persist.

In the course of his Night Journey, the Prophet was offered wine, water and milk, and chose the milk.[29] Drink will also be offered to the *sālik*. He must accept only water, milk or honey, on their own or mixed together, but must not drink the wine 'unless it is mixed with rainwater'. Ibn ʿArabī says that he wrote an opuscule, now lost, on the subject of these symbolic drinks (which are related to the four rivers of

Paradise, Qur'ān 47:15-16).[30] But in the *Kitāb al-Isrā'*,[31] he describes his own 'night journey' during which he was offered wine and milk: *fa sharibtu mīrāth tamām al-laban*, 'and I drank the prophetic heritage of milky perfection; but I abstained from the wine for fear of unveiling the secret under the influence of intoxication, in which case he who followed me would lose himself and become blind.' Honey too is dangerous, for it leads to a rejection of the revealed Law 'because of a secret in the bee'. Milk, says a *ḥadīth*,[32] symbolizes both knowledge and the *fiṭra*, the original pure nature. Honey is a 'remedy for men' (Qur'ān 16:69). But the 'secret of the bees' which may cause him who drinks it to reject the Law, is found in verse 16:68 ('And your Lord revealed to the bees . . . .'), in which the verb *awḥā* is the same as the one used of the prophetic revelation (*waḥy*). This is a reference to what is communicated directly by God to all beings, quite apart from any law brought by a prophet, and which may also cause spiritual 'intoxication'—a fact implied in another *ḥadīth* which says that an intoxicating drink is sometimes made out of honey.[33] With regard to water, one must distinguish between rainwater, which is heavenly and pure and a symbol of the divine *Raḥma*, and the water of rivers, which is earthly and tainted.[34] To consider these as mere allegories, comparable to the rhetorical dangers marked on the 'Carte du Tendre',[35] would be to understand nothing of Ibn ᶜArabī's teaching. For him as for all Ṣūfis they are real ordeals, which the traveller must experience of necessity and, on occasion, with pain.

Common temptations have long been overcome. Those that remain are the more formidable in that they are more subtle:

> Next, God will test you by displaying before you the levels of His kingdom. If He shows them to you in order, first will come the secrets of stones and minerals. You will thus learn the secret of each stone and its useful or harmful properties. If your desire is aroused by this mineral world, you will be kept there and therefore rejected [by God]; His protection will be withdrawn from you and you will perish. However, if you detach yourself from it and persevere in your invocation, and take refuge with Him who is invoked, this category of unveiling will be taken away from you. Then the vegetable world will be unveiled. Each plant will call out to you to tell you what useful or harmful properties it contains.[36]

The same goes for the animal world. 'And each of these worlds will also teach you its own way of praising and glorifying God.' Here again, Ibn ᶜArabī is making an implicit reference to his personal experience, as some passages in the *Futūḥāt* confirm: 'We heard the stones invoking

God . . .. Each species of God's creatures constitutes a community and God has so created them that they worship Him each with its own form of worship.'[37] 'At the beginning of our spiritual life, we heard the stones glorifying and invoking God.'[38] The Epistle, however, wisely and prudently warns against the aberrations of the imagination:

If you consider that the worlds invoke God with the same invocation as you, your unveiling is imaginary, not genuine, and you are quite simply seeing your own condition in created beings. However, if you perceive in them the diversity of their invocations, then your unveiling is genuine.

This journey through the four 'kingdoms' of the sublunary world (mineral, vegetable, and animal, the human kingdom being represented by the *sālik* himself) corresponds to the first stage of the ascent proper, leading to 'the heaven of this world below'. It also corresponds to the first phase of the progressive laying bare referred to above: the traveller, according to what Ibn ᶜArabī says in the autobiographical account in the *Futūḥāt*,[39] has now left behind him the four elements of earth, water, air and fire. This is why, at this point in the journey, the *Epistle* points out that the ascent (*miᶜrāj*) described is an ascent of dissolution (*miᶜrāj taḥlīl*) and proceeds in a specific order (*tartīb*), which is the order of the levels of existence in the universe. First to be 'dissolved' are the elemental 'coverings', which are symbolic of all that makes up the human condition. This initiatic death, which is a necessary prelude to palingenesis, is a painful operation: 'You will be in a state of contraction (*qabḍ*) all the way as you pass through these successive worlds.'

For a detailed description of this first heaven, where the traveller has just arrived, we must turn to the first-hand account in Chapter Three Hundred and Sixty-Seven of the *Futūḥāt*. Here Ibn ᶜArabī, having shed his corporeal nature (*nash'atī al-badaniyya*), meets Adam and finds that he is simultaneously in front of him and on his right. Adam, with a smile, says to him: That is how I was as well at the time of the primordial Covenant: both in front of God and in His right hand with my sons. 'I and my sons', he adds, 'are all in Allāh's right hand', and thus all vowed to felicity. In reply to a question from Ibn ᶜArabī, he explains that this felicity is eternal, even though the places where created beings will dwell after the last Judgement—that is, Paradise or Hell—are different: 'Allāh will furnish each of these two dwellings with whatever is needful for the happiness of those who inhabit it, but each of them must be inhabited.' The divine wrath will be extinguished on the Day of Judgement and universal Compassion (*al-raḥma al-ʿāmma*) will have the last word. This universal Compassion, which rules out eternal punishment in Hell, is a basic element of the Shaykh al-Akbar's doctrine.[40] The knowledge imparted to him about it is identified here as belonging to the 'heritage' of Adam.

Like Chapter Three Hundred and Sixty-Seven, but this time in an impersonal way, Chapter One Hundred and Sixty-Seven also describes the journey through the heavenly spheres, employing two characters in the process. One of these is the *tābiʿ*, he who 'follows' a prophet and conforms to his Law, and the other is the *ṣāhib al-naẓar*, the philosopher who, in his search for truth, relies on speculative thought alone. In each heaven, the former converses with the prophet who dwells in it (in this case Adam) and receives spiritual knowledge from him, whereas the latter speaks only with the ruling angel of that sphere and receives only cosmological knowledge from him. From the angel of the first heavenly sphere, whom Jīlī identifies, in the language of the philosophers, with the tenth intellect, the *ṣāḥib al-naẓar* receives only the knowledge of the 'world of generation and corruption'.

The next paragraph of the *Epistle*—'After this it will be revealed to you how the life of causation is diffused within living beings, and the effect that it produces within each essence in accordance with the predispositions of that essence'—signals the arrival at the second heaven, which is the heaven of Mercury (*ʿUṭārid* or, especially for the Maghrib, *al-kātib*, the 'scribe', which is the form preferred by Ibn ʿArabī). According to Chapter One Hundred and Sixty-Seven, this is the 'dwelling of eloquence' from which the inspiration of orators comes. The *kātib* or angel of the second heaven confirms the truthfulness of the Prophet by demonstrating the unsurpassable nature of the Qur'ān, and also teaches the knowledge of signs, which enables one to act 'through the letters and the Names', and the secret of the *kun*!, the 'fiat!' which bestows existence. But this is also the heaven of Jesus and John (Yaḥyā), who are associated here as they are in sacred history because Yaḥyā, whose name, taken etymologically, symbolizes life, and Jesus, whom the Qur'ān calls *rūḥ*, or spirit (Qur'ān 4:171), are inseparable: where there is spirit there is life. Chapter Three Hundred and Sixty-Seven represents Yaḥyā as a theophany of the divine Name *al-Muḥyī*, 'He who quickens'; whence, according to one *ḥadīth*, it will fall to him on the Day of Resurrection to put death to death (which will appear in the form of a ram).[41] Jesus, for his part, has the power to bring the dead back to life and to bestow life on the birds of clay (Qur'ān 3:49). The connection of these two prophets with the diffusion of the 'life of causation' in living beings is obvious.

The next lines of the *Epistle* are more obscure, and on one point Jīlī himself is at a loss:

> If you do not stop at that point, the glow of the Guarded Tablet will be revealed to you. Terrifying voices will call out to you. Your spiritual state will undergo changes. A wheel will be set up for you, where you will see the forms of metamorphoses: you will see how the gross becomes subtle and the subtle gross, how the first becomes last and the last first (literally: how the head becomes the tail and the tail the head), how man becomes an animal and how the vegetable becomes man, and other similar things.

Our translation of *al-lawā'iḥ al-lawḥiyya* (two words with the same root) as 'the glow of the Guarded Tablet' is merely conjectural: Jīlī says that he does not know the meaning of the phrase. The word *lawā'iḥ* in Ibn ᶜArabī belongs to a family of technical terms which designate spiritual phenomena of a luminous nature, which differ from each other in intensity and stability (the *lawā'iḥ* are 'fleeting as lightning'). These phenomena also find mention in earlier authors such as Qushayrī,[42] for whom they are confined to beginners (*ahl al-bidāya*). The *lawā'iḥ*, explains the Shaykh al-Akbar, are 'that which radiates from the Light of the Essence and the burning Glories of the Face, viewed in terms of their positivity and not of their negativity, to the gaze (*baṣar*) when it is no longer conditioned by the limitations of its physical organ.' Every *lā'iḥa* (singular of *lawā'iḥ*) comes as the result of passing from one state (*ḥāl*) to another, and involves an increase of knowledge.[43] In short, what is in question is a mode, as yet very imperfect, of perceiving theophanies. But what is the meaning, here, of the adjective *lawḥiyya*? It is derived from *lawḥ*. Now the *lawḥ maḥfūẓ*, a Qur'ānic phrase (Qur'ān 85:22) meaning the 'Guarded Tablet', is a symbol in Islamic cosmology of the Universal Soul. Upon this 'tablet' the Calamus—itself a symbol of the first Intellect—engraves in indelible fashion all that will come to pass until the Day of Resurrection. Thus, its connection with the 'wheel' of becoming, with the 'metamorphoses', and with the manifestation of life-giving power associated with the second heaven, would seem logical.[44] We may notice that in the definition of the *lawā'iḥ*, it is made clear that this 'glow' is perceived by the gaze (*baṣar*) and not, as one might expect, by the inner vision (*baṣīra*). But this gaze is not 'conditioned by the limitations of its physical organ'. Just as the body of the resurrected elect is a glorious and transfigured body, the gnostic's eye is also 'glorious' and transcends the limitations of the human condition. The continuing use of the terms 'eye' and 'gaze' serves to emphasize the fact that we are speaking here of a perception which has the force and the immediacy of visual perception. The object of this perception is the divine perfections in their positive aspect—that is to say, inasmuch as they are what they are, not inasmuch as they express God's transcendence with regard to imperfection. The gaze perceives the fact of Beauty; the intellect, left to itself, can know this Beauty only as the negation of all ugliness.

If you do not stop at that point, a light will appear to you which throws out sparks in all directions, and you will wish to protect yourself. But fear nothing and continue your invocation: if you do, no harm will come to you.

If you do not stop at that point, you will see the Light of the Rising Suns appear, and the form of the universal composite. You will see what the appropriate rules are that must be observed in order to attain to the divine Presence, to stand before God, and then to go out of His Presence and return to created being, and what it is to contemplate God perpetually in the infinite variety of His Faces, whether visible or invisible. In this way you will come to know the perfection that it is not given to all to know: for that which is missing from the visible face of a thing is captured in the face which is invisible. Since the visible and the invisible have but one Essence, there is no imperfection present. Similarly, you will learn how to receive divine knowledge from God Himself and what predispositions are required on the part of him who receives it. You will come to know the rules of taking and giving, of contraction and expansion, and you will learn how to preserve the heart from consuming itself to death. You will also see that all paths go in a circle and that not one is straight; and many other things that cannot be contained in this epistle.

The sparks mentioned in the first of these paragraphs proceed, says Jīlī, 'from your own being'. The invocation of God then causes them to disappear. On the other hand, the 'light of the Rising Suns' (*al-ṭawāliʿ*) is the 'light of divine Unity (*al-tawḥīd*) which rises over the heart of the gnostic and extinguishes all other lights'[45]—particularly the 'light of rational proof',[46] which is now useless and which furthermore can lead only to a negative knowledge, and thus ultimately to a conflict with revealed fact. An example of the latter is a reference to God's 'Hands' or 'Feet'. For rational speculation, these attributes are incompatible with divine transcendence: at best one may ascribe an allegorical meaning to them. But the gnostic *sees* God's Hands or His Feet; he knows by direct vision how, in spite of human logic, these attributes can be divine. His knowledge of God never opposes or separates the *tanzīh* from the *tashbīh*, transcendence from immanence or likeness.[47] This synthetic knowledge alone is in conformity with the 'appropriate rules' which must be observed in order to attain to the divine Presence.

Our translation takes account of only one of the possible meanings of the word 'faces' (*wujūh*), which Ibn ᶜArabī almost always uses in a deliberately ambivalent way. The *wujūh* are simultaneously the 'Faces of God', the visible or invisible forms of the phenomenal world, and the modes of contemplation: all these different meanings, moreover, are obviously related. Similarly, the 'perfection that it is not given to all to know' is the perfection of God; but it is also the perfection of each thing inasmuch as what is manifest in it is the 'Apparent One' (*al-Ẓāhir*), that is to say the divine Reality itself. This is a fleeting allusion to a theodicy that Ibn ᶜArabī develops elsewhere, and according to which the 'imperfection' of created being is a necessary element of the perfection of the universe.[48] At this point Jīlī employs two expressive images: when, he says, the visible face of the moon is waning, its hidden face is waxing in the same proportion, and vice versa; when the day (*nahār*) becomes shorter, the night (*layl*) becomes longer, but the duration of the nychthemeron (*yawm*) never changes.

The part of this passage about the 'circularity' of paths may also appear enigmatic. Ibn ᶜArabī makes the meaning clear in a chapter of the *Futūḥāt* where he represents manifestation in symbolic form by a circumference whose starting point (the first Intellect or Calamus, the first being in creation) coincides with its final point (Perfect Man).[49] The 'path' which leads from the Principle to the ultimate frontier of creation ('the lowest part of the abyss', *asfal al-sāfilīn*, Qur'ān 95:5) leads back from this extreme limit to the place of origin—symbolized in the same *sūra* by the 'land made safe', (*al-balad al-amīn*)—which souls yearn after. 'If the path were straight', writes Jīlī, 'there would be no finishing point for created beings to reach; and once they had "gone out" of the Presence of God, they would never go back to Him.' The statement that 'all returns to him' occurs in different forms over and over again in the Revelation (cf. Qur'ān 24:42, 42:53, etc.). But owing to divine Infinity, which precludes all repetition,[50] the return cannot be a simple reversal of the process of going away: created beings do not retrace their steps. It is the curvature of the spiritual space within which they move which brings them back to their point of departure.

After this second heaven, where the *sālik* also learns 'how beings are generated by the reciprocal influence of the world of spirit and the world of flesh', the journey continues to the third heaven, 'the world of formation, of ornamentation and of beauty. This is the level from which inspiration comes to poets, whereas the inspiration of orators comes from the previous heaven.' It is the heaven of Venus (*Zuhra*) and its resident prophet is Yūsuf (Joseph): a double reference to beauty because traditionally, and on the basis of *sūra* 12 which bears his name, Yūsuf is considered to represent the perfection of the human form. According to Chapter One Hundred and Sixty-Seven of the *Futūḥāt* (henceforth we will refer to this chapter as *Fut.* A, and to Chapter Three Hundred and Sixty-Seven as *Fut.* B), from this heaven proceeds the harmony (*niẓām*) of the four elements and the four humours which form the structure of the sublunary world. Here again, the philosopher is instructed only in the cosmological knowledge that corresponds to this sphere, whereas Yūsuf, the interpreter of dreams *par excellence* and the decipherer of forms, imparts to the *tābiᶜ* the knowledge of the imaginal world, symbolized by 'the earth which was created out of what remained of Adam's clay.'[51]

If you do not stop at that point, you will find out what the levels are of the Pole's office. Everything you had contemplated hitherto came from the domain of the Imām of the left. But the place where you are now is the heart. When this new universe is made manifest to you, you will learn the secret of the reflections [of divine perfection] and also the secret of the permanence of what is permanent and of the eternity of what is eternal. You will become acquainted with the hierarchy of beings and with how Being is distributed among them. Divine Wisdom will be granted to you as well as the strength required to preserve it and the faithfulness necessary to impart it to those who are worthy of it. You will receive the gift of symbols and of synthetic knowledge and the power to veil or unveil.

The *sālik* now enters the fourth heaven, which occupies the central position (the 'heart') in the hierarchy of the planetary spheres, and is therefore the heaven both of the Sun and of Idrīs, the Pole of the universe.[52] From Idrīs, the traveller who follows the way of prophecy (*Fut.* A) receives the knowledge of the perpetual revolution of the divine realities (*taqlīb al-umūr al-ilāhiyya*)—the knowledge, that is, of the infinite diversity and the eternal renewal of theophanies. At this stage of his ascent, he sees 'how the night conceals the day and the day the night, how each of them in relation to the other is sometimes male and sometimes female, the secret of their union, and what they engender' (day and night here represent, respectively, the manifest and the non-manifest). He learns the difference between the 'children of day'—those whose spiritual perfection is visible—and the 'children of night', the *malāmiyya*, whose sainthood is hidden from men's eyes. During his own *miʿrāj* (*Fut.* B), Ibn ʿArabī was received on the threshold of this heaven by Idrīs, who saluted in him 'the Muḥammadan heir *par excellence*': a recognition on the part of the supreme Pole that he was in the presence of the Seal of Muḥammadan Sainthood. A dialogue ensues in which Idrīs says that God 'conforms to all that is said about Him'. This is one of the great themes in Ibn ʿArabī's writings: he maintains that all perception, whether of the intellect or the senses, and whether one knows it or not, is perception of an aspect of the divine Reality, for things are simply places of manifestation (*maẓāhir*) for theophanies. All error, therefore, is relative (*al-khaṭa' amr iḍāfī*, as Idrīs says). Thus, every statement about God is accurate in terms of what it includes, and false in terms of what it excludes.[53]

Ibn ʿArabī tells Idrīs of his meeting in front of the Kaʿba with a person from one of the human races which preceded our own,[54] and asks him the following question: before this world existed, was there another dwelling place? 'The dwelling place of existence (*dār al-wujūd*)', replies Idrīs, 'is unique. This world is only the world below because of you, and the future world is only different from it because of you.' The realities of Paradise are present, here and now, for him who has eyes to see them.

If you do not stop at that point, you will see the world of combative fervour, of anger and of burning zeal, and you will learn the origin of the seeming divergences in the universe and of the diversity of forms, as well as many other things.

This is the fifth heaven, the heaven of Mars (*al-Aḥmar, al-Mirrīkh, al-Naḥs al-Aṣghar*), which Ibn ʿArabī (*Fut.* A) describes as the heaven of terror, fear, affliction—in a word, of all the manifestations of divine Severity. From here the *sālik* derives the necessary strength to resist his adversaries, both inner and outer. His conversation with Hārūn (Aaron), the prophet of this heaven is chiefly concerned with one of the most controversial points of Ibn ʿArabī's doctrine: the posthumous fate of Firʿawn, the Pharaoh who was Moses' enemy, and whose act of faith, uttered *in extremis*, precludes the possibility that he is doomed to damnation, because 'the Mercy of God is too vast not to accept even faith under duress'.[55] Severity itself is merely a veil over Compassion—something which is also implied in the rule, laid down by Hārūn for the *tābiʿ*, 'to let the blood flow in ritual sacrifices so that the animals may attain to the level of human beings': a painful but necessary alchemy which integrates creatures of a lower order to the nature of the Perfect Man and enables them to share in his destiny.

In the autobiographical account (*Fut.* B), other conversations take place, first of all with Yaḥyā (John). Ibn ʿArabī had already met him in the second heaven at the side of Jesus, and meets him again with Hārūn. 'I didn't see you on the path. Is there then another path?' he asks. 'Everyone has his own path, on which he walks alone', replies Yahyā: 'every being is unique and his relationship with God is likewise unique.' Next follows a dialogue with Hārūn who, like Idrīs, greets the 'heir of Muḥammad' in Ibn ʿArabī, and in reply to a question affirms the reality of the world that is denied by 'certain gnostics'. The 'imperfection' of their knowledge, says Hārūn, 'may be measured by the extent to which the world is veiled from them: because for him who has knowledge of God, the universe is nothing other than His epiphany.' In connection with this same text,[56] we drew attention elsewhere to the radical opposition on this point between Ibn ʿArabī's doctrine and the doctrine of the so-called school of 'Absolute Oneness' (*al-waḥda al-muṭlaqa*), whose most famous teacher was Ibn Sabʿīn.

The traveller now comes to the sixth heaven, the heaven of Jupiter (*al-Birjīs* or *al-Mushtarī*) where Moses resides:

> If you do not stop at that point, you will behold the world of jealous Love and of the perception of Truth in its most perfect forms. You will learn which opinions are valid, which points of view correct, and which Laws are truly revealed. You will see a world which God has embellished in the most beautiful fashion by endowing it with knowledge most sacred. No spiritual station will be unveiled to you which does not receive you with respect, dignity and honour, inform you clearly of its degree in relation to the divine Presence, and desire you with all its being.

At this point of his ascent, he who has renounced the speculative way of the philosophers and has followed the path of prophetic teaching, receives from Moses 'twelve thousand forms of knowledge'—an implicit reference to verse 2:60 in which twelve rivers flow out of the rock that Moses strikes with his rod, corresponding to the twelve tribes of Israel or, in other words, to so many aspects of the *walāya mūsawiyya*[57] (*Fut.* A). Moses also teaches him that 'theophanies occur only in the form of beliefs (*al-iʿtiqādāt*) and of needs (*al-ḥājāt*)', in allusion to two other verses (Qur'ān 28:29-30) which refer to the episode of the Burning Bush. According to Ibn ʿArabī, it was because Moses was in search of a fire, as these verses tell us, that the voice of God came to him out of a tree on fire.[58] Each time we think about what we need (in either a material or a spiritual sense), we are thinking, whether or not we know it, about God, for 'all need is need of God'.[59] He who desires something for its beauty is in love with the divine Beauty which exists in it. But he will know no more of divine Beauty than what this object can contain. It is plain that, in the language of the Shaykh al-Akbar, the word *iᶜtiqādāt* covers a great deal more than 'beliefs' in the sense of articulated expressions of faith, and extends to all the limited representations that we form of whatever we aspire towards. The theophany will be in the image and the measure of our desire.

From the prophet of the sixth heaven, the traveller also learns how substances (*al-jawāhir*) can be stripped of their forms and clothed in other forms without any change taking place in their essential reality. An example of this is the rod of Moses, which looks sometimes like a rod and sometimes like a serpent, even though its essential nature is not affected by these metamorphoses. Armed with this knowledge, the *walī* can no longer be duped by the illusion of the phenomenal world, but perceives the Oneness of Being in the multiplicity of beings: 'Say [when you see something]: this is God! or: this is the world! or: this is I! or: this is you! or: this is He! all these designations are simply pronouns [*ḍamā'ir*, in place of the Name], and only the points of view are different. [In this knowledge of the One beneath the diversity of appearances] there are brimming oceans, shoreless and bottomless!'

The question of the vision of God is at the heart of Ibn ᶜArabī's conversation with Moses (*Fut.* B).[60] In a famous episode in the Qur'ān, Moses asks God, 'Oh my Lord, appear to me, that I may look on You!' and hears the reply, 'You shall not see Me!' (Qur'ān 7:143). 'God singled you out among men in making you His Messenger and by speaking with you, and yet you asked to see Him', says Ibn ᶜArabī in the course of this conversation, 'but Muḥammad said, "None of you will see his Lord before he dies".' 'That is so,' replies Moses. 'When I asked to see Him, He granted my wish. I fell down in a faint and I saw Him—may He be exalted!—while I was unconscious.' 'So you were dead?' 'I was dead!' says Moses, who goes on to explain that he is one of those who will not have to die when the trumpet of Isrāfīl sounds on the Day of Judgement: he who has experienced initiatic death already shares in the eternal life of the elect. For such a man, 'death is dead', just as it will die for all created beings at the end of time, slain by Yaḥyā (John), 'he who is alive'. Once again, we may observe the close correspondence that exists between initiatic and eschatological doctrine: the apocalypse (in its real sense of 'revelation') is a posthumous *fatḥ* or illumination, and the *fatḥ* of the *walī* is an apocalypse in advance.

The conversation continues. When you asked to see Him, did you in fact not see Him? asks Ibn ᶜArabī. 'I was already seeing Him,' says Moses, 'but without knowing that it was Him I saw!' The difference between the layman and the gnostic does not lie in what is seen. What distinguishes the *ᶜārif* is the fact that he knows *whom* he is seeing.

After this world, ruled by 'jealous Love'—the love that impels Moses to destroy the golden calf (Qur'ān 2:51-54, 92; 4:153; 7:148-152; 20:85-97)—the *walī* arrives at the seventh heaven, the heaven of Saturn (*Kaywān, Zuḥal*), which is 'the world of gravity, serenity, stability and of the divine ruse'. Whereas the reigning angel of this sphere instals the philosopher (*Fut.* A) 'in a dark house', which is no other than his own ego, the *tābiᶜ* is greeted by Abraham, whom he finds (as did Muḥammad during his own *miᶜrāj*) leaning against the *Bayt al-maᶜmūr*, the 'Visited House', which is the goal of the eternal procession of the angels as well as the heavenly prototype of the earthly Kaᶜba.[61] 'Make your heart like this House by being present to God (*bi-ḥuḍūrika maᶜa 'l-Ḥaqq*) at every moment', enjoins Abraham.

As in the preceding planetary heavens, each traveller receives instruction here according to the purity (*takhlīṣ*) of his being; but whereas the *tābiᶜ* is invited to enter the 'Visited House',[62] the philosopher learns that he has arrived at the end of his ascent and that he will have to wait here for his companion to return. Despite appearances, they are not 'brothers'; for, says Abraham, only the 'brotherhood of milk' is important, which unites those who have drunk the same drink—that is to say, who have imbibed the same knowledge. The philosopher then declares that he submits to the prophetic Law and claims the same status as the *tābiᶜ*. But this conversation does not happen here: first he will have to go back down, for it is on earth that man, created of earth, must accept faith and the Law.

As the text of the *Epistle* says, it is from this heaven of serenity and stability (*thabāt*) that 'divine ruse' (*makr, istidrāj*) paradoxically proceeds.[63] But this is a paradox only in appearance: stability closes what is open, limits what is infinite. It is merely a dangerous illusion, the highest and most fatal of temptations. Spiritual perfection involves *ḥayra*—stupefaction, perplexity, a perpetual marvelling at the incessantly changing theophanies, each of them bringing a new knowledge which is never the *nec plus ultra*.[64] The description of the next stage of the *miᶜrāj*, therefore, should come as no surprise:

If you do not stop at that point, you will be shown the world of perplexity, deficiency and impotence, as well as the treasure-house of actions, that is to say [what the Qur'ān, 83:18-21, calls the *ʿIllīyūn*.

This stage marks the arrival at the 'Lote-tree of the Boundary' (*sidrat al-muntahā*, Qur'ān 53:14), the point where Jibrīl, the angel of the Revelation, stopped during the Prophet's *miʿrāj*, leaving Muḥammad to continue his ascent alone. It is also the stopping point for the pious actions of created beings, which the angels 'carry' each day to God. From this tree, the *tābiʿ* (*Fut.* A) sees a great river welling up, out of which arise three smaller rivers and innumerable streams. The great river is the Qur'ān, the other three are the Torah, the Psalms (*al-zabūr*) and the Gospel (*al-injīl*), and the streams represent the *ṣuḥuf* ('leaves'), or minor revelations. He who drinks one of these waters is the heir of the prophet corresponding to it. But the Qur'ān, the river of Muḥammad, contains all the other Books, and he who drinks from it receives the fulness of all the prophetic inheritances.

In Chapter Three Hundred and Sixty-Seven of the *Futūḥāt*, the detailed description of the ascent (a description continued in Chapter One Hundred and Sixty-Seven and in the *Kitāb al-Isrā'*) ends at this point on a note of glory. Ibn ʿArabī sees the Lote-tree surrounded by a dazzling light, and he himself becomes a being altogether of light. Then, he says, 'God caused to descend upon me [*anzala ʿalayya*: the verb used here is used in the Qur'ān of the "descent" of the Revelation][65] the verse: "Say: we believe in God, and in what has been revealed to us, and in what was revealed to Abraham, Ishmael, Isaac, Jacob, the tribes [of Israel] and in what was given to Moses and Jesus . . . ." (Qur'ān 3:84). And in this verse He gave me all the verses . . . and He made it the key to all knowledge.' Ibn ʿArabī interprets this divine communication as an indication that he has attained to the 'Muḥammadan station'. He continues, 'During this night journey, I acquired the meanings of all the divine Names. I saw that all these Names had reference to one Named One and to one Essence. This Named One was the object of my contemplation and this Essence was my own being. My journey took place only within me and I was guided towards myself. And hence I knew that I was a servant in the pure sense, and that there was not the least trace in me of sovereignty.' These few lines contain the whole secret of the *walī*'s ascent: he has visited his own inner planets, met with the prophets of his own being, ascending in this way from heaven to heaven towards the summit of himself, at which point, with his ontological destitution fully and finally laid bare, the infinity of God is revealed to him.[66]

Whereas the autobiographical account in the *Futūḥāt* condenses the last stages of the *miʿrāj* into a few lines,[67] the *Epistle of the Lights* describes the last phases of the journey in a way equally cursory but more explicit, intersecting—in reverse order since the ascent of the *walī* is a de-creation—the successive levels of Ibn ʿArabī's cosmology.[68] The 'Lote-tree of the Boundary' is at the highest point of the 'world of generation and corruption' (*ʿālam al-kawn wa 'l-fasād* or *ʿālam al-shahāda*) of which the planetary spheres are part. Thus the traveller will have to cross the sphere of the fixed stars (*falak al-kawākib al-thābita*), then the 'heaven without stars' (*al-falak al-aṭlas*), both of them part of the 'World of Creation' (*ʿālam al-khalq*), as are the Footstool (*al-kursī*) and the Throne (*al-ʿarsh*). He will then go up through the levels of the 'World of the Commandment' (*ʿālam al-amr*), which are, in ascending order, the 'Universal Substance' (*al-jawhar al-muẓlim al-kull*);[69] Nature (*al-ṭabīʿa*), in which sensible forms are contained *in potentia*; the Guarded Tablet or Universal Soul; and lastly the Calamus, identified both with the First Intellect and with the Muḥammadan Reality or Perfect Man. Leaving behind the World of Command, he enters next what is termed the Primordial Cloud (*al-ʿamā'*), which is produced by the Breath of the Merciful One (*nafas al-Raḥmān*),[70] and enters the divine Presence.

The lower part of the heaven of the fixed stars is the 'roof of Hell', and its upper part is the 'floor of Paradise'. This geography determines the landscape revealed to the *walī* after the stage of the Lote-tree of the Boundary has been passed:

> If you do not stop at that point, the paradises will be revealed to you in the ascending order of their levels, and how they fit into each other, together with the hierarchy of their felicities: all this will be revealed while you are standing on a narrow path. Then you will see Hell and its levels in descending order . . . .[71] If you do not stop at that point, you will be shown spirits annihilated in their contemplation, who are lost and intoxicated in it, for the power of ecstasy has overcome them . . . .[72] If you do not stop at that point, a light will be revealed to you in which you will see nothing but yourself. Thereupon you will be seized by a divine ecstasy and a mad love and you will experience a joy in the power of God such as you have never previously known . . . . If you do not stop at that point, the Bed of the Majesty of Compassion will appear to you. All things are there. There you will see all that you had seen before and much more besides. There is no reality which you cannot contemplate

there, whether it be present only in the divine Knowledge or whether it is endowed with existence. Seek for your own reality among all these things: when your glance falls on it you will recognize your goal, your spiritual dwelling-place and your ultimate level. Then you will know which of the divine Names is your Lord, which portion of knowledge and sainthood is yours, and in what you are unique.

Akbarian eschatology is outlined in several chapters of the *Futūḥāt*, in which the maps of Paradise and Hell are described and clarified by diagrams. Without giving a summary of it here, we will single out two concepts which throw light on the nature of the traveller's experience at this stage of his journey. 'Know', says Ibn ʿArabī, 'that the Paradise which is pre-destined for those who will come to it in the next life is before your eyes already, this very day . . .. You are there now . . . but you do not know it.'[73] This is why the Prophet was able to say that the space contained between his tomb and his pulpit is 'one of the gardens of Paradise':[74] whereas the simple believer is content to accept this statement through an act of faith, the 'men of unveiling' (*ahl al-kashf*), when they look at this part of the mosque in Medina, actually see one of the gardens of Paradise, here and now. The ascent of the *walī* is an apotheosis of his sight, whereby a reality is revealed to him which has always been present to all beings, but which the majority of them will not perceive in this world unless they have learned how to 'die before death'. What another passage in the *Futūḥāt* says about Hell[75] confirms that the difference between the *walī* and the ordinary man lies entirely in their way of seeing things: for Ibn ʿArabī, Gehenna was created out of the essential reality (*ḥaqīqa*) which finds expression in the *ḥadīth qudsī* where God, addressing the sinner, says, 'I was ill and you did not visit Me. I was hungry and you did not feed Me . . .. I was thirsty and you did not give Me anything to drink . . ..' He goes on to explain to the bewildered sinner ('How could I have visited You who are the Lord of the Worlds?'), 'My servant "so-and-so" was ill and if you had visited him you would have found Me at his side . . ..'[76] Thus, Hell is nothing other than the blindness which prevented the man from seeing God in all His forms, from perceiving His presence in all things, all beings, all places, at all times. This blindness of him who looks at theophanies without seeing them is the root of sin and the very substance of its punishment. Only the man escapes it who is aware of 'his own reality', his eternal haecceity (*ʿayn thābita*)—the man, that is to say, who knows himself to be the theophany of a divine Name and its place of manifestation (*maẓhar*).[77] To his own transparency corresponds the transparency of things.

At this point of the journey of initiation, the saint attains to the level of the *lawḥ maḥfūẓ*, the 'Guarded Tablet'—a synonym in Ibn ᶜArabī for the Universal Soul—on which the divine Calamus has engraved indelibly that which is, was or will be ('all things are there'). The ascent is approaching its end:

If you do not stop at that point, the teacher and instructor of all things [i.e. the Calamus or Universal Intellect] will appear to you. You will see the line he traces and you will become acquainted with its message. You will see how he changes direction,[78] how he receives knowledge, and then how that which he has received in synthetic mode from the angel of the *Nūn* becomes differentiated.[79]

If you do not stop at that point, you will see that which moves [the Calamus]—that is to say, God's Right Hand. At this level the traveller is shown the world of the angelic spirits overcome by Love (*al-muhayyamūn*), who in Islamic tradition are usually called the Cherubim (*al-karūbiyyūn*), and one of whom is the Calamus. Lost in their contemplation of the divine Beauty and Majesty, these *muhayyamūn* 'are not even aware that God created the world'. The same is true of the *afrād*, who are their equivalents on the human plane—unless, that is, they have been assigned a task, like the Calamus, which obliges them to turn towards created being. As we saw earlier, the Pole—among others—is one example of this.

If the *walī* has been able to resist the temptation to stop at each successive stage of his journey (a danger to which our attention is insistently drawn by the first line of every paragraph of the *Epistle*), he has now arrived at the 'Station of Proximity' (*maqām al-qurba*), at the fulness of sainthood which Jesus will seal at the end of time. The only thing forbidden to him, since the disappearance of the Seal of Muḥammadan Sainthood, is the position at the centre, reserved in this *maqām* for those who are 'heirs of Muḥammad' in the fullest sense. But to know that one is near is still to know that one is—it still implies, for created being, a degree of ontological autonomy. True Proximity is consummated only in the total de-creation of what has been created, when all that survives is the Divine Oneness (*al-waḥda*).

If you do not stop at that point, you will be blotted out, extinguished, obliterated, annihilated.

Then, when this erasure and all that follows it—occultation, extinction, obliteration, annihilation—have worked all their effects in you, you will be affirmed, made present, existent and reassembled.

Here the loop of becoming has come full circle: the palingenesis is complete. At the end of this *miʿrāj*, man is reduced to the indestructible divine secret (*sirr ilāhī*) which was lodged in him at the beginning of time by the breath of the Spirit (*nafkh al-rūḥ*) breathed into Adam's clay.[80] 'Then', says Ibn ʿArabī in his *Kitāb al-Isrā'*, 'the even and the odd come together, He is and you are not . . . .. And He sees Himself through Himself.'[81]

However, even though the 'arrival' at God (*al-wuṣūl*) is the final point of the ascent, for the most perfect it is not the end of the journey. The Arabic word *miʿrāj* may be translated as 'ladder': but in this case the ladder is a double ladder. The *walī*, having reached the summit, must go back down by rungs which are different but symmetrical to those by which he climbed up.

> Next, you will be sent back on your way and you will see again what you saw previously, but under different forms; and in this way you will return to the limited, terrestrial world of your senses. At least, this is what will happen if you do not cling on to the place where you were occulted.

The *walī*, then, will travel once more through the levels of universal existence and re-visit, in reverse order, the hierarchy of the heavens. All that he saw he will see again. But the same things will have 'different forms', because what he used to look at 'with the eyes of his ego' (*bi-ʿayn nafsihi*) he now contemplates with 'the eyes of his Lord' (*bi-ʿayn rabbihi*). At each stage of the descent, he will take up again the part of himself that he had left there. This progressive recovering of what he had left behind is not a regression, however: to employ Jīlī's beautiful image in his commentary,[82] each 'tunic' that he took off on the way up was by the same token turned inside out, like a garment which one pulls over one's head hem-first. Thus, the wrong side is now the right side; what was hidden has become visible. The *walī* 'reclothes himself' on the way back with all the elements of his being that he had returned earlier to their respective worlds; but, through being turned inside out, these elements have undergone a metamorphosis. Not all the *awliyā'* arrive at the highest level, represented by the *maqām al-qurba*, and not all of them 'return' to created being. Furthermore, at every stage there are different modes of spiritual realization, which correspond strictly to the different prophetic types inherited by the saints. These features of Akbarian hagiology are reaffirmed in the following passage:

For each traveller, the journey's end depends on the road he has taken. Some will be spoken to in their own language, others in a language which is different from theirs. Each will be the heir of the prophet who corresponds to the language he has had spoken to him. This is why you will hear the People of the Way saying, 'So-and-so' is *mūsawī*, or *ᶜīsawī*, or *ibrāhīmī*, or *idrīsī*.

Here, each 'language' represents a particular form of the revelation (*waḥy*) or inspiration (*ilhām*) which descends from God upon the heart of the servant and which determines, in return, a specific form of knowledge and worship. As we know, however, the same person can accumulate many inheritances:

But there are some among them who will be spoken to in two languages, or three, or four, and so on. Perfect among them is he who is spoken to in all languages: this is the exclusive privilege of the Muḥammadan.

The model *par excellence* of this Muḥammadan who is spoken to 'in all languages', and who as a result is the only qualified interpreter of Universal Truth in all its aspects, is Ibn ᶜArabī himself. We referred in Chapter Five to his *Kitāb Al-ᶜAbādila*, a highly enigmatic work which, as far as we know, has never been studied. The very word *ᶜabādila*, which is rarely employed, is an irregular plural of *ᶜAbd Allāh*, 'servant of God'. Throughout this curious work, utterances of a metaphysical or initiatic nature are put into the mouths of about a hundred people who are called by strange and obviously symbolic names. It would be futile to attempt to identify these characters with known Ṣūfī figures: as we are given to understand by the allusions in the preface, the voice which speaks from beneath all these masks is Ibn ᶜArabī's, 'servant of the Name which encompasses all Names', 'totalizing son of a limited father' (*ibn jāmiᶜ ᶜan ab muqayyad*), 'interpreter of all languages'.[83]

For as long as the traveller remains at the end point of his journey and does not retrace his steps, he is called *al-wāqif*, 'he who has come to a standstill'. Some, indeed, are permanently obliterated at this station, such as Abū ᶜIqāl and others.[84] These will die and be resurrected at this station.

Some, on the other hand, are 'sent back'. He who is sent back in this way is more perfect than he who comes to a standstill and is annihilated, always provided that their spiritual stations are similar . . . otherwise he who is sent back has to live until the moment when he reaches the same level as he who is annihilated: when this happens he will be above him as regards the approach (*tadānī*) and the descent (*tadallī*) and will outmatch him in terms of ascent (*taraqqī*) and reception (*talaqqī*).[85]

We must distinguish between two categories of those who are 'sent back'. He who belongs to the first category is sent back for his own sake, as in the case discussed above. He is termed a gnostic (*ᶜārif*), and in order to perfect himself he returns by a different way from the one he took before.

But there is also he who is sent back to created beings in order to direct and guide them by his words. He is the wise man (*alᶜālim*) through inheritance.[86]

We have drawn attention several times to the importance of the concept of 'return' (*rujūᶜ*). Here, we see once more that it occupies a central position in the definition of sainthood. On this point the Shaykh al-Akbar's doctrine is forcefully expressed from his earliest writings onwards. In the *Risāla fī 'l-walāya*, written when he was thirty years old, Ibn ᶜArabī makes the same distinctions: 'Among them', he writes, 'are those who are sent back [to created being], those who are not sent back, and those who are left to choose. He who is not sent back is called in our technical vocabulary by the name of *wāqif* . . .. He who is sent back specifically [i.e. for his own sake] is called an *ᶜārif*. He who is sent back in a general sense [i.e. in order to guide created beings] is called *ᶜālim* and *wārith*.' But although Ibn ᶜArabī is the first to explain this concept and to bring out its implications clearly, both as regards the course of sainthood and in the *walī*'s personal experience, it must be stressed that it is already present in the teaching of earlier *awliyā'*, and above all that, like all the other aspects of *walāya*, it is included within the Muḥammadan paradigm. The rest of the text just quoted alludes to a very significant statement made by Shaykh Abū Madyan: 'To flee from created being is one of the signs of a novice's sincerity. To reach God is a sign of the sincerity of his flight from created being. To return to created being is a sign of the sincerity of his having reached God.' This return, comments Ibn ᶜArabī, represents 'the perfection of the Station of Inheritance (*wa huwa kamāl maqām al–wirātha*)': in fact, he says, withdrawal from created being corresponds to the period in the Prophet's life which preceded the Revelation. The Revelation marks the end of the phase of ascent following which Muḥammad is 'sent to all created beings'. The 'perfection of the Station of Inheritance' implies that there is a strict equivalence between the journey of the heir and that of the Prophet whose heir, directly or indirectly, he is.[87]

The 'heirs' who call [created being] to God in this way do not all possess the same rank . . .. Some of them call created being in the language of Moses, of Jesus, of Shem, of Isaac, of Ishmael, of Adam, of Idrīs, of Abraham, of Aaron or of other prophets. They are the Ṣūfīs, who, in comparison with those of us who are the perfect Masters, are termed *aṣḥāb al-aḥwāl*, the 'People of the Spiritual States'.

Others of them call created beings to God in the language of Muḥammad. They are the 'men of blame' (*al-malāmiyya*), the People of Immutability and Essential Truth.

What distinguishes the *malāmī* from the *ṣūfī* and explains the 'blame' that attaches to him is, as we said, his refusal to free himself from secondary causes, to tear the veil beneath which God conceals the mystery of His presence. Because he preserves God's incognito, God preserves his. Because he has knowledge of God, he perceives Him in all things. But because the Law prescribes servitude, he keeps his Lord's secret: it is the transparency of his own being which reveals him to those who have eyes to see. Only the *malāmī*, through his total acceptance of the order of things in this world, fully satisfies all the conditions of the return to created being, in the absence of which the saint is only half a saint. This expression may appear to be an exaggeration, but it merely transposes what Aaron (Hārūn) says to his visitor in the fifth heaven, or, even more directly, what Ibn ᶜArabī himself says in the *Fuṣūṣ*. 'Elijah', he writes, 'possessed only half of the knowledge of God', because he was 'a pure intellect emancipated from all passion' (*ᶜaqlan bi-la shahwa*).[88] God was therefore known to him only in His transcendence (*tanzīh*) and not, simultaneously, in His similitude (*tashbīh*). Yet God is both the First and the Last, the Invisible and the Visible. The *wāqif*, who remains forever motionless at the highest point of the ascent, knows God only in terms of the first two of these four Names, which in the Qur'ān form inseparable pairs. The world was not created in vain (*ᶜabathan*, Qur'ān 23:115), it is not an illusion (*bāṭilan*, Qur'ān 3:191): it is the theatre of theophanies, it displays the 'Hidden Treasure' to which God compares himself in a *ḥadīth qudsī*,[89] it is the place where one acquires that other half of the knowledge of God which is the essence of sainthood. In this way the 'two bows' are joined together, and the *walī* arrives at that indescribable 'nearer', *qāb qawsayn aw adnā*, evoked in the *sūra* of the Star (Qur'ān 53:9). This necessary complementarity finds figurative expression in the rites of the pilgrimage—another symbol of the journey of initiation in the course of which the believer, after completing the *ṭawāf*, the act of circling the Kaᶜba or *bayt Allāh*, the dwelling of the One who has no second, must return to duality by making a journey in a straight line between the hills of Ṣafā and Marwa.[90]

The title as a whole of the *Epistle of the Lights* suggests a treatise on the *khalwa*, retreat in a cell. But although monastic solitude appears at the beginning of the text to be a necessary preliminary to the journey, it is radically opposed to the state of perfection to which it should lead. The place of the living saint is among men; and when he is dead he will continue, through his *rūḥāniyya*, or spiritual presence, to mingle with them and watch over their fate. His true 'retreat' consists in concealing himself while remaining visible, *khalwa fī jalwa*, also expressed in a Persian formula, which occurs among the eleven cardinal rules of the *ṭarīqa naqshbandiyya*, as retreat among the crowd (*khalvat dar anjumān*).[91] Like the architecture seen in certain dreams, his *mi*ʿ*rāj* is a stair which ascends downwards; for 'all roads are circular'. His exile, prefigured by the exile of the Prophet when he was driven from the Sacred Territory, separates him only in appearance from the goal of his search: he who has arrived at the centre knows that the points of the circumference are all equidistant from God, and that this distance is no distance, for 'He is with you wherever you may be' (Qur'ān 57:4).

Walāya is, literally, proximity. But this proximity is twofold: the *walī*, close to God, is not wholly a *walī* unless he is also close to created being. Ibn ʿArabī identifies the Perfect Man with the tree[92] 'whose root is firm and whose branches are in heaven' (Qur'ān 14:24). Earthly as well as heavenly, the saint is he who brings together the high and the low, the *Ḥaqq* and the *khalq*. Like the Muḥammadan Reality whose heir he is, he forms the 'isthmus' (*barzakh*) of the 'two seas'. Even though he is the guarantor of cosmic order, and thus ultimately the instrument of divine Severity, his function—whatever rank he holds in the hierarchy of initiation—is first and foremost to be the agent of 'the Compassion which embraces all things' (Qur'ān 7:156). This is why his 'heroic generosity' (*futuwwa*) extends 'to minerals, to plants, to animals and to all that exists.'[93]

Although properly speaking the role of *axis mundi* belongs to the Pole, every *walī* shares in it to some degree. But although the *walāya* exists forever in the life to come, here below it comes, of necessity, to an end. With the coming of the first Seal, its most perfect forms were placed out of reach for ever. The coming of the second Seal will close off permanently the *maqām al-qurba*, the highest degree of proximity. When God 'seizes the soul' of the third Seal, who will also be 'the last-born of the human race', 'men will be like beasts'.[94] Then the Qur'ān, 'brother' to the Perfect Man, will also be erased in the space of one night from the hearts of men as from their books.[95] Empty of all that united heaven with the earth, an icy and insane universe will sink into its death. The end of the saints is nothing less than another name for the end of the world.

Notes to Chapter Ten

1. *Futūḥāt*, I, p. 735; III, pp. 127, 159, 288; IV, p. 235; *Fuṣūṣ*, I, p. 202; *Kitāb al-ʿAbādila*, p. 200.

2. A start has been made in studying this theme by Nazeer El-Azma in his article 'Some notes on the impact of the story of the Miʿrāj on Sufi Literature', *The Muslim World*, LXIII, April 1973, pp. 93-104. We have not been able to consult the work by Qassem al-Samarrai, *The Theme of Ascension in Mystical Writings*, Baghdad 1968. See also in C. Kappler *et al.*, *Apocalypses et voyages dans l'au-delà*, Paris 1987, pp. 167-320, the articles by E. Renaud and A. Piemontese on an Arab version and a Persian version of the *miʿrāj*. If we are more in favour here of the spiritual journey described in the form of a *miʿrāj*, because of its clarity and synthetic character as well as its unequivocally Muḥammadan references, it is none the less true that Ibn ʿArabī's work is susceptible to other modes of representation, based (as suggested by the six-section structure of the *Futūḥāt*) on the classic Ṣūfī distinctions: *aḥwāl* (states), *maqāmāt* (stations), *manāzil* (dwellings), etc.

3. The place and date of writing are given in one of the manuscripts listed by Osman Yahia, *Histoire et classification*, I, p. 162, R. G. no. 33, MS Şehit Ali 1344. The authenticity of this treatise is established by Ibn ʿArabī's references to it in the *Fihris* and the *Ijāza*, and finds ample confirmation in the style and ideas.

4. Damascus 1329AH (with the commentary by ʿAbd al-Karīm al-Jīlī), Cairo 1322 AH, and Hyderabad 1948.

5. This is the MS Bayazid 1686 (written in 667AH), fos. 21 b-26. We have also referred at times to a later manuscript (MS Yahya Ef. 2415, fos. 86 b-90b, dated 1293 AH), which has the advantage of being largely vocalized. There are two translations of this text into Western languages: one is by Asín Palacios (*El islam cristianizado*, Madrid 1931, pp. 433-49), later re-translated from Spanish into French (*L'Islam christianisé*, Paris 1982, pp. 321-33), in a form which is incomplete and unannotated; while the other, in English, is by Rabia Terri Harris, *Journey to the Lord of Power*, New York 1981, the accuracy of which leaves much to be desired (see our review of this translation in *Bulletin critique des Annales islamologiques*, XXI (1985), pp. 278-82). The commentary by Jīlī, published in Damascus in 1329AH, and the attribution of which is confirmed by—among other things—the mention on p. 29 of his *Kitāb al-Insān al-Kāmil*, is entitled *al-Isfār ʿan risālat al-anwār fī mā yatajallā li ahl al-dhikr min al-anwār* ('The removal of the veil from the *Epistle of the Lights*: on the light which appears to those who devote themselves to the *dhikr*').

6. The two chapters of the *Futūḥāt* ('On *khalwa*' and 'On giving up *khalwa*') have been translated by Michel Vâlsan in *Études traditionelles*, no. 412-13, March-June 1969, pp. 77-86. They centre on the metaphysical meaning and the principles of the *khalwa*, but refer only briefly to practical rules or effects. The *Kitāb al-Khalwa*, which is much more technical in character, is in the same collection (Bayazid, 1686, fos. 6b-11) as the manuscript of the *Risālat al-anwār* which we are using here, and alludes to this last fo. 10b (*wa-qad dhakarnā tartīb al-fatḥ fī risālat al-anwār). The Kitāb al-Khalwa* was written (cf. *Futūḥāt*, I, p. 392) in response to a

question from someone whom we have already encountered, Abū l-ʿAbbās al-Tawzarī (cf. note 2, chapter 9).

7. On the Muslim sources dealing with the Prophet's *miʿrāj*, see *EI*[1], s.v. the article by J. Horovitz. The version by Ibn ʿAbbās, which was far and away the most popular, has been through many editions. The *Kitāb al-Miʿrāj* by Qushayrī, Cairo 1954, is of interest in that it has all the versions that were in circulation during the fifth century of the *hegira*.

8. Ibn ʿArabī (*Futūḥāt*, II, pp. 380-82) distinguishes four types of *sālik (bi-rabbihi, bi-nafsihi, bi 'l-majmūʿ, sālik lā sālik*) and five types of *sulūk (minhu ilayhi* (from theophany to theophany), *minhu ilayhi fīhi* (from Name to Name within a name), *minhu lā fīhi wa lā ilayhi, ilayhi lā minhu wa lā fīhi* (of which the model in the Qur'ān is the flight of Moses), *lā minhu wa-lā fīhi wa lā ilayhi* (this is the case of the ascetic, *al-zāhid*).

9. On the *rujūʿ*, the return to created being, which will be discussed again later, we refer the reader as before to chapter 45 of the *Futūḥāt* (I, pp. 250-53), and to the *Risāla fī' l-walāya*, pp. 25 and 27. See also Junayd, *Enseignement spirituel*, transl. R. Deladrière, Paris 1983, pp. 45-46 (pp. 53-54 of the Arabic text in A. H. Abdel-Kader, *The Life, Personality and Writings of Al-Junayd*, London 1962).

10. Cf. *Futūḥāt*, IV, p. 67. On the theme of the veil, see also *Fuṣūṣ*, I, pp. 54-55; *Futūḥāt*, IV, pp. 39 and 72. Besides the reference to Qur'ān 6:103, there is an allusion here to the *ḥadīth* on the seventy thousand veils of light and darkness (Ibn Māja, *Sunan*, I, 44; cf. Ghazālī's commentary in *Mishkāt al-anwar*, trans. R. Deladrière, *Le Tabernacle des Lumières*, Paris 1981, pp. 85 ff.).

11. On the *mīthāq*, see *Futūḥāt*, II, p. 247; III, p. 465 (where Ibn ʿArabī explains that at the moment of theophany in the life to come, created beings would recognize their Lord if He showed Himself to them in the form in which He had appeared at the time of the *mīthāq*); IV, p. 58 and 349.

12. On the *barzakh*, see *Futūḥāt*, I, pp. 304-7.

13. The four levels or forms of initiatic death are distinguished in *Futūḥāt*, II, p. 187.

14. Cf. ibid., I, pp. 307-17.

15. The description of Hell occurs in *Futūḥāt*, I, pp. 297-304, that of Paradise at ibid., I, pp. 317-22.

16. *Futūḥāt*, I, p. 320; III, p. 465; IV, p. 15; *Kitāb al-Tarājim*. Hyderabad 1948, p. 27. The *kathīb* is situated in Eden, which is the citadel of Paradise.

17. Contemplation (*mushāhada*) is different from vision (*ru'ya*). In fact, 'it is preceded by knowledge about the Object of Contemplation, and this is the knowledge envisaged when speaking about beliefs (*ʿaqā'id*, a term whose etymology suggests a limitative representation). Consequently, the Object contemplated can be either affirmed [i.e. if He conforms to our previous idea of Him] or denied [i.e. if He does not], whereas in the case of vision, properly speaking, there can be only affirmation . . .. All contemplation is vision but not all vision is contemplation' (*Futūḥāt*, II, p. 567; see also *Futūḥāt*, II, pp. 494-96; *Iṣṭ.*, definitions §§60 and 188).

18. *Fuṣūṣ*, I, p. 113.

19. On the concept of *khalwa*, see the article by H. Landolt in *EI*[2], s.v. In spite

of Ibn Taymiyya's criticisms, who saw it as a reprehensible innovation (*Majmūʿat al-rasā'il wa 'l-masā'il*, ed. Rashīd Riḍā, v, p. 85), the retreat, whose Islamic prototype lies in the practice of the Prophet himself prior to the Revelation, has a long history in Sufism. Cf., among others, Abū Saʿīd al-Kharrāz, *Kitāb al-Ḥaqā'iq*, quoted by Nwyia, *Exégèse coranique . . .*, p. 303; Muḥāsibī, *Kitāb al-khalwa*, ed. Abdo Khalife, *al-Mashriq*, 1955, XLIX, pp. 43-49; Abū Nuʿaym al-Iṣfahānī, *Ḥilyat al-awliyā'*, Beirut 1967, VI, p. 376; IX, p. 356; Qushayrī, *Risāla*, Cairo 1957, pp. 50-52; Hujwīrī, *Kashf al-mahjūb*, trans. Nicholson, pp. 51 and 324; Ghazālī, *Iḥyā'*, Cairo, n.d., II, pp. 221-41; Suhrawardī, *ʿAwārif al-maʿārif* (vol. 5 of the edition of the *Ihyā'*), pp. 121-31, in which chapters 26, 27, and 28 discuss the *arbaʿīniyya*, the forty-day retreat.

20. Scrupulousness (*waraʿ*) and the abandoning of scrupulousness (*tark al-waraʿ*) form the subject of chapters 91 and 92 of the *Futūḥāt* (II, p. 175). The author explains that in the case of the gnostic, the abandoning of scrupulousness comes about because his gaze falls not on things but on the Face of God within those things: as he cannot escape the evidence of this theophany, he is unable to perceive the signs which might cause him to have scrupulousness—might cause him, that is, to renounce that which might be, legally speaking, suspect. To renounce what is lawful but superfluous is a result not of scrupulousness but of ascesis; whereas to renounce what is lawful and necessary is disobedience pure and simple.

21. On ascesis (*zuhd*), see *Futūḥāt* II, p. 177.

22. *Tawakkul* (*Futūḥāt*, II, pp. 199-202) 'consists in the heart's leaning on God alone and remaining untroubled by the absence of the secondary causes which are [divinely] established in the universe and on which souls are in the habit of depending.'

23. On *karāmāt*, see *Futūḥāt*, II, pp. 369, 374-75; IV, p. 65. *Karāmāt* can be either sensible (*ḥissiyya*) or spiritual (*maʿnawiyya*). The latter are all, essentially, a question of greater knowledge. The former consist in the suspension of secondary causes (*kharq al-ʿawā'id*); they may conceal a divine ruse (*makr*) for testing the servant, who will be questioned about the use he made of them. The true *kharq al-ʿawā'id*, in accordance with the literal meaning of the expression, is the unloosening of the bonds of habit, and being aided by grace in full observance of the Law and in the acquisition of noble character (*makārim al-akhlāq*).

24. Tirmidhī, *tafsīr*, s. 11; Ibn Ḥanbal, IV, pp. 11-12.

25. Cf. *Futūḥāt*, III, p. 523 ff.

26. Ibid, I, p. 616.

27. The distinctions between *wāridāt* (or *khawāṭir*) are classic in Sufism. Cf. Junayd, *Enseignement spirituel*, trans. R. Deladrière, Paris 1983, pp. 74-79 (pp. 58-62 of the Arabic text in A. H. Abdel-Kader, *The Life . . . of Al-Junayd*); Qushayrī, *Risāla*, Cairo 1957, p. 43; Suhrawardī, *ʿAwārif*, pp. 221 (chapter 57). In the work of Ibn ʿArabī, cf. *Futūḥāt*, I, pp. 281-84; II, pp. 77-78 (the 55th question of Tirmidhī), pp. 563-66. Like earlier teachers, Ibn ʿArabī usually distinguishes between four kinds of *wārid: rabbānī* (lordly), *malakī* (angelic), *nafsī* (proceeding from the soul), and *shayṭānī* (satanic). Let us note that, as an example of the way in which satanic suggestions may enter the soul under cover of feelings which are themselves praiseworthy, Ibn ʿArabī cites the case of the Twelver Shīʿites

(*al-imāmiyya*) whom the demons have led astray through their (legitimate) love for the *ahl al-bayt*. To persist in seeing the author of the *Futūḥāt* as a Shīʿite at heart is indeed something of a paradox.

28. 'If the forms—be they spiritual, corporeal or conceptual—which appear to you also speak to you', notes Jīlī in his commentary, 'it is because the divine Ipseity is diffused in all manifested beings; for within all beings, God has a Face which is His own' (on this concept of Face, cf. note 1, chapter 6). For Jīlī, the formula 'Glory be to God' avoids the error of immanentism, while the utterance 'You are *through* God' avoids the error of transcendentalism.

29. Bukhārī, *anbiyā'*, 24, 48, etc.; Ibn Hishām, *Sīra*, Cairo 1955, I, pp. 397-98. Cf. also *Futūḥāt*, III, p. 341.

30. *Futūḥāt*, III, p. 346.

31. *Kitāb al-Isrā'*, p. 10.

32. Bukhārī, *faḍā'il aṣḥāb al-nabī*, 6.

33. *Inna min al-ʿasal khamran*: Abū Dāwūd, *ashriba*. Jīlī interprets honey as a symbol of the path of wisdom (*al-ʿulūm al-ḥikmiyya*) which leads to a claim of autonomy with respect to the prophetic Law. Nevertheless, honey can also signify something wholly positive: not merely a remedy (apart from Qur'ān 16:69, cf. Bukhārī, *ṭibb*, 14), but a symbol of the Qur'ān, and thus of the *prophetic way* (Dārimī, *ru'ya*, 13).

34. Jīlī warns specifically at this point against well water, symbol of the *ʿilm fikrī* or speculative knowledge, which is particularly dangerous when mixed with wine (*ʿilm al-aḥwāl*, uncontrolled ecstatic knowledge).

35. A famous allegorical rendering in *La Clélie*, a seventeenth-century French novel by Mademoiselle de Scudéry. The lover travels from 'New Friendship' through 'Sweet Verses', 'Gallant Notes', and 'Generosity'; he must avoid 'Negligence' and 'Lightheartedness' which would take him to 'the Lake of Indifference', but also 'Grief' or 'Calumny' which would attract him to the 'Sea of Enmity', and so on. It is thus a profane version of Bunyan's *Pilgrim's Progress*.

36. As far as Ibn ʿArabī is concerned, there are no inanimate beings. The beings that are called mineral and vegetable also possess spirits (*arwāḥ*) which are not normally perceived, except by the People of the Unveiling (*ahl al-kashf*) (*Futūḥāt*, I, p. 147). This position is based on various Qur'ānic verses, particularly Qur'ān 17:44, 13:13, 24:41, 59:24, 62:1, as well as on personal experience, as we shall see.

37. *Futūḥāt*, I, p. 147.

38. Ibid., I, p. 382.

39. Ibid., III, p. 345.

40. Ibid., I, p. 656; II, p. 408; IV, p. 248; *Fuṣūṣ*, p. 94 (the verse), etc.

41. Bukhārī, *tafsīr*, s. 19, 1; Muslim, *janna*, 4, etc.

42. Qushayrī, *Risāla*, p. 40.

43. *Futūḥāt*, II, pp. 498-99. Cf. *Iṣṭ.*, definitions §§87, 88, 89. (The technical terms which belong to the same family are *al-ṭawāliʿ* and *al-lawāmiʿ*).

44. Without going into further detail, let us note at this point that Ibn ʿArabī (*Futūḥāt*, III, p. 61) makes a distinction between *al-lawḥ*, in the singular, and the plural form *al-alwāḥ*, the use of which, for him, has reference to a cosmological level below that of the Tablet. What is engraved on the Tablet is engraved indelibly.

What is engraved on the tablets generally may, possibly, be rubbed out (*maḥw*) or abrogated (*naskh*).

45. *Iṣṭ.*, definition 88.

46. *Futūḥāt*, II, p. 389.

47. This point is further emphasized by the verses, quoted by Jīlī in his commentary, on the concept of the Universal Composite (*al-tarkīb al-kullī*), which is the 'manifestation of God in the form of created being':

Do not look on God (*al-Ḥaqq*) and strip him of created being (*al-khalq*)
Do not look on created being and clothe it with something other than God.
Affirm both His transcendence and His likeness
And stand in a place of truth [a reference to Qur'ān 54:55].

The need to know God under both these aspects simultaneously is a recurrent theme in the Shaykh al-Akbar's doctrine. Cf. *Fuṣūṣ*, *faṣṣ Nūḥ* (I, pp. 68-75), and the numerous passages in the *Futūḥāt* which comment on verse 42:11 (*Laysa ka mithlihi shay'un . . .*): I, pp. 62, 97, 111, 220; II, pp. 129, 510, 516-17, 541, 563; III, pp. 109, 165, 266, 282, 340, 412, 492; IV, pp. 1325, 141, 306, 311, 431.

48. Cf. in particular Ibn ʿArabī's commentaries on Ghazālī's famous phrase: *Laysa fī 'l-imkān abdaʿ min hādha 'l-ālam*, *Futūḥāt*, I, p. 259; III, pp. 11, 166, 449; *Fuṣūṣ*, I, p. 172; *Tadbīrāt*, p. 106. The basic idea is that God manifests His Infinity by bestowing existence on all possibilities, including the possibility of imperfection. This idea is expressed in the verses quoted by Jīlī in his commentary:

If imperfection were not well established in the universe
The Being of God would thereby be imperfect
It is through me that God possesses perfection.

On the question of theodicy in Islam, cf. Eric L. Ormsby in his *Theodicy in Islamic Thought*, Princeton 1984, and our review in *Bulletin critique des Annales islamologiques*, XXII (1986).

49. *Futūḥāt*, I, p. 125.

50. Cf. the references given in note 1 above.

51. Chapter 8 of the *Futūḥāt* (I, pp. 126-31) concentrates on this earth which is the place of theophanic visions. Henry Corbin has translated part of it in his *Spiritual Body and Celestial Earth*, Princeton 1977.

52. Idrīs (who is mentioned twice in the Qur'ān, in verses 19:57-58, and 21:85-86), is identified in Islam sometimes with Enoch, sometimes with Elijah (Ilyās), sometimes with al-Khaḍir, and in addition is often assimilated to Hermes. On Enoch, the father of Methusalah, cf. Genesis 5:21-24, where we are told that all the days of Enoch were three hundred and sixty-five years—a statement that has an evident connection with solar symbolism. The same passage adds: 'And Enoch walked with God: and he was not; for God took him', which corresponds to the observation in the Qur'ān about Idris: 'Then We took him up to a sublime place' (Qur'ān 19:58). On the person of Idrīs in Ibn ʿArabī's work, see *Fuṣūṣ*, chapter 4 (I, pp. 75-80), partially translated by Burckhardt (pp. 62-67), translated in its entirety by Austin (pp. 82-89), and chapter 22 (I, pp. 181-87; Austin, pp. 228-35), whose subject is Elijah but in which the latter is identified with Idrīs. Ibn ʿArabī speaks of his own arrival in the fourth heaven in the *Kitāb al-Isrā'*, p. 21, where he is greeted

as the master of saints (*sayyid al-awliyā'*)—a reference to his office of Seal, an equivalent to which comes in the account in chapter 367 of the *Futūḥāt*.

53. Cf. *Futūḥāt*, II, pp. 219-20; III, pp. 132, 162, 309; IV, pp. 142, 165, 211-12, 393; *Fuṣūṣ*, I, pp. 113, 122-24, etc. The scriptural backing which is usually given for this is the *ḥadīth qudsī* which says: 'I conform to the opinion that My servant has of Me' (Bukhārī, *tawḥīd*, 15, 35; Muslim, *tawba*, 1, *dhikr*, 3, etc; this *ḥadīth* appears under no. 19 in Ibn ʿArabī's *Mishkāt*).

54. This account, which corresponds to *Futūḥāt*, III, p. 348, occurs at the end of the same volume, p. 549.

55. On the question of the fate of Firʿawn, see the article by Denis Gril, 'Le personnage coranique de Pharaon d'après l'interpretation d'Ibn ʿArabī', *Annales islamologiques*, XIV (1978), pp. 37-57.

56. Cf. our introduction to the *Épître sur l'Unicité absolue* by Awḥad al-Dīn Balyānī, Paris 1982, pp. 32-37.

57. The transition from twelve to twelve thousand in this context signifies the *tafṣīl*, the setting forth in detail of the forms of knowledge under discussion: the learning imparted to the *walī* is not only synthetic but distinctive.

58. This theme is discussed in the chapter of the *Fuṣūṣ* on Moses (I, pp. 212-13).

59. *Futūḥāt*, III, pp. 208, 265; IV, pp. 221, 318.

60. On the question of the vision of God, see also *Futūḥāt*, IV, p. 2.

61. According to some traditions, the *bayt al-maʿmūr* (which is mentioned in Qur'ān 52:4) is no other than the primordial Kaʿba, which was taken up to heaven at the time of the Flood.

62. Unlike the seventy thousand angels who enter the 'visited House' each day by one door and leave it by another, never to return, the *tābiʿ* (who is destined to return to it) enters and leaves by the same door. On this stage of the *walī*'s ascension, cf. the very beautiful passage, in verse and prose, in the *Kitāb al-Isrā'*, pp. 28-34.

63. On the divine *makr*, cf. *Futūḥāt*, II, pp. 529-31, and IV, pp. 144-45. The nature of this problem in Islamic theology is discussed more generally by R. Brunschvig, 'De la fallacieuse prospérité' in *Studia Islamica*, LVIII (1983), pp. 5-33.

64. The doctrine of *ḥayra* (the epokrasis of the Greek fathers) is discussed repeatedly in the *Futūḥāt* (I, p. 270 ff; II, p. 607; 661; III, p. 490; IV, p. 43, 196-97, 245, 280) and in the *Fuṣūṣ* (I, pp. 41, 78, 113, 200).

65. This phenomenon of the descent, in the absence of any intermediary, upon the *awliyā'* of the Revelations received by the prophets is described in the *Futūḥāt*, II, p. 506; III, pp. 94, 181; IV, p. 178. With regard to the specific event described here, we learn from the *Kitāb al-Isrā'* that it took place in Fez in 594/1198.

66. The doctrine of the inner prophets was to be made explicit in the works of ʿAlā' al-Dawla Simnānī (died 737/1336). Henry Corbin gives a summary of it in his *The Man of Light in Iranian Sufism*, London 1978.

67. The rest of chapter 367, however, includes four very dense pages which list the forms of knowledge acquired by the *walī* during this phase of his journey: knowledge of the acquiring of the divine character traits (*al-takhalluq bi-akhlāq Allāh*)—that is to say, knowledge of 'deification'; knowledge of the correspondences between the Qur'ān and the Perfect Man; knowledge of the final return of all things to the divine Compassion (which consequently rules out eternal punish-

ment); knowledge of the secret of man's pre-eminence over woman (which is accidental, not essential); knowledge revealing that Allāh is the One who is worshipped in everything that is worshipped (*huwa 'l-maʿbūd fī kulli maʿbūd*), whether or not the worshipper is aware of it, etc. For an explanation of the relationship between these sciences and the *manzil* (spiritual abode) described in this chapter, see our book, *Un océan sans rivage, Ibn ʿArabī, le Livre et la Loi*, Paris, chapter 3.

68. The cosmological order is described in the *Kitāb ʿUqlat al-mustawfiz*, edited by Nyberg in his *Kleinere Schriften*, Leiden 1919, pp. 41-99 of the Arabic text, and in chapter 295 (II, pp. 674-79) of the *Futūḥāt*. The geographical distribution of the levels of existence is illustrated by a series of diagrams in chapter 371 (III, pp. 416-55). Cf. also M. Asín Palacios, *El mistico murciano Abenerabi*, IV, *Su teologia y sistema del cosmos*, Madrid 1928; Titus Burckhardt, *Clé spirituelle de l'astrologie musulmane*, Milano 1974; Naṣr Ḥāmid Abū Zayd, *Falsafat al-ta'wīl*, Beirut 1983, pp. 45-149. The twenty-eight levels of universal existence (*marātib al-wujūd*) correspond to the twenty-eight letters of the Arabic alphabet (cf. *Futūḥāt*, II, p. 395), which are themselves connected with the spiritual categories (cf. *Futūḥāt*, II, p. 591).

69. The names given by Ibn ʿArabī to the *marātib al-wujūd* are variable and, in the event, interchangeable. The level attributed here to the universal substance is sometimes attributed to the universal Body (*al-jism al-kull*) and sometimes to *habā'* ('Dust') or *materia prima* (*hayūlā*). But at times Ibn ʿArabī speaks of Nature (*ṭabīʿa*) and *habā'* as two twins who engender between them the universal Body (which is then no longer the lowest level of the World of the Commandment but the highest level of the World of Creation).

70. Akbarian cosmology is characterized by the recurrence of quaternate series in the successive worlds described, the last (fourth) term of each series being the first of the next. Even though the term *al-ʿamā'*, the Cloud, can be used in a global sense to mean the ontological level which is in a certain way intermediate between the absolute, single, unconditioned Essence and the world of multiplicity, it is also used by Ibn ʿArabī to mean the second of the four aspects of this level. The level is then made up of *al-ulūha* (the divine function, the Essence considered from the point of view of its inner determinants—the divine Names—and thus as involving multiplicity), *al-ʿamā'*, the Cloud or divine Reality out of which all things are created (*al-ḥaqq al-makhlūq bihi*), the *ḥaqīqat al-ḥaqā'iq* or Reality of Realities, and finally the *ḥaqīqa muḥammadiyya*, the Muḥammadan Reality, which is thus the *barzakh*, the term which is common to this quaternate series and to the one after it that makes up the level of the World of the Commandment.

71. A detailed description of posthumous dwelling places is found in chapters 61-65 of the *Futūḥāt* (I, pp. 297-322). Cf. also the diagrams in chapter 371 (III, pp. 423, 425, 426).

72. The ecstatic intoxication of these spirits is also caused by the joys of Paradise and must not be confused with that of the *muhayyamūn* (the spirits overcome by love) or their equivalents on the human plane, the *afrād*, whom we encounter later.

73. *Futūḥāt*, III, p. 13.

74. Ibn Ḥanbal, III, p. 64.

75. *Futūḥāt*, I, p. 297.

76. Muslim, *birr*, 43; Ibn ʿArabī, *Mishkāt al-anwār*, *ḥadīth*, no. 98.

77. On the divine Name which is the Lord of each being, cf. our introduction to Balyānī's *Épître sur l'Unicité absolue*, p. 30. For Ibn ʿArabī, no created being possesses more of God than his own Lord (*Fuṣūṣ*, I, p. 90). Only the Muḥammadan saint, whose Lord is the totalizing Name (*al-ism al-jāmiʿ*) attains to God 'through all the Names at once'.

78. The Calamus is alternately active and passive. When it is turned towards God, it receives from Him in synthetic mode the knowledge that, having changed direction, it proceeds to inscribe on the Guarded Tablet in specific mode.

79. There seems to be a contradiction between this reference to the angel of the *Nūn* (*al-malak al-nūnī*) and the statement made elsewhere (*ʿUqlat al-mustawfiz*, ed. Nyberg, p. 55) according to which there is no intermediary between the Calamus and God. The *Nūn*, which is both a letter in the Arabic alphabet and a name for the divine Inkwell (which contains the letters that the Calamus will write on the Guarded Tablet) should not in fact be considered as a separate entity, but as a symbol of the Calamus itself inasmuch as it contains synthetically (*ijmālan*) what it will proceed to inscribe in detail (*tafṣīlan*). On this distinction, see *Iṣṭ.*, definitions §§138 and 140. On the symbolism of the letter *nūn*, cf. *Futūḥāt*, I pp. 53-54; René Guénon, *Les Symboles fondamentaux de la science sacrée*, Paris 1962, chapter 23.

80. On the *nafkh al-rūḥ*, cf. *Futūḥāt*, I, p. 168.

81. *Kitāb al-Isrā'*, p. 44.

82. See his introduction, p. 33.

83. *Kitāb al-ʿAbādila*, Cairo 1969, p. 39.

84. This ecstatic saint who lived in chains (whence his name meaning 'man of bonds') at Mecca for several years without eating or drinking is mentioned several times by Ibn ʿArabī. Cf. *Futūḥāt*, I, pp. 248 and 251; *Mawāqiʿ al-nujūm*, p. 81.

85. On these four technical terms which designate the modes of spiritual realisation, see *Futūḥāt*, chapter 331 (III, pp. 115-19), and *Iṣṭ.*, definitions §§123, 124, 125, 126.

86. Unlike the majority of authors, Ibn ʿArabī generally puts *ʿilm* (knowledge), which is a divine attribute, and the *ʿālim* (the wise man) higher than *maʿrifa* (gnosis) and the *ʿārif* (the gnostic). Cf. *Futūḥāt*, II, p. 318; but see also ibid., I, pp. 636, 712.

87. *Risāla fī 'l-walāya*, pp. 25-28.

88. *Fuṣūṣ*, I, p. 181.

89. On this *ḥadīth*, which is often quoted by Ibn ʿArabī, see in particular *Futūḥāt*, II, pp. 232, 399; III, p. 267.

90. Verse 2:158, which institutes the ritual of the journey (*saʿī*) between al-Ṣafā and al-Marwa, has been the object of esoteric commentaries which we cannot analyse here (cf. *Futūḥāt*, I, pp. 708-11; Qāshānī, *Tafsīr*, Beirut 1968, I, p. 100). We will draw attention briefly to two essential aspects of this text from the Qur'ān. Firstly, al-Ṣafā and al-Marwa are defined as part of the *shaʿā'ir Allāh*—that is to say, in accordance with the etymology, the sacred places *insofar as they are modes of knowing God*. Secondly, only he who completes the pilgrimage

to the House or the visit may come and go with impunity (*lā junāḥa ʿalayhi*) between the two hills: duality is without danger only for him who returns from Unity and never ceases henceforth to behold It in multiplicity.

91. Verse 95:5 ('Then We sent him back to the lowest depths of the abyss') can be interpreted as referring to this necessary return to created being: although, taken in its obvious sense, as we said above, it expresses man's fall from Eden, esoterically speaking it expresses the perfection of the being who, by redescending to the world, takes on the divine Lieutenancy (*khilāfa*) in all its fulness.

92. *Iṣṭ.*, definition no. 116.

93. *Futūḥāt*, II, p. 283. See also ibid., I, p. 244.

94. See note 32, chapter 8, for the reference to this passage of the *Fuṣūṣ*.

95. This erasing of the Qur'ān is one of the signs of the Hour foretold by the Prophet (Ibn Māja, *fitan*, 26). Cf. Shaʿrānī, *Mukhtaṣar tadhkirat al-Qurṭubī*, Cairo, n. d., p. 272. On the identification of the Qur'ān and the Perfect Man as two brothers, see note 39, chapter 4.

Index

Khirqa: 44, 45, 99n. 8.
Khirqa akbariyya: 135, 140.
Khirqa khaḍiriyya: 141n. 2.
Khirqa qādiriyya: 12n. 27.
Khoury (R.G): 62n. 6.
Khuldī (Jaᶜfar al-): 35.
Konya: 6, 148.
Kraus (P.): 81n. 15.
Kubrā (Najm al-Dīn): 39, 40.
Kufr: 46.
Kun: 39, 156.
Kursī: 166.
Kutubī: 83n. 24.

Landolt (H.): 16, 46n. 61, 81n. 16, 143n. 36.
Laṭā'if al-asrār: 72n. 46.
Laugier de Beaureceil (S. de): 39n. 36.
Lawā'iḥ: 157.
Lawāmiᶜ: 177n. 43.
Lawḥ al-maḥfūẓ (al-): 157, 168.
Laylat al-qadr: 87, 113.
Lings (M.): 82n. 22.
Littmann (E.): 84n. 25.
Logos spermatikos: 64.
Loubignac (V.): 74n. 2.
Luqmān: 48, 85n. 28, 87n. 30.

Maᶜrifa: 42.
Maḥabba: 42.
Mahdawī (ᶜAbd al-ᶜAzīz al-): 7, 8, 47n. 2, 48n. 2, 53n. 14, 72n. 47, 142n. 13.
Mahdī: 118, 119, 121, 122, 136, 137, 144n. 40, 145n. 46, 145n. 47.
Maḥmūd (ᶜAbd al-Ḥalīm): 34n. 19, 34n. 21.
Maimonides: 83.
Majmaᶜ al-baḥrayn: 70.
Makr: 46, 164, 176n. 23.
Malāmī, pl. *malāmiyya*: 47, 109, 110, 111, 113, 161, 172.
Malatya: 3, 118n. 4.
Manbijī: 14.
Manzil, pl. *manāzil*: 7, 8, 53, 116, 128, 174n. 2, 180n. 67.
Manzil al-qutb (Kitāb): 95, 96, 100n. 19, 101n. 39.
Maqām, pl. *maqāmāt*: 6, 41, 55, 58, 72, 82n. 20, 93, 105, 106, 151.
Maqām al-ᶜiyān: 122.
Maqām al-khilāfa: 44.
Maqām al-maᶜrifa: 44.
Maqām al-qurba: 55, 57n. 26, 58, 114, 137, 138, 168, 169, 173.
Maqām al-wirātha: 172.
Maqām Ibrāhīm: 129.
Maraboutism: 12.
Marātib al-wujūd: 180n. 67.
Marcais (G.): 75n. 2.
Margoliouth: 99n. 8.
Marrakesh: 6, 58.
Martin (R.C.): 12.
Marwa: 172.
Masā'il (Kitāb al-): 107n. 7.
Massignon (L.): 4, 9n. 19, 22n. 19, 28n. 8, 63n. 12, 64, 66n. 20, 66n. 22, 70n. 36, 81n. 15, 82n. 17, 83, 98n. 4, 142n. 20.
Mawāqiᶜ al-nujūm: 72n. 44, 75n. 2, 100n. 19, 101n. 32, 101n. 40, 181n. 84.
Mawlā: 24n. 23.
Mawlid, pl. *mawālid*: 8, 10, 14n. 31, 67.
Mawt: 150.
McCarthy (R.): 32n. 14, 105n. 5.
Mecca: 6, 7, 43, 95, 99n. 8, 104, 108, 112, 128, 129, 130, 131, 134, 141n. 2.
Medina: 167.
Meier (F): 39n. 18.
Memon (M.U.): 8n. 17, 98n. 3.
Miᶜrāj, pl. *maᶜārij*: 52, 80, 87, 108, 112, 147, 148, 155, 161, 164, 165, 166, 169, 173, 174n. 2, 175n. 7.
Michon (J.L.): 16, 26n. 3.
Minna: 29.
Miquel (A.): 101n. 31, 103n. 1.
Mirrīkh (al-): 161.
Miṣbāḥ: 66.
Mishkāt al-anwār: 25n. 25, 25n. 27, 110n. 13, 179n. 53, 181n. 76.

Mithāl: 76.
Mīthāq: 66. 175n. 11.
Mo'in (M.): 41n. 45.
Monteil (V.): 98n. 4.
Montgomery Watt (W.) 62n. 6.
Morris (J.W.): 4, 16, 48n. 2.
Moses: 19, 37, 43, 44, 50n. 7, 59, 74, 81, 103, 107, 118, 161, 162, 163, 164, 171, 175n. 8, 179n. 58.
Mosul: 6, 7.
Muᶜammar: 79, 84n. 25.
Muᶜāwiya b. Yazīd: 95.
Muᶜjiza, pl. *muᶜjizāt*: 32, 105.
Mubārak (Aḥmad b. al-): 13n. 30.
Mubāyaᶜat al-qutb: 100n. 19.
Mudabbir (*al-*): 21.
Muḥāḍarāt al-abrār: 75n. 2, 78n. 11, 100n. 24, 106n. 6.
Muḥammad (the Prophet): 17, 18n. 10, 30, 43, 48, 49, 50, 57, 59, 60, 61, 63, 65, 66, 71, 72, 73, 76, 77, 78, 80, 87, 89, 91, 93, 94, 96, 110, 114, 116, 117, 118, 120, 121, 122, 124, 125, 129, 130, 131, 132, 134, 138, 141n. 11, 162, 163, 164, 165, 168, 171, 172.
Muḥammad al-Bāqir: 65n. 18.
Muḥammadan Reality: 60, 67, 68, 69, 130, 147, 166, 173, 180n. 70.
Muḥarram: 49, 58.
Muḥāsibī: 176n. 19.
Muhayyamūn: 101n. 34, 107, 114, 168, 180n. 72.
Mujāhada: 150.
Munajjid (S.): 9n. 20.
Munāwī: 108n. 10.
Munāzalāt: 152.
Munson Jr. (H.): 12.
Muqarrabūn: 26, 33, 58,95, 115.
Muqātil: 24.
Murcia: 5, 6.
Mūsawī: 74, 77, 80, 83, 106, 162, 170.
Mushahada: 42, 175n. 17.
Mushtarī (*al-*): 162.
Muslim: 65n. 17, 79n. 12, 177n. 41, 179n. 53, 181n. 76.
Mutawakkil: 95.

Nabhānī (Yūsuf): 8n. 17, 84n. 25, 108n. 10, 143n. 38.
Nābulusī (ᶜAbd al-Ghanī al-): 136.
Nadla b. Muᶜāwiya: 78.
Nafas al-Raḥmān: 69, 166.
Nafs: 26, 35.
Nā'ib: 93, 140.
Najīb, pl. *nujabā'*: 104, 107.
Najm al-Dīn b. al-Ḥakim: 19.
Naqīb, pl. *nuqabā'*: 104, 107.
Naqsh al-fuṣūṣ: 110n. 13.
Naqshaband (Bahā' al-Dīn): 146n. 58.
Naqshabandiyya: 12, 13n. 28, 82, 146n. 57, 173.
Nasab al-khirqa (*Kitāb*): 99n. 8. 141n. 2.
Nāṣir (*al-*): 21.
Nāṣir Li-Dīn Allāh (caliph): 14.
Naṣr: 55.
Nicholson (R.A.): 3, 26n. 5, 28n. 8, 34n. 19, 45n. 59, 70n. 36.
Nihāwand: 91.
Niyāba: 147.
Noah: 85n. 28, 86, 96.
Nora (P.): 16.
Nubuwwa ᶜāmma : 51, 114, 137.
Nubuwwa muṭlaqa: 54, 114, 138.
Nūn: 65, 168.
Nūr aṣlī: 53.
Nūrāniyya: 65.
Nūr muḥammadī: 61, 63, 64, 65, 66, 67.
Nuṣra: 26, 42.
Nwyia (P.): 23n. 19, 24n. 22, 65n. 18, 144n. 45, 176n. 19.
Nyberg (H.S.): 3, 69n. 30, 71n. 38, 180n. 68, 181n. 79.

Ormsby (E.): 178n. 48.

Paraclete: 145n. 47.
Pharaoh: 19, 37, 161.
Piemontese (A.): 174n. 2.

Tozeur: 129.
Tradition (Great-Folk): 12.
Ṭūl: 81.
Tunis: 6, 8.
Tustarī (Sahl al-): 18n. 8. 27, 58, 65, 66, 69n. 30.

ᶜUbaydallāh Aḥrār: 82.
ᶜUbūda, ᶜubūdiyya: 29, 39, 43, 51, 96, 109, 111, 112.
Ulūha: 180n. 70.
ᶜUmar (caliph): 78, 95, 107, 123.
ᶜUmar b. ᶜAbd al-ᶜAzīz: 95.
Ummahāt: 85.
Uns: 26.
ᶜUqlat al-mustawfiz: 180n. 68, 181n. 79.
ᶜUryabī (Abū l-ᶜAbbās): 17, 77, 80.
ᶜUṭārid: 156.
ᶜUthmān (caliph): 95.
Uwaysiyya: 146n. 58.
ᶜUzayr: 50, 85, 86, 87n. 30.
ᶜUzla: 148, 151.

Vajda (G): 100n. 20.
Valensi (L.): 16.
Vâlsan (Michel): 15, 81n. 14, 82, 83, 100n. 19, 104n. 3, 113n. 25, 130,. 134, 141n. 12, 174n. 6.
Verus propheta: 62, 64, 65.
Vollers (K.): 84n. 25.

Wafā (ᶜAlī): 135.
Wafā (Muḥammad): 135, 140.
Waḥdat al-wujūd: 149.
Wahy: 142n. 14, 154, 170.
Wajh bi-lā qafā: 96, 98n. 2.
Wajh khāṣṣ: 89, 98n. 1.
Walāya (Risāla fī l-): 48n. 2, 53n. 14, 72n. 44, 72n. 47, 111, 113n. 25, 171, 175n. 9.
Wāqif, pl. *wāqifūn*: 113, 114n. 26, 170, 171, 172.
Waraᶜ: 176n. 20.
Waraqa b. Nawfal: 62.
Wārid, pl *wāridāt*: 153, 176n. 27.
Wārith: 47, 171.
Warrāq (Abū Bakr al-): 27, 34.
Watad, pl. *awtād*: 54, 91, 93, 94, 97, 100n. 18, 102n. 41, 103, 106, 107, 108, 113, 142n. 13.
Weir (T.H.): 3.
Wensinck: 25n. 24.
Wirātha: 71, 75, 82, 147.
WLY (root): 21, 23, 25, 26, 137.

Yahia (O.): 5, 18n. 8, 19, 20, 28, 29n. 9, 31, 32n. 13, 40n. 42, 47n. 2, 52n. 13, 68n. 29, 100n. 19, 110n. 13, 117n. 3, 136, 141n. 7, 174n. 3.
Yaḥyā (John the Baptist): 117, 156, 162, 163.
Yasaᶜ: 48, 86.
Yathrib: 72n. 44.

Zayn al-ᶜĀbidīn: 107.
Ziyārat al-qubūr: 8, 45.
Zubayr b. al-ᶜAwwām: 105n. 5.
Zuḥal: 164.
Zuhd: 37, 176n. 21.
Zuhra: 160.
Zurayb b. Barthalmā: 78, 79.
Zurqānī: 63n. 13.